3/24

Best

$£ 1:99$ 3/1.

BY BIKE TO BUDAPEST

ELIZABETH HILTON

MINERVA PRESS
MONTREUX LONDON WASHINGTON

BY BIKE TO BUDAPEST
Copyright © Elizabeth Hilton 1996

ISBN 1 85863 965 4

First Published 1996 by
MINERVA PRESS
195 Knightsbridge
London SW7 1RE

Printed in Great Britain by
Antony Rowe Ltd., Chippenham, Wiltshire

BY BIKE TO BUDAPEST

For our courageous children,
Anna, Alexander, Krister and Oliver.
Thank you for making us so proud of you.

THE COMPLETE JOURNEY
JUNE — AUGUST 1994

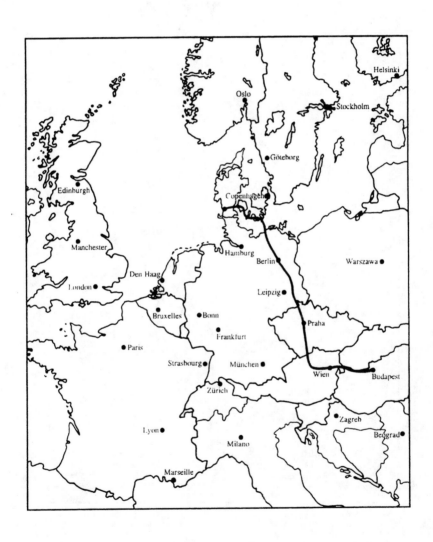

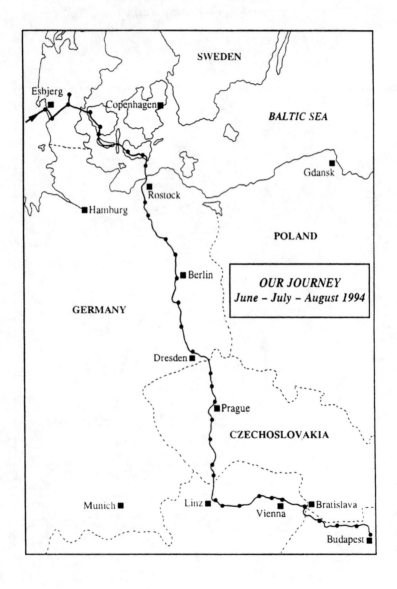

NORTHERN GERMANY

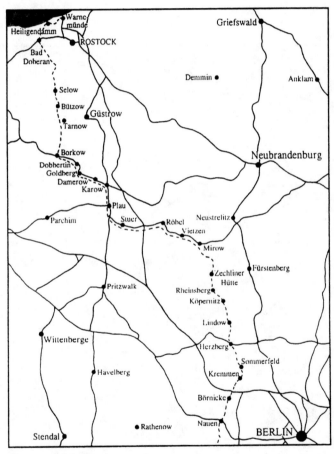

Heiligendamm
Warne-münde
ROSTOCK
Bad Doberan
Selow
Bützow
Güstrow
Tarnow
Borkow
Dobbertin
Goldberg
Damerow
Karow
Plau
Parchim
Stuer
Röbel
Vietzen
Neustrelitz
Mirow
Zechliner Hütte
Fürstenberg
Pritzwalk
Rheinsberg
Köpernitz
Lindow
Wittenberge
Herzberg
Sommerfeld
Havelberg
Kremmen
Börnicke
Stendal
Rathenow
Nauen
BERLIN
Griefswald
Demmin
Anklam
Neubrandenburg

——— Major Roads
- - - - Route

SOUTHERN GERMANY

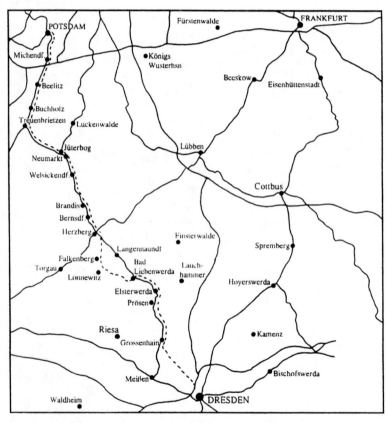

POTSDAM

Fürstenwalde

FRANKFURT

Michendf.

Königs
Wusterhsn

Beeskow

Eisenhüttenstadt

Beelitz

Buchholz

Treuenbrietzen

Luckenwalde

Jüterbog

Lübben

Neumarkt

Welsickendf.

Cottbus

Brandis

Bernsdf.

Herzberg

Finsterwalde

Spremberg

Langennaundf.

Falkenberg

Bad
Liebenwerda

Lauch-
hammer

Torgau

Lönnewitz

Hoyerswerda

Elsterwerda

Prösen

Riesa

Kamenz

Grossenhain

Bischofswerda

Meißen

Waldheim

DRESDEN

——— Major Roads

- - - - Route

CZECHOSLOVAKIA

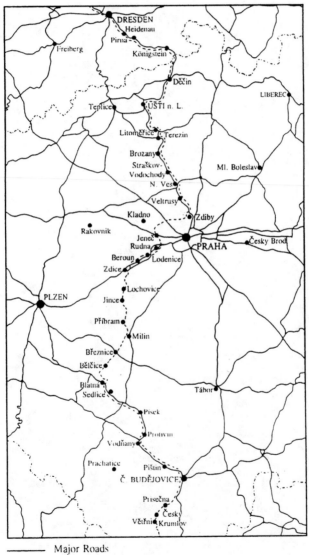

——————— Major Roads

– – – – Route

· – · – · Border

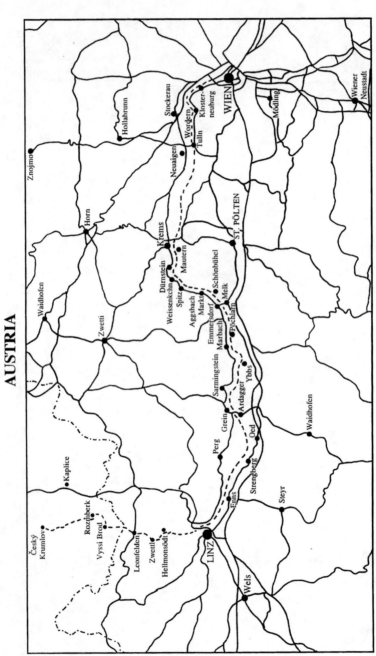

AUSTRIA

Český Krumlov
Kaplice
Rožjnberk
Vyssi Brod
Lconfelden
Zwetil
Hellmonsödit
LINZ
Wels

Znojmo
Horn
Waidhofen
Zwettl
Perg
Grein
Ardagger
Ocl
Strengberg
Enns
Steyr
Waidhofen

Hollabrunn
Neuaigen
Krems
Dürnstein
Weissenkchn
Spitz
Aggsbach
Markt
Emmersdorf
Marbach
Sarmingstein
Ybbs
Mautern
Schönbühel
Melk
Pöchlam
ST. PÖLTEN

Stockerau
Wordern
Tulln
Klosterneuburg
WIEN
Mödling
Wiener Neustadt

——— Major Roads
- - - - Route
· — · — Border

HUNGARY

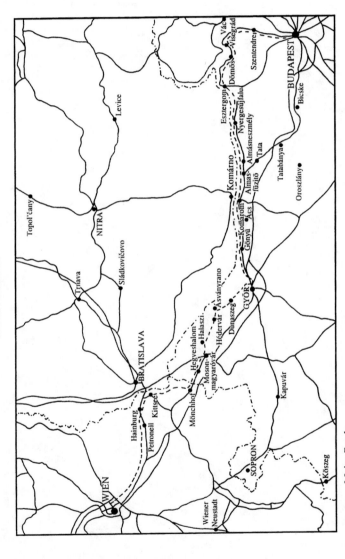

Major Roads ——
Route – – –
Border – · – ·

Chapter 1

The Great Idea

October 1993 – another bleak, rain-lashed Saturday in our suburban house in Swansea. Our four children were, as usual, doing their best to avoid even thinking about, let alone starting the pile of weekend homework. Anna at sixteen seemed to spend hours in her room doing her hair, while the three boys – Alexander, Krister and Oliver, at fourteen, eleven and just eight respectively, were either fighting or more likely lying slumped in front of the latest ghastly computer game which to my inexpert eye looked and sounded like all the others.

"Turn that wretched thing off and do something USEFUL," I shouted for the third time that afternoon while passing their door with yet another huge basket of soaking washing, wondering where on earth I was going to hang it.

A chorus of, "Oh Mum, we've only been on it five mins – give us a break," followed me into the living room where I slumped into a chair – the back of which was covered with drying washing – and started to sink into my usual winter depression.

We really had everything. A lovely house, four super children, security – my husband Peter was a doctor at the local hospital – and most importantly good health. Admittedly our eldest children appeared to be struggling with the ever-changing demands of the educational system, but then so had I. Why oh why was I falling into this awful gloom? Looking back now the answer was obvious, but looking back I suppose the answer always is. At the time it seemed that we were all on a merry-go-round which was impossible to get off – school, housework, piano on Monday, Karate on Tuesday and Thursday, on-call for Peter, cooking, homework – ending with a weekend which was not really any different, and so on. Oh well, best not to dwell on things – what can I think of for supper that hasn't appeared for the last week?

Talking to Peter later that night as we stirred our coffee, he came up with the unoriginal suggestion that we needed a holiday. We'd had some lovely summer holidays and as I pointed out, had only been back six weeks from the previous one which had involved driving to

Provence and staying in a rented villa complete with a swimming pool. Yes, it had been a long drive and Monaco had been heaving with people, but the long hot days lazing by the pool must have recharged our batteries – surely? Well, I suppose the boys had been a little bored and Anna did read the same *Just 17* magazine for two weeks and it really had been incredibly expensive and the pool did give us all ear infections and... We both had to admit that another standard holiday was not much to look forward to and to be honest not much to look back on either.

"In any case," I said, "Anna probably won't want to come anyway."

This statement was undoubtedly true, but nevertheless also a shock – the first of our children leaving the nest and it only seemed like yesterday that we were reading her bedtime stories.

"Well then, I reckon that whatever we plan next year has got to be pretty special," Peter said, "not just an ordinary holiday, but something we can all remember."

Easy enough to say, but what were we actually going to do? He had just finished reading a book entitled *Paddle Down The Amazon*, the story of a Canadian family who had planned and undertaken an incredible canoe journey. This had taken two years, nearly killed them several times and left them broke and unemployed, but they did achieve it and the two teenage sons had something to look back on with pride for the rest of their lives.

"We have got a canoe," I reminded him. "Although it's only got two seats!"

We briefly considered the major rivers of the world before coming back to reality and asking the fundamental question of how long could we be away for? GCSEs were imminent, including resits and with already lowish achievement levels, we both felt, perhaps incorrectly, that a year out of school would be unwise. Apart from anything else, how on earth could we afford it?

"What about working abroad for a year?" Peter suggested. "I could almost certainly arrange a job swap with someone in New Zealand."

We both sat and pondered about this and not for the first time considered the problems of emigrating, even if only temporarily. Peter was always coming up with suggestions like this and we had at various times in the past been almost en route for places as diverse as

South Africa, Australia, New Zealand, Canada and even the Gilbert Islands. Indeed, ten years previously, when the children were a great deal younger, we had managed to spend a glorious year in Swedish Lapland and really had wanted to travel again ever since. The problem now, however, apart from the huge cost of flying six people to the southern hemisphere, was that the children were right in the middle of exam courses and would no doubt blame it all on us if they did badly – I have to say that they blame us anyway, but that's another story. Even if we did take the plunge, so much of the time would be spent working that there would be little left for serious travel.

What we seemed to need was an experience longer than our usual holiday but less than a year, which didn't interfere with school, was a real adventure and which ensured continued payment of salary as well as being cheap!

I'm surprised that it took so long to consider a cycling holiday. Both Peter and I had possessed mountain bikes for several years and used them fairly regularly for short spins around the Gower Peninsula. We had even been on a family cycling holiday in Ireland – well, actually we had taken a car and done short day trips, but it was great fun. All the children had bikes in various stages of disrepair and occasionally used them for Sunday outings on the local cycle path.

The more we thought about it, the more it seemed to fit the bill and very slowly over the next few weeks, the GREAT IDEA took shape.

Chapter 2

The Route is Planned

Like all great ideas this one was not original, but for our family it would form the basis of a tremendous adventure which we could all take part in and which we could remember and talk about for years to come. It would also probably be the last time that we would all holiday together, so even more important to make it memorable.

In essence, we would undertake an unsupported bicycle ride across Europe, carrying all our equipment, not just for two weeks but for three months. We would rely on nobody but ourselves and would aim to see countries and cities never previously visited and which we would be unlikely to visit again as a family. Three months was a compromise in that it would be long enough to forget normal life but short enough not to interfere too much with it. Spread over the Summer we calculated that the children would miss the last two weeks of the Summer term and the first week of the Autumn term – surely they could cope with that. Peter with luck could lump all his leave for the year into one giving a period of about eight weeks and the rest taken as unpaid, if the hospital and his colleagues agreed – there was no guarantee that they would, but it was certainly worth trying.

And so our thoughts raced along on that autumn evening. We started planning in the most ridiculous detail, until by the time we staggered up to bed way past midnight, we both felt that the ride itself was a mere formality. Peter especially had been poring over maps, covering hundreds of miles of seemingly flat country in one sweep of his finger and talking of "a few days" to travel across a succession of land-locked and apparently small European countries. It all sounded so easy, and dreaming of sun-drenched, traffic-free rural roads, with a ready supply of cold drinks, delicious food and cheap but spotless hotels, we were soon asleep.

The following morning, strangely enough, we both seemed reluctant to broach the subject, as though half-hoping that the other had forgotten all about it. My mood had lifted and escaping no longer seemed so necessary or even so desirable and it was probably not until our afternoon walk that Peter said,

"Are you still keen then? – on the trip I mean."

"What trip?" chorused the kids, with Anna in particular looking rather worried.

Our explanation was greeted enthusiastically by the boys – not so by the one and only daughter who proceeded to go into what can only be described as a decline. Although I said the children all had bikes, Anna had only ridden hers once and any form of physical exercise was complete anathema to her. Ignoring her wails for the time being, we tried to explain to the boys the GREAT IDEA and waited for their response.

"We'll never go," grumbled Alexander. "You promised we could go to South Africa and we never did."

This was undoubtedly true, and one of Peter's faults – he hasn't got many – is that his enthusiasm for ideas leads him to suggest things that never quite happen. There had indeed been other 'South Africas'.

"There's no point in even talking about it," continued Alex with a look of deep gloom on his face, "cos we'll never ever go."

A look of hope came into Anna's face at this point, as she considered that her brother, for once in his life, was probably right.

He would have been right had we not made the fatal mistake of **telling** our friends and relatives of our plans. Initially it was necessary for Peter to ask his colleagues and the hospital manager about his leave, but word soon spread and before long we were being quizzed on an almost daily basis. Our position quickly became one of 'no retreat' when the local press somehow got hold of the story and published a rather stirring but not entirely factual account of our exploits. I say 'exploits' because the way it read suggested that we had already accomplished the adventure and were looking for some further challenge. Constantly over the next few months, Peter and I were asked:

"What was it like?" "How did the children cope?" "How many miles did you do?"

It was bad enough saying, "Well, actually, we haven't been yet!" without adding, "And I don't think we'll bother either."

So before we knew it, locum arrangements had been made at the hospital and we were faced with the prospect of having to go – at least somewhere. In our panic, we did in fact toy with the idea of cycling out of Swansea and then hiding in mid-Wales in a cottage for the duration, having previously arranged for strategic postcards to be sent to our friends and families but no, we were made of sterner stuff and so without quite the enthusiasm of that first night, we looked again at our large map of Europe.

Where to start? Where to finish? Straight line or circle? Avoid the Alps or relish their glorious scenery? Go south to ensure good weather or stay north to avoid being fried? For some peculiar reason, Peter had a fixation about ending our journey in Istanbul, 'The Gateway to Asia'. It certainly sounded romantic and impressed everyone.

"We're cycling to Istanbul you know."

"Gosh, who's looking after the kids?" was the usual reply.

"Oh they're coming as well!" we would answer with just a hint of smugness, leaving the other person with an expression combining admiration and pity.

It looked straightforward. Ferry to Roscoff in Brittany and head east through the Loire Valley – stopping for the odd croissant and Château – nip through Switzerland and the Austrian Alps before picking up the Danube in Vienna and following it through Hungary, Romania and Bulgaria to the Turkish border and Istanbul! Two thousand five hundred miles of pure pleasure. Peter even had the proposed route highlighted in lurid yellow – it certainly looked impressive, but could we do it?

"Of course we can," he said, "only 25 miles a day for 100 days."

Put like that it did seem possible; after all, Peter and I often did that on our Gower spins. Would the children cope though day after day and where would we stay and what would we eat and what if we were ill and, and, and... Secretly I was getting worried, but not wanting to appear negative, I decided, strangely for me, to keep quiet, at least for the time being.

My salvation came in the unlikely form of my brother Steve. I say unlikely, because Uncle Steve saw us about once every eight years when passing through the UK on his travels around the world. He was currently living in Los Angeles but had flown over for a few weeks and was able to spend a weekend with his adored niece and nephews. Steve was one of those people with the extraordinary knack of making you think that you only saw him yesterday and within two minutes of arriving was completely at home and relishing his position as favourite uncle.

Later on that evening, he listened to our plans with obvious misgivings. He had travelled extensively through all the proposed countries and it appeared that as one went east, life for the traveller got harder and harder. Interesting maybe, but hard undoubtedly.

"You and Pete could cope," he said, "but I really wouldn't be happy about the children."

Romania was very unstable with poor medical facilities and Bulgaria seemed worse. As for Turkey, the roads were poor, the driving appalling and there seemed to be every chance of losing one of our blond-haired children to some vice ring. Listening to this from anyone else, we would probably have laughed and ignored it, but as I have said, Steve had travelled widely. Over the past fifteen years he had done it the hard way, with pack and no money – a bit like our proposition really – he wasn't exaggerating and I felt relieved that he had said it and not me. Peter looked a bit glum but cheered up when Steve offered to help him plan an alternative route. This they proceeded to do until three o'clock in the morning with the help of a nearly full bottle of whisky – this probably explains some of the resulting twists and turns.

Essentially, after briefly looking at a southern option through Italy and Greece which was considered to be too hot for the children, they transferred their attentions to the top of the map. Our problem was that we wanted to see Eastern Europe before it changed out of recognition. We had been to Western Europe, particularly France, and although beautiful and ideal for cycling with good food, accommodation and medical facilities, it could hardly be described as an adventure. How then, did we get to Eastern Europe without spending the first three weeks in countries that we already knew?

Look at a large scale map of Europe and the answer becomes immediately clear. Scandinavia, largely forgotten by sun-seeking holiday makers, is the obvious gateway to the old Eastern block. Denmark was immediately attractive since we had never been there, it lay in close proximity to the old East Germany, had ferry connections to the UK, but most importantly appeared to be completely flat. It seemed the ideal place to start. Where next? Denmark to my surprise was made up of an archipelago of islands and the furthest east of these – excluding Bornholme – was not far away from the major port of Rostock, on Germany's Baltic coast. A quick look at our AA road atlas confirmed that there was a ferry crossing – we were on our way. From Rostock the route more or less designed itself. Berlin was a must – so were Dresden and Prague. From Prague, either south to the Danube or south-east to Vienna. From Vienna to Hungary and Budapest. From Budapest to...

"Hang on," said Steve, "I think Hungary will be fine, but any further and you will start finding it harder. Romania is a different kettle of fish altogether. The route we have so far is interesting; you will see a lot of the old communist countries, but it is also pretty safe."

So we left it at that. A few days later Steve flew back to the States and we were left to get down to the detailed planning. Well, actually we did nothing at all for the next few months. Christmas came and went and it wasn't until January that Peter announced:

"We really must start getting organised," and that he, "wasn't going to do it all," and that, "we will have proper meetings every month involving ALL the family."

I can only remember one of these meetings, although the children claim there were more. What is incontrovertible, however, is that the first meeting did not go well. It started smoothly enough with a typed agenda and Peter assuming the role of chairman. Order didn't last though and it wasn't long before Anna was in another of her 'declines' refusing to come, refusing to talk about it and refusing if we did take her, to cycle at all.

"Right," said Peter, "if you don't want to come, we're not going to force you. Sort something out by the next meeting that is acceptable to your mother and me and you can stay."

A loud cheer from the boys made her even more moody and she spent the remainder of our meeting muttering to herself things like:

"Stupid idea," and, "Why do I have to belong to this family – they're mad!" Leading to the oft repeated refrain, "And why did I have to have three brothers in the first place?"

We knew from experience that this would go on for some time, so quietly ignoring her we looked at the rest of the 'agenda'. We had only got as far as 'Dates of Tour' before Anna's protests and the next was 'Approximate Route'. The boys listened intently as the list of countries we intended crossing was reeled off.

"That's only five," said Alexander. "That's pathetic – I thought we were going to do much more than that."

"Yeah, that's pathetic!" piped up Oliver, who on principle agreed with everything that his big brother said.

We patiently explained that it was the distance that mattered, but they remained unimpressed – after all, some of the countries did look remarkably small on our 1:3 million map. Krister, normally quiet on these occasions, had, however, been taking it all in and putting up his hand as though in class asked what turned out to be a very perceptive question.

"How are we going to come home Daddy?"

How indeed.

"Oh we don't need to worry about that now," said Peter. "We can fly, or take a train, or if there's enough time we could even cycle back!"

The last few agenda items 'Bicycles', 'Method of Carrying Kit' and 'Camping?' nobody seemed too interested in and as *You've Been Framed* was starting – I felt we had been – the Chairman having got absolutely nowhere, disappeared into the kitchen to find a bottle of cold white wine.

Chapter 3

Bikes and Equipment

Although the children didn't appear to be interested in the fine details of our adventure, the question of equipment was an important one. We all had mountain bikes, but it had to be said that Oliver's infantile version was unlikely to last long, as well as being incredibly heavy.

For those biking aficionados reading this, I can report that the problem of providing an eight year old boy with a decent bike was solved by the purchase of a 14" Kona with a steeply sloping top tube to allow a low saddle height. This, with its normal 26" sized wheels proved ideal for him, and he probably coped better than anyone. The rest of us had standard mountain bikes of various types – well actually mine was not quite standard as it was a man's bike with a 23" frame, a fact that would bring the tears to my eyes later on.

These were not ideal touring bikes, but who can afford six brand new purpose-built machines? They would have to do. To make life a little easier, Peter fitted them all with low resistance 'Slick' tyres and to make life a little harder fitted them all with load carrying racks. The baggage we took depended largely on whether or not we were going to camp. Plan A involved stopping each night at a cheap hotel/B+B but it did not take too much mental arithmetic to work out that the cost of this over twelve weeks would be prohibitive. Camping it was then. At a stroke, this realisation vastly increased the amount of equipment we would have to take – tents, sleeping bags, sleeping mats, cooking gear etc. How on earth were we going to carry enough for six people on our bicycles without weighing the children down to the point of exhaustion? Talk to any cycle tourist and there is only one answer – travel very light and use panniers. Well, all I can say is that we would have needed panniers the size of dustbins – try as we might we could not reduce our pile of 'essentials' to anything less than a mountain. Well a hairdryer and ladyshaver are essential aren't they?

Peter solved the problem by buying a bicycle trailer made of fibreglass (The Freedom Trailer, Squirrel Trailers, Ipswich). He assembled this in our hall and spent the next few months wheeling it around (empty of course) and declaring how light it was, and how easy it was going to be. It had to be said that there were advantages. Firstly I didn't have to carry much and secondly the trailer was supposed to be 100% waterproof, as opposed to panniers which never are. It still looked a bit small though and no doubt we would have to take some panniers as well. Our clothes we decided, would fit in the trailer in individual stuff sacks – we had tried this system on previous caravanning holidays and it worked well. In addition, we took an extra sack for dirties. I mostly packed T shirts and shorts, but for those hopefully infrequent cold and rainy days we each had a Buffalo Jacket. For those unfamiliar with outdoor clothing please look no further – these are extremely light, very warm as well as windproof, waterproof, permeable to sweat and cheap! They proved to be fantastic.

Our caravanning sleeping bags were far too bulky for a trip of this kind, and so we had to invest in six new lightweight ones as well as six self-expanding sleeping mats (Thermarest). These latter inventions were worth their weight in gold, and made sleeping on the ground positively enjoyable. It is an interesting side issue to report that although the above amounted to a combined order of £800 at our local camping shop, it took over three months and constant telephone calls to ensure delivery four days before we left. So much for British industry.

The final major decision was, which tent? There are literally hundreds to choose from, with Himalayan expedition models at one end of the scale, to cubscouting weekenders at the other. The only factor we were interested in was ease of putting up and taking down. It was bad enough camping at all at the end of a long day, without struggling for an hour with poles and flapping fabric. Again, for those with little knowledge or interest in these matters, there is in our view only one choice. The Khyam range of tents all have an ingenious integral pole system, which allows them to be erected in, it is claimed, twenty seconds. We usually took about a minute, but even so our arrival and setting up at a campsite proved to be an impressively speedy affair which generated lots of interest. We took two of these tents – one for the teenagers and one for Mum, Dad and the little ones.

Additional kit included a small petrol stove (Whispalite) which was just fantastic, a medical box (complete with suturing material!) and a container full of cycle tools. Peter, I am forced to admit, came up with the perfect solution to the problem of maps. Normally paper ones disintegrate with overuse or rain, and in any case are so big as to be virtually useless. He overcame this by buying 1:300,000 maps to cover the whole route, which he then highlighted with a marker. The maps were then cut up into strips (leaving approximately 50 miles on each side of the route to allow for deviations) and then laminated to form stiff weatherproof sheets of a manageable size, which were then numbered in sequence. Only one sheet needed to be used at a time and this could be strapped to his handlebars.

As the fateful day grew nearer, a large pile of camping kit began to accumulate in our hall, and Peter could often be found either staring at this with a rather anxious expression, or trying to load it into his trailer to test the 'nose weight' as he put it. Despite my hints, he seemed remarkably reluctant to actually try it out on a road and I do believe that if I hadn't put my foot down, he would still be staring at it now. So one sunny Saturday, the six of us sallied forth with a very under-loaded trailer, for a twenty mile round trip with hopefully a pub lunch at the half-way stage.

Anna insisted that we shouldn't go anywhere near her school, her friends' houses, or any centre of population in case she met anyone she knew. This and the fact that she remained about two hundred yards behind throughout (pretending not to be with us) made life rather difficult. I don't think we looked that odd anyway – well perhaps Peter did. He had a six foot orange flag on the end of a pole attached to the trailer and it did make him rather conspicuous.

"Well that's the whole idea," he said. "Be seen, be safe."

"But Dad," groaned Anna for the umpteenth time. "You look like a wally – what will my friends think?"

Peter did seem to be attracting all sorts of funny looks, but as he pointed out, they were probably jealous of the image of freedom that we represented. That also must have explained why a car full of 'young men' slowed down beside him, wound down their window and started shouting things – I couldn't quite hear what they said, however, and Peter didn't seem to want to tell me either.

Despite these early interruptions, the day was a great success and by lunchtime we were sitting in the sunshine enjoying a well earned pint and admiring the simplicity of our mode of transport. We had already cycled ten miles and the trailer appeared to be a most useful container for our jumpers, anoraks and the odd tin of fizzy drink.

Peter seemed to have got the hang of towing it, and was even managing to go up hill. The big question remained, however; could we survive day after day, miles away from home and would we have sufficient desire and determination to keep going?

Only time would tell, but we all felt pretty confident as we wobbled our way home – next stop Denmark.

Chapter 4

Departure

The final few weeks sped by as I packed and repacked the clothes bags, trying to be ruthless and considering the worth of every single item. However, as fast as I abandoned things, others came to take their place and Peter still ended up having to squash the trailer lid down rather like a suitcase.

Poor Alexander's bike was laden with two enormous panniers full of dehydrated food, tins of ham and pots of honey and jam. We also took enough tea and coffee for the duration, dried milk and a huge pot of Marmite – we didn't intend to starve. My panniers were full of shampoo and washing up liquid and Anna had all the sandals for wearing in the evening – we rode in stiff soled cycle shoes since ordinary trainers cause all sorts of aches and pains. In addition, we all had our sleeping bags and mats rolled up and attached by elastics to the rear racks.

The children made valiant attempts to include cuddly toys, computer games and a badminton set, but finally realised we were serious about travelling light and resigned themselves to their fate. Anna, however, as well as trying to bring a mountain of perfume, moisturising creams and sanitary towels, also seemed to be going through premature withdrawal symptoms at the prospect of leaving behind her newly acquired boyfriend, 'Duncan'. This enigmatic character we had never set eyes on, as whenever he came to pick up our daughter for the evening, he lurked about out of range until she left the house. We had tried of course.

"Bring Duncan to the house darling, why don't you ask him in for a drink?" but Anna went to the most extraordinary lengths to avoid this.

We finally pinned him down on the evening before we left by the simple expedient of keeping his 'date' well and truly grounded. Shortly after the appointed time, a greasy-haired adolescent slouched up our drive and Peter, in a misguided effort to make him feel at home, started showing him our equipment, which at that precise moment he was trying to cram into the back of a hired minibus.

"Well Duncan what d'you think – quite a trip eh?"

Duncan's gaze took in the chaos in front of him before giving his considered reply in a slow, flat monotone.

"Rather... you... than... me."

These pearls of wisdom were all that he ever did say, but they seemed to impress Anna considerably from the adoring look she gave him. Honestly, you put in seventeen years of hard work and then some yobbo comes along and... oh why worry!

Tuesday, June 28th dawned bright and sunny and we rushed around, turning off water and gas before Brian arrived. Brian was my great photographic friend and as well as driving the minibus back from Harwich, he was also going to look after the house and animals while we were away. We had spent every Monday evening for the past nine months attending 'A' Level evening classes in photography and had sat the exam only a few weeks previously. Although I still felt deep misgivings about our whole enterprise, it certainly provided a marvellous photographic opportunity for me – the only problem was, how much equipment could I take? This is the one area that most sensible cycle-tourists either forget about completely or restrict themselves to a small compact. Not me. I took an enormous camera bag full of lenses, filters, films as well as a 35mm SLR. This just fitted into a wire shopping basket on the front of my bike, but so altered the steering and handling characteristics that I could hardly ride it. Lets hope the results are worth it – after all, photographs are all we have left when memories fade.

We were all dressed in lightweight clothes and wearing our new cycle shoes which in Alexander's case were a lurid pink and yellow. The van was packed with the six bicycles and trailer, leaving very little room for the passengers and so, squeezing in to avoid protruding handlebars and oily chains, we took a final look at the house before Peter started up the van and pulled away. Five hours later we arrived at Parkeston Quay in Harwich and there was the ferry already beginning embarkation for the crossing to Esbjerg.

I looked in disbelief at the mounting pile of equipment as Peter and Brian off-loaded the van. Were we really going to take this lot to Budapest – we could hardly hold it all upright let alone cycle with it.

"Take care," said Brian after lining us up for a group photograph. "If you really get into trouble, I'll come and rescue you."

With this comforting thought we waved our goodbyes to Brian before Peter led us all in a wobbling line to the check-in desk.

"Oh you must be the Hiltons," said the pleasant girl behind the counter, staring incredulously at the spectacle we represented. "We've been waiting for you, stick these on your bikes and queue in Line 1."

The car drivers waiting in the other lines also seemed to stare and nudge their passengers so we stared back – something we were going to get pretty good at over the coming months. Within minutes we were beckoned forward to board – cyclists first seemed to be the rule and continued to be so all through Europe, whether on boats or crossing borders. Unfortunately what also seemed to be true throughout Europe was that cyclists are expected to help themselves, so while the cars were being carefully shepherded into position, we were left to tie up the bikes and trailer with some filthy oil encrusted ropes covering ourselves with muck in the process.

We appeared to be the only cyclists on the boat, until at the last minute a young Swede shouting and waving, just managed to push his machine up the gangplank before the ship left. Peter got into conversation with him later in the voyage, "to pick his brains" as he put it, but returned looking rather gloomy. The Swede had been cycling for three weeks, it had poured with rain every day, he had nearly been killed in Germany and Belgium and was now returning to Gothenburg (by train) for treatment to the pressure sores on his backside and hands prior to booking a package holiday in Greece to recover. Also depressing was the fact that his gleaming aluminium bike was dripping with every gadget imaginable designed to make the cyclist's life comfortable and enjoyable and probably cost more than all of ours put together.

Feeling not a little apprehensive, we sent the children off to the ship's cinema to see their last entertainment for a very long time, while Peter and I found the bar and sat looking at a beautiful sunset on a flat calm sea while we 'considered our position' and drank some very pleasant Danish lager.

To be quite honest, following the one and only bike meeting in January when our route had been vaguely discussed, I had not given it a second thought – until now.

"Where exactly are we going tomorrow?" I asked Peter as he returned to our table with another foaming tankard. "Can you show me on the map?"

He nearly fell over. I don't think that ever before in eighteen years of marriage had I asked to look at a map, but to be fair, never before had it involved me in such a direct way. When he was convinced that I was serious, the table was cleared and the first laminated map was unrolled covering the middle of Jutland from Esbjerg to Kolding.

"We'll be arriving at about 2 p.m. tomorrow," said Peter, "and I thought we would head south on the coast road for about nine miles to this campsite here," and he stabbed his finger at the map.

"Well that's not very far," I said. "Can't we keep on going towards Germany?"

Peter seemed rather uncomfortable at this point and it took some time to find out why. It appeared that in an attempt to quell revolution in the children's ranks at the prospect of this trip, he had promised them a trip to Legoland, which lay about forty miles to the north-east of Esbjerg.

"But that's miles out of our way," I moaned, "and besides I hate theme parks – this is supposed to be freedom and adventure, not Disneyworld!"

It was true, I did loathe anything resembling a funfair, and while other families flew to Florida for successive years of thrills and spills, we had never even been to Barry Island which was just up the road.

"I've heard it's very educational," continued Peter in an effort to placate me, "with amazing models built entirely of LEGO."

I was forced to remind him that unlike most of the precocious children we knew who seemed to spend their entire lives creating beautiful art forms in plastic, our slow plodders had never shown the slightest interest in the stuff. Unless toys flew, exploded, or made terrible noises the boys soon became bored – they certainly wouldn't have contemplated sitting quietly with LEGO bricks unless allowed to throw them at each other.

Ignoring this setback for the moment, we looked at the rest of the proposed route through Denmark ending at the port of Gedser on the island of Falster. I must say it looked incredibly far on these larger scale maps and I began to realise for the first time what we had undertaken.

"How far do you think we'll manage each day?" I asked Peter.

"Oh about twenty to thirty miles I should think, perhaps more if we get up early," he replied.

"But what's that on the map" I persisted, hoping it equalled at least two of his laminated sheets (maps as I've said, have never been a strong point). When he only indicated a distance of about 3" on sheet one, I felt what is commonly known as a 'sinking feeling'.

"How many sheets have you got?" I asked, my voice quivering just a little.

"Well to reach Budapest, I think it's about nineteen," Peter said in a nonplussed sort of way. "But some are shorter than others," he added encouragingly.

"NINETEEN – you're mad. We'll never do it. We're not the Tour de France and have you forgotten that Ollie is only eight?"

"Look, if you're going to worry about anybody, I reckon it should be me," Peter retorted with an injured expression. "I'm the one who's lugging half a ton of unnecessary rubbish behind me. You didn't *have* to bring four changes of clothes for everyone and as for the hairdryer..."

"You can talk – you would be the first to complain if I hadn't brought enough and come to think of it what about those books? You must have at least ten of them. I hardly think *Crime and Punishment* is essential reading."

"Well I bought it ages ago – I've just never had the time to read it."

"Well don't think you're going to have any spare moments on this trip," I answered with feeling. "You'll be spending all your time pedalling by the looks of things."

After thirty minutes of this, feelings had been aired and we both agreed that what we needed was an attainable target – Budapest was simply too far away to contemplate. I secretly felt that getting across Denmark would be more than enough of an achievement, but in the end we settled on Berlin.

"We'll try and get to Berlin then," Peter summarised, "and then have a good rest before making any more plans."

This seemed a little more reasonable, so as we could see the children running towards us from the cinema, we left it at that and began to think about supper.

Chapter 5

Denmark

After the last night in beds for sometime, we awoke to a rather grey day with the sea and clouds merging into one. It was also rather chilly and before long a thin drizzle began to fall.

The boat docked at 2 p.m. giving us glimpses before she did so of a flat featureless landscape, with clouds scudding across it. We arrived on the car deck to find that many of the car drivers had already started their engines and some were revving them as if on the starting grid at Le Mans. As levels of carbon monoxide rose, I began to seriously wonder if we'd ever get off alive. Eventually the bow doors opened and paying little heed to instructions, the cars at the front of each line vied with each other to be first out. We all stood pinned against the side, until an officer taking pity on us waved us on and in a few minutes we were pushing our bikes on to Danish soil.

The car drivers were now competing with each other to be the first through passport control and one middle-aged British driver who was gripping the wheel like grim death and peering through his windscreen with fierce determination, seemed so intent on getting there first that he drove straight into the back of our trailer.

"Hey," shouted Peter, "what the hell do you think you're doing? Are you blind?"

I think he was deaf as well, for completely ignoring us he seized his chance and made straight for a new gap that had opened up. What an inauspicious start; damage appeared superficial, but on closer inspection there appeared to be a small buckle in the trailer wheel. Lesson number one; when a car hits a bike, the bike comes off worse.

A friendly Danish policeman waved us through the main gates and stopping to put on our waterproofs, we pedalled off, trying to keep as far in to the right as possible. A few hundred yards along on the main road to Ribe we discovered a cycle path with its own signposting, proving beyond doubt that Denmark is a cyclist's Utopia. We simply followed the signs towards Ribe and were led along a network of paths and minor roads which avoided most of the traffic. We soon adopted the pattern that was to remain with us for the next three months; Peter in front with the trailer and map followed by Ollie and Alexander.

Anything from fifty yards to half a mile behind Alex came Anna and Krister, with me bringing up the rear. Although this system made communication between front and back rather difficult, it avoided us bunching up and made it easier for cars to overtake. It also allowed for the differences in our natural speeds. Although we had all laughed at Peter's orange flag, it did prove to be highly visible and I could always tell where he was from my position as 'tail end Charlie'.

During one of our fairly frequent stops to check the map or have a swig from our water bottles, I asked Peter what time he had told the site we would arrive.

"What time?" exclaimed Peter. "They don't even know we're coming; in fact I'm not even sure if they're open."

"Oh that's just great," I retorted. "Next you'll be telling me that you're not sure if there's a site there at all."

"Well, to be honest, I'm not," he mumbled defensively. "But there is a little red triangle on the map."

So all that lay between us and utter homelessness was a 'little red triangle on the map'; great, what fantastic planning. Since we were more than halfway to the little red triangle we pressed on through flat coastal scenery to Store Darum and as we crossed the main road to enter the village, Peter gave a shout and pointed at a camping sign. Five minutes later and we pedalled into Darum Camping which appeared to be completely deserted and covered with puddles from a recent downpour. Leaning our bikes against a fence – where they promptly fell over – we all trooped into a wooden chalet which served as the camp's reception and pressed the bell. A middle aged Dane with a smiling face soon booked us in, told us all about his site of which he was clearly very proud and asked us where we were going.

"BUDAPEST! From here? On bicycles? With children? I simply don't believe it – that's incredible!" And he shook his head slowly to emphasise his amazement.

Now we were 'on the road' so to speak, I didn't really believe it either, especially as we appeared to be relying on nebulous little red triangles, but it certainly sounded impressive and as we had just seen, produced rather satisfying reactions.

Picking up our bikes, we picked our way through the puddles to find a place for the tents. We were to become very adept at this as the weeks went by. The ideal place would be free of stones, slightly sloping (so our heads would be higher than our feet – we didn't have pillows) at least twenty yards away from any other camper, reasonably close to loos and showers, have a tree nearby to lean the bikes against, a trestle table to eat off and most importantly, would benefit from a nice view! I must at once confess that when it comes to campsites I am very, very fussy and, oh alright I admit it, I change my mind. As I explained countless times over the holiday to a fuming husband, "For me, it's got to be right." On this particular occasion, I think it was the third pitch which was presented to me for consideration that finally met with my approval.

"Thank God for that," sighed Peter, who had been pulling the trailer through muddy paths after me, "and which way would Madame like the tents facing pray?"

Ignoring this, I left the boys to sort things out while Anna and I went off to inspect the showers.

We returned twenty minutes later to find the tents up, the bikes neatly stacked, the beds made and everything shipshape.

"Anyone for tea?" said Peter as he put the kettle on our little stove. "This is really the life; it's so easy getting things out of our trailer I'm surprised that nobody else has thought of it."

At that precise moment, a tandem pedalled by two elderly Danes purred past us towing a very sturdy little trailer. With a cheery "Goddag" and an expertise that indicated years of experience, they proceeded to extract several large bottles of Danish beer from the trailer and consume them before attempting anything. How sensible.

As we sat on our foam mats drinking our tea and enjoying the afternoon sun that had just appeared, I think we realised for the first time that this was how it was going to be. Fresh air, each other's company and a very simple life using the few things that we had brought. Our main concerns would be weather, food, planning the next twenty to thirty miles of route and finding campsites at the end of each day; nothing else mattered and home, school and work were already receding. While the children tried out the tiny swimming pool which had been built inside what looked like a greenhouse, I started our instant risotto supper and Peter pored over the map.

He did this for hours at a time and I must say that I found it mildly irritating. Watching someone reading a book and turning the odd page is one thing, but staring fixedly at a single sheet of paper with nothing but lines on it struck me as slightly absurd. Even though Peter always said, "A little time spent now could save hours tomorrow," we still seemed to get lost.

We turned in just after dark at about 9 p.m. and there were excited giggles from the children as they snuggled down into their new bags and tested the sleeping mats. The inside of the tents were faintly illuminated with an eerie greenish light by another of Peter's gadgets. This was a cycle lamp powered by five light emitting diodes which as far as I could see was completely useless.

"But you don't understand," Peter explained. "This will work continuously for three weeks."

"So does a firefly," I replied, "and it's about as much use."

After writing up my diary with great difficulty, the 'firefly' was extinguished and we lay back to listen to the gentle sound of – Krister's incessant coughing. It went on and on and every so often he sat up to give a really good hack. Nothing seemed to help, not that we had brought anything for coughs, and as the hours of the night ticked by Peter and I lay listening to the flapping of the tent caused by what appeared to be a force ten gale.

I suppose we must have dropped off eventually, but it didn't seem like it and all too soon the sky began getting light. Six o'clock and Peter put his jacket on in order to go outside and make the tea. I would like to record here and now, formally and publicly, the immense debt of gratitude I owe to my husband in his role of early morning tea maker. He carried out his duties unflinchingly and cheerfully and with a smiling face and steaming mug, made a wonderful start to the day. There, I've said it.

The day was overcast and threatening more rain, but we were keen to get going and after rousing the children had a cereal breakfast and packed up. This took about two hours and however hard we tried, this time could not be much improved on. At least half an hour of this was spent rolling up bags and mats and expelling the air from the latter forced Peter into such extraordinary contortions that the rest of us usually fell about laughing.

Eight-thirty a.m. and we were finally off, waving to the remaining campers. The Danish tandemists, after restocking their trailer with beer, had been up and away in minutes. Remembering to cycle on the right again, we turned out of the camp gates and headed along a quiet farm road for our first day of real cycling. A few miles later, the quiet farm road became a muddy farm track which became totally impassable.

"I don't think this is right," said Peter, stating the obvious and at the same time slamming on his brakes so that Oliver crashed into the back of the trailer and we all crashed into the back of Oliver.

"When you stop, would it be possible to warn us?" I shouted at him in with just the slightest hint of exasperation. "And could you do it slowly next time?"

"You lot should be paying attention and not be so close behind," Peter countered. "I've got enough to do finding the right road without acting as nursemaid – we'd better turn round."

So it was that fifteen minutes later we pedalled past the campsite we had left earlier that morning. Unfortunately the owner was there to witness this and you could almost hear him thinking,

"If they can't find their way out of here, Budapest doesn't have a hope."

Finding the right road at last, we spent the morning travelling along the most picturesque quiet country roads which were virtually free of traffic. This part of Jutland appeared to be one vast farm and we knew we were close to the source of Danish bacon by the occasional and overpowering pong of pigs – the children spent these nasally challenging episodes blaming each other for the smell!

We began to feel decidedly peckish at eleven o'clock and arriving at Agerbaek we leant our bikes against the church wall before raiding the local supermarket. Bread and butter, cold meat, crisps, fruit, chocolate and biscuits with plenty of lemonade, eaten sitting on the wall in the sun watching the world go by. And what a quiet world it was. The odd car, the odd pedestrian but virtually no noise or industry to spoil our growing feeling of peace and freedom. We had covered about eighteen miles and were more than halfway to the next little red triangle already.

Leaving Agerbaek at about 12:30 the countryside began to change and become much more wooded. It also, to our dismay, became rather hilly.

"I thought Denmark was supposed to be flat?" I panted at Peter.

"Pardon?" his voice drifted back.

"I thought Den... oh forget it." I pulled into the side while Peter and the children struggled up what appeared to be a never-ending incline.

The trailer was lurching from side to side as he stood on the pedals and I watched with interest as he disappeared from view around the next bend. Left alone for a little while in this leafy lane with fields and woods stretching away on either side and a pretty red wooden farmhouse about a mile distant, the wind blowing through the trees and bird life all around it seemed almost magical just to be alive – this really was the way to travel. To feel the breeze, to smell the air, to listen to every little sound and somehow be a part of it all.

They were waiting at the top and I smilingly put up with their accusations of being unfit. I had after all ridden up – Anna had walked. This small ridge actually marked the high point of Jutland and we freewheeled down the other side to Vorbasse where we had planned to stop. Just as we emerged from the woods, Peter gave another shout of glee as a camping sign came into view – this was going to be easy and the little red triangles on our map so far appeared to be very reliable.

Camping Vorbasse in retrospect was one of the nicest places we stayed at during the entire trip and after checking in we pitched the tents in a field that satisfied all our stringent requirements, including a picnic table. The time was 2:30 p.m. and we had covered thirty three miles – I record this since it was the only occasion that we ever arrived at a destination so early. Not that we subsequently did enormous mileage – we just left later and later.

The afternoon was spent lazing around and the boys discovered a Moon Car track. Moon Cars I must explain are sturdy four wheel drive and four wheel steered pedal cars which can be driven at furious pace around a suitably bumpy track and raced against other Moon Cars. Suffice to say that they could not be torn away – what a simple idea and what's more, it was free!

Much to our amusement, several more bicycle trailers arrived later and one home-made model even had a lid, which when fully open acted as a table. Cycle touring seemed to be a popular way of having a holiday, although it must be said that none of the groups we saw were blessed with four children.

After supper we strolled around the little town admiring the neatness and cleanliness of the houses and shops. Stopping in a park, we were somewhat alarmed to see the conning tower of a German submarine, complete with number U 35, protruding above the surface of the duck pond. Closer inspection revealed that this wasn't a horrendous navigational error, but in fact a sculpture by a local artist. It looked faintly sinister until a duck hopped on to the deck casing and settled itself down in what was obviously a favourite spot. Other sculptures were dotted around, but none had quite the impact of the first one – it was clearly the pinnacle of the artist's career.

We walked back as dusk was falling and a gorgeous sunset gave us hopes of a fine day for our trip to Legoland on the following day. We all slept better, although my diary notes it was a bit cold around 4 a.m.

Even leaving the tents behind and just taking the bikes, we didn't leave until 9.30 partly because time was wasted looking for Alexander's water bottle. The boys had been squirting each other with them the previous day and surprise, surprise his was nowhere to be seen. It sounds a small thing – they are only £1.50 – but we didn't have a replacement and they are essential for cycling. Peter spent a few minutes 'bending the children's ears' about the importance of looking after their kit and the difficulties of replacing it and how they should be more responsible etc., etc. They all listened with what looked like serious expressions on their faces – but it could have been resignation – and promised to be more careful. Needless to say the list of missing equipment grew and grew over the weeks until I seriously began to wonder if we would be taking anything home at all.

The ride to Billund was lovely, particularly since we were unencumbered by baggage and the weather was perfect. Alexander and Ollie were mucking about cycling with their hands in the air and Anna not to be outdone also had a go.

"Look Daddy," she crowed. "This is easy!"

The crash that followed was really rather spectacular, with Anna somersaulting over the handlebars and landing in a ditch. The boys chortled and pointed, while Peter ran over to see if there was any damage – to the bike! Anna, as usual, was more embarrassed than hurt and was looking quickly around to make certain that nobody else had witnessed the event, especially any young men. Shortly after this, Peter was passing a solitary parked car when the driver's door was suddenly thrown open and a doddery Dane climbed out, nearly causing a nasty accident.

The perils of cycling, as well as the pleasures, were rapidly becoming apparent.

A busy main road took us the last few miles to Legoland, where, instead of queuing to enter the vast car park, we were able to cycle right up to the front gate and lock our bikes in a special area. We all felt a bit apprehensive leaving them there – if any one, let alone all, of them was stolen, that would spell the end of our trip as well as stranding us far away from the tents. Entry was £10 each, but I'll be the first to admit that we had a super day.

The main attraction for us all was the series of models made entirely out of LEGO – this sounds tedious, but the incredible thing was that everything worked. A LEGO airport complete with taxiing planes and firetenders running around was next to a harbour with boats docking, cranes lifting and lorries loading. A cabin cruiser moved up a series of four locks in a canal system, with water rising and falling appropriately in each section and a wonderful model of old Amsterdam had cars being carried across water – and driving off the other side – by an ingenious chain ferry, while tourist boats motored past. There were sound effects also and it was possible to become completely immersed in the miniature scenes for quite some time.

"Gosh, it's lush," said Alexander, using the latest schoolboy expression of commendation. "Can we get some LEGO – there's a shop selling it over there."

It took some time pointing out to the boys that Amsterdam could not be built from a box the size of a small book for £2.50. Therein lies the problem of LEGO – to get enough of it to make one of these models, you'd probably have to take out a second mortgage, as well as employ twenty full time labourers. As well as the working models, there were some scaled reconstructions of famous buildings – the Statue of Liberty stands out in my memory as does an amazing rendering of Sitting Bull's head set into an artificial hill. I think the latter required three million of the tiny plastic bricks to complete.

Since we had become wise to Danish prices, lunch consisted of fresh bread and peanut butter – a combination we would grow used to. We found a table near the Legoland Railway, which meant that a miniature 'steam' engine driven by the most bored looking man I have ever seen in my life, passed our way every few minutes pulling carriages full of excited tourists, who seemed intent on taking pictures of everything – including us. Just beyond our table was a bridge and it was clearly part of the engine driver's instructions to ring the bell as he passed underneath, thus adding an air of jollity to the whole occasion. I often think of that engine driver and wonder if he's still there, going round and round ringing his bell under the bridge. Perhaps he's revolted and is ringing it at some other part of the track – that would be something to tell the wife when he got home wouldn't it?

It was while we were there, watching the train and wondering if we could possibly have another slice of bread, that I saw one of the saddest sights of my life. A mother with two children, a boy and a girl aged about ten and twelve, were looking at one of the marvellous models – I think it was the Norwegian harbour scene – but no matter, what struck me was the fact that with her head bent low she talked to them both almost continuously. They were both completely blind and as they turned away and came towards us the brother and sister held hands and tapped their way through the crowd with white sticks, their mother still explaining what they couldn't see. Why oh why are some people so selfish, when others have such immense courage?

More marvellous models and rides awaited us in the afternoon, including one in a revolving tower that gave a bird's eye view of the whole park. Krister especially loved the Lego Safari which took him through a jungle full of life-size LEGO animals. So, if you're near Billund go there and have a treat.

We left at 4:30 p.m., greatly relieved to find our bikes intact and bypassing the traffic jam were soon on the main roads back to Vorbasse. Stopping only to buy some provisions for supper at a small country shop, we covered the ten miles in just over an hour, talking excitedly about all that we had seen and done. It had been a great day, made more pleasurable and memorable by the fact that we had got there ourselves.

We now began to take more than a passing interest in Peter's maps and after supper sat in a circle discussing the next day's destination. To our surprise we learnt that the following evening would find us right across Jutland and on the next island of Funen – this after only two proper days of cycling. Most fit cyclists could actually do it in one, but who wants to rush through this lovely country? Despite the lure of this achievement, we were late leaving and spent more time stocking up in the local supermarket. Peter had fitted an elastic net to the lid of the trailer and under this were crammed jackets, loaves of bread, bottles of drink, fruit, biscuits and for lunch today a large sticky Danish pastry. Groaning and swaying – the trailer not Peter –

we set off and sticking to quiet roads, were soon in gorgeous countryside interspersed with small villages – Fitting, Vester Torsted, Jordrup.

Peter had decided to avoid the centre of Kolding and we made a detour to the North. This was, in retrospect, a mistake. Large Danish cities all have excellent cycle paths running through them and it would have shortened our journey considerably. The day was blisteringly hot and it was with relief that we found a patch of shade to have lunch and gallons to drink in the pretty town of Vester Nebel. Some of the signposting was a bit 'iffy' and dare I say it but we went wrong later on that afternoon, which added a bit more to our mileometers. The problem was that all the motorways, railways and roads in this part of Denmark funnel through a very small space as they cross from Jutland to Funen – we too were crossing that very small space while trying to avoid the worst of the traffic. Apparently stranded on the wrong side of this 'spaghetti', we sat in a field during the afternoon and devoured the most delicious cake I have ever had – who cares when you're burning it all off?

Well Peter was caring very much at the moment, not just about the route but also about the large and increasing buckle in the nearside trailer wheel. This was inauspicious to say the least after only fifty miles (only 1450 to go) and was due to a combination of the prang and the immense weight.

"If you had left that blasted hairdryer behind, this would never have happened," he fumed, as he gloomily spun the wheel, his eyes flickering like someone demented as the dent whizzed past with each turn.

"So much for your trailer," I replied. "It can't be much cop if it packs in at this stage."

This seemed to incense him even more, so I tidied up the remains of the cake while he inspected the trailer from every conceivable angle, presumably looking for further evidence of failure.

We pressed on after our break, until Peter spied an elderly Dane wobbling along on a bicycle.

"I'll ask him," he said. "He looks like a local, so is bound to know the way."

"Jag hampter Gudso," Peter started in his appalling rusty Swedish. "Kan du hjalp mej?"

The old man looked at him in surprise but without any comprehension in his eyes and I began to wonder if Peter's claim that "Danish, Swedish and Norwegian are all the same" was strictly correct. It was only by repeating Gudso in every conceivable phonetic variant, that one of them at last registered. Pointing down the road he waved us on our way and fifteen minutes later we were cycling up the steep railway cutting at the top of which was our first view of the Baltic Sea. There is something rather emotional about the sea and although our crossing from the North Sea to the Baltic had only been sixty miles, we felt an absurd sense of achievement.

A major road running by the water brought us eventually to a spectacular bridge linking Jutland to Funen. Being Denmark, there was a cycle path across it, but its great height gave us all a queasy feeling even though there was a guard rail. Peter had planned to stop at a site just on the other side, near the town of Middlefart, so we dutifully followed him down a long hill to Kolding Fjord. There was the site and it was absolutely packed with Dutch campers, easily recognisable by the yellow number plates on their cars and the fantastic array of leisure equipment.

Now I have nothing personal against the Dutch, but my heart sank at the all too familiar spectacle in front of us. They seem to camp in huge extended family groups with hundreds of little white-haired children and this place was obviously booked up for the duration. Their requirements are sun, water (for windsurfing and swimming) and beer and wherever you find these three essentials, I guarantee you will find the Dutch en masse. I don't know what the population of Holland is, but there can't be many left there in July. You'll never see a Belgian, rarely the French, and Italians hardly at all, but the Dutch...

"This looks fine," beamed Peter. "I'll go and check in."

Peter, I swear, would put up with anything, which is either a vice or a virtue, depending which way you look at it. On this occasion we unanimously thought it was the former and by the time he returned carrying a little metal tag we were united.

"We're not staying here," I said as elected spokesperson. "It's ghastly."

To the children's eternal credit, there was not a single murmur of complaint as we all laboured back up the hill, leaving the Dutch to their frites and late night discos. We found another site fairly close by and this was the complete opposite – barely half-full, quiet, trees, lovely views and a nice mixture of nationalities. What's more, it was cheaper.

"Gosh this is nicer," said Alexander.

"Yes, this is lovely," agreed Anna.

It must be said that if two teenagers can think like that, then we must have succeeded somewhere.

We celebrated our good fortune during supper with a bottle of wine – well we would have done had we brought a corkscrew, but this most vital bit of equipment had been left behind. We eventually borrowed one from a party of young Germans who spent the evening crammed into a Campervan watching the World Cup on a tiny television and drinking large amounts of ale. Every so often one of them would dive out of the side door, run around to the boot, extract another six cans and run back again. Occasionally this foray would be interrupted by excited shouts from inside the van and the beer would be left or dropped as a frantic attempt was made to get back into the 'cinema'.

By 9:30 p.m. we were also making frantic attempts to get into our accommodation, driven not by the urge to entertain ourselves, but by clouds of mosquitoes. Only by keeping up a constant shaking movement of head and all four limbs was it possible to avoid being bitten and this looked peculiar to say the least. Our marvellous tents had insect screens, so once inside and zipped in we were theoretically safe – apart of course from the ones zipped in with us. These had to be eliminated if we were to avoid the dreaded high pitched whine of mozzies circulating around our ears all night. The trick was to nobble them before they nobbled you – not that a few bites mattered much, but squashing an engorged insect on the tent material left a horrible blood stain. We often weren't very successful in this regard and by the end of the trip the inside of the tent looked like a film set for the *Texas Chainsaw Massacre*.

The following day was a Sunday and not wanting to strain ourselves, we declared it a rest day. The children spent most of it leaping up and down on the biggest inflatable mattress I've ever seen – their energy was unbelievable. I took lots of colour slides of them, since the mattress was a bright orange and in photographic parlance 'provided plenty of contrast' while Peter made valiant attempts to straighten the now badly bent trailer wheel. To do this it was emptied and turned upside down and various spokes loosened or tightened with a spoke spanner from the spares box. To those not expert in this technique, (Peter for example), it is fraught with pitfalls – altering tension in one part of a wheel causes another area to bulge and before long, what was one simple bend looks like a concertina. For enthusiasts who really want to try this out at home, the secret is to individually mark the spokes and carefully record what is done to each one, so at least you can get back to where you started.

Learning the hard way, Peter sat on the ground for at least two hours, spinning the wheel like some travelling knife grinder – all you needed to complete the picture was a shower of sparks. Eventually, a young Dane, presumably unable to stand the sight of this any longer, came over and offered his assistance. It turned out that he was a Formula 1 motor mechanic and had worked in England for ten years. Had we had trouble with a computerised fuel injection system, or needed our suspension tuning, he might have been of some help but I'm afraid that a mangled bicycle wheel was completely beyond him. It was so simple that it was impossible – that's progress.

It was another bright, hot day and we lunched on Danish crispbread and cheese at a table under a copse of beech trees. There was lots of bird life and the woods around us were apparently full of deer. Another cycling couple had arrived late the previous night towing a trailer which consisted of a large canvas bucket suspended on a tubular steel frame. We watched with interest as they packed up, as first of all they filled several large panniers with their equipment before putting these in the canvas bucket. This strange method of loading resulted from the early part of their holiday when they discovered that panniers made their bicycles so ungainly as to be practically unrideable. A quick trip to a Danish cycle shop had provided the trailer which eased their problems considerably – perhaps we'd made the right choice after all.

Unable to tear the children away from their frenzied bouncing, Peter and I spent the afternoon exploring the beautiful peninsula on our bikes. Lovely views, water, yachts, fishermen's cottages with nets drying in the sun, forests and small quiet country roads combined to give us a blissful couple of hours. On the way back we passed an imposing eighteenth-century country house with formal gardens leading down to the fjord, which had recently been used as a venue for EEC foreign ministers. As mere tax paying peasants, all we could do was drool at the thought of spending a weekend there, but then politicians are very clever people who lead very stressful lives and I'm sure they deserve these little luxuries.

On returning I discovered that my film hadn't wound on correctly and that all my carefully composed photos of the last few days had sadly not been recorded for posterity. I was fuming, with myself really but I would never admit it and Peter didn't exactly help by rubbing my nose in it.

"It's all very well knowing about depth of field and bracketing," he chortled. "But didn't you have a lesson on putting a film in?!"

We left this haven with regret – we could have stayed much longer but strangely all felt keen to push on with our journey and enjoy once again the freedom of 'the road'. It was hot by 8:30 a.m. without a breath of wind, but the roads were quiet as we headed south-west across Funen. By 11 a.m. we were parched and out of water so it was with some relief that we came across a roadside 'Polser' kiosk. You find these throughout Denmark selling drinks and hot-dogs and although I normally would have avoided such a place like the plague, it now seemed like an oasis in the desert.

"What's everybody having to drink?" said Peter, precariously balancing his bike against Alexander's.

"Coke please Dad!" chorused four voices in unison.

I groaned inwardly. Coke was more or less a banned substance in our house ever since I had been told by my dentist that it dissolved teeth. There is no doubt however, that when it comes to quenching a paediatric thirst, there is nothing to match it. Even Peter succumbed, but I held out and ordered a lemonade.

"Anyone peckish?" Continued Peter, running his eye down the chalked menu board. "I think I'll have a hot-dog."

"That's ridiculous," I replied. "It's not even lunchtime."

He never listens to me, so a few minutes later he was back with an absolutely delicious looking hot-dog.

"Mmm this is gorgeous," he mumbled through a mouthful. "Can you believe it, they baked this roll especially and then spiked it on this hot prong thing and then put a blob of Danish butter in it and..."

I was off, saliva flowing, towards the serving hatch which was staffed by three of the fattest girls I've ever seen. The children, sensing sustenance, had also gathered round and were excitedly pointing out various options. Eventually we decided on three more hot dogs and two fish and chips. I watched in amazement as les girls swung into action – one produced fillets of FRESH fish, one started to make a batter while the third sliced up potatoes. In the odd spare moment, rolls for the hot dogs were popped in the oven and sausages put to sizzle. About ten minutes later we were sitting down to the most delicious fish in a gorgeous crispy batter and thick golden chips – it was wonderful. Les girls also presumably thought it was wonderful which probably explained their shape – well, at least they seemed happy.

Well fortified by this, we continued on our sizzling way, gratefully stopping in every available patch of shade. Anna was beginning to 'play up' and stops to allow her to catch up were becoming more and more frequent. She had the most extraordinary way of cycling with her legs moving at exactly the same ponderous rate irrespective of the terrain. This may have been due to the fact that she couldn't work the gears, or it may have been due to her extremely high handlebars, or the panniers but I suspect the real reason was lack of fitness. Well, we'd sort that out over the next few weeks.

We were all suffering from sunburn to some extent despite the frequent application of cream, so after thirty-one miles we called it a day and cycled into the quiet rural campsite at Gummerup. The warden wasn't due until 5 p.m., so finding an unoccupied corner near some very old and interesting buildings, we set up camp. It was only later that we realised our mistake – the tents were in the grounds of a medieval farming museum complete with medieval farm. The museum curator also doubled as camp commandant and was not best pleased.

"I inzist zat you vill go by zeben in zee morgan," she answered in response to our plea not to have to move the tents.

It was a lovely spot with two ponies in an adjoining field – Krister spent most of his time feeding them with grass. Peter and Ollie pedalled a few miles to a supermarket we had passed and returned with salad, cold meats and new potatoes which we ate sitting in a circle on our mats, enjoying some Danish beer and the evening sun.

"Showers please," I called to the children after the meal. So far we had managed at least one shower a day (I think Anna had about three) which considering the Danish shower system was quite an achievement. In all the sites visited so far, there was a system of tokens purchased from reception which when placed in the shower control, gave you hot water for varying periods. I say 'varying', but in reality it seemed to be decreasing. Four minutes for twenty kronor in Darum, three minutes in Vorbasse and here it was down to two minutes.

"This is ridiculous," complained Peter. "I suppose by the time we get to Gedser it will be reduced to milliseconds."

It was really quite an art. Clothes off and out of shower range, shampoo and soap easily accessible, temperature controls set to what you hoped was about right, token poised to be inserted and you're off! The timer made an ominous ticking noise while you frantically washed and scrubbed wondering if you had enough time to get the soap out of your hair. The children became very adept at this with one of them calling out the times.

"Nearly halfway Zands," Ollie would shriek jumping around, his little white bum contrasting sharply with the ever deepening tan elsewhere. "Ten seconds left Zands; ten, nine, eight," he would chant until a mechanical click indicated time up.

"I've still got soap in my eyes," Alexander would wail. "Can you put your token in Ollie?"

"NOooo, itser moine," Ollie would reply, parodying his hero 'Mr Bean'.

Why on earth they couldn't have given us a decent ten minute shower was beyond us – considering the camping fees it should have been free. I can now publicly admit that I often took TWO tokens just for me – well, I did all the cooking didn't I?

At first light the next day we were woken by high winds and emerged to find grey, threatening thunder clouds scudding across the sky. It was also rather cold. The weather appeared just as changeable as at home in Wales and indeed our little guide book confirmed June and July as the wettest months of the year. While wondering whether we could pack and be away before it rained, the heavens opened and down it came. Quickly stuffing the clothes bags into the trailer and putting the panniers in the tent porches, we dived back inside hoping it wouldn't last long. So much for leaving at 'zeben'.

After four hours of monsoon conditions, it was clear that this was no local shower and since Anna and Alexander's tent resembled a paddling pool we decided to warm ourselves up with some hot soup. Although their shower arrangements are not ideal, Danish sites are all equipped with communal kitchens with gas or electric rings and sinks – a real help to the cycle tourist, particularly wet ones. The campsite was now one large bog and splodging our way through the puddles to the kitchen, we shut ourselves in and turned on as many rings as we could find. Such do your relative values change on a journey like this, that standing in a steamy kitchen with a plastic mug of soup warming your fingers is pure luxury – you're happy and content because immediate needs are taken care of. Tomorrow is impossibly far away so you don't need to worry about it.

What we did worry about was whether it would ever stop raining and how we were going to dry our kit. After a few false stops, the rain moderated to a thin drizzle and we decided to make a run for it. Anything would be better than spending another four hours cooped up in the tents. Everything in the trailer was bone dry but everything else was soaking, so it was a matter of throwing it all in plastic bags and sorting it out later. So, with the remaining happy campers peering at us through the windows of their caravans, we weaved through the worst of the mire and headed for the main road to Faborg.

Cycling in the rain is not pleasant. As Peter put it "my rear mechanism gets filthy". Well my rear mechanism got filthy as well, but I don't think it was quite what he meant. The spray from the back wheel went all over my shorts and top and if you ventured too close to the bike in front you got an eyeful from their wheel as well. Cars and even worse, lorries, sent up clouds of spray as they passed, often far too close, so we were well and truly soaked after only a few miles.

Stopping only to take a picture of a Grubbe Molle (old windmill), we covered the distance to Faborg in a couple of hours.

Faborg is a lovely old town and two hundred years ago was one of the most important in Denmark. Picturesque cobbled streets crowded down to a pretty little harbour full of fishing boats, and churches were still the tallest buildings to be seen; no industry, no high rise development, no ghastly office blocks faced with reflective glass. Architects over the last fifty years have been simply appalling in the aesthetic impact on our lives. They seem to have ignored completely what has gone before – 'carbuncle' is absolutely right; our towns are peppered with them like some horrible septic rash.

There was a Youth Hostel in Faborg and having asked the way from some helpful shop assistants, we pushed our bikes through the jolly streets until we found it; the sky still looked very threatening and we didn't fancy a night in soaking tents. On the way there, a Danishman seeing the large GB sticker on the trailer laughingly shouted at us:

"I can see you've brought your own weather with you!"

Youth Hostels have been around for a long time, but I'm afraid their original purpose of providing cheap accommodation for young (well youngish) walkers and cyclists seems to have been lost. Now they are no longer cheap and will accept anyone. Businessmen and well-heeled couples were disgorging themselves from expensive looking cars and checking their bookings with the reception – they really had struggled to get there hadn't they? When our turn came, a pleasant man looked sympathetically at our wet children and perhaps remembering how it used to be, promised to do his best.

"Come back in an hour," he said, "and I'll see what I can do."

Leaving our bikes, we were able to explore Faborg more carefully on foot. We were particularly impressed with the graveyard of the large red brick church which was laid out like a beautiful garden. Instead of huge morbid headstones and bare white gravel with weeds growing through, each plot was a well tended window box of colour with flowering shrubs and plants. You can always tell a people by their graveyards and here were the Danes – neat, individualistic, bright and happy.

True to his word, the youth hostel man had reorganised everyone else and had found us a large family room across the road in an old half-timbered annexe. We lugged our bags over and revelled in the space and comfort, while the children fought over possession of the three bunk beds. Soon, wet clothes were drying on radiators and we were enjoying the luxury of hot, tokenless showers – fabulous! Dressing in the single pair of trousers we had each brought, and putting our Buffalo jackets over a clean T shirt we were ready for our meal out. What a treat!

The meal that night was simply delicious – well, we were all starving but I think it really was good. We ate it in a simple candlelit restaurant with a lovely view of the old town, while the rain drizzled down outside. Peter and I shared a bottle of wine and let the big two have some as well. Scrummy ice-creams and fragrant Danish coffee to finish with and we were all feeling pretty content.

So far so good – we were making progress, supporting each other and really enjoying our adventure. I still had pangs of doubt about the rest of the journey and Eastern Europe might be impossible and... oh but why worry. Take things a day at a time. Tomorrow we would be taking a ferry to the most beautiful of all Denmark's islands – Aero. Let's just look forward to that and face any other problems if and when they arise.

After supper, the rain had stopped so we walked down to the harbour to check on the ferry times. The sky was clearing rapidly, and the sea more settled in its motion as the winds died away although there was still quite a swell. We eventually found a ferry timetable on the wall of the shipping line office and huddled round to read it.

"Ah ah," exclaimed Peter. "This is fascinating – it's called the Sommerfartplan!"

Krister and Ollie immediately went off into fits of giggles and Peter, warming to his theme, carried on.

"You see Sommer means Summer," he explained, "and Fartplan means, well, er, Fartplan."

Leaning forward and pointing at the timetable he continued,

"Now let me see – ah yes, Ollie goes at 8 a.m., Krister at 9 a.m., Alexander every hour and Anna apparently not at all. Daddy, however, can go whenever he likes."

With this he let rip the most monumental gust of wind I've ever heard. It seemed to go on and on and reverberated around the empty harbour. Well it had been empty, but the middle aged bespectacled lady now peering at the timetable over Peter's left shoulder really did appear to have materialised from nowhere. The children and I quietly slunk away in horror, but Peter still immersed in his little joke (it was probably all that wine) continued talking to us blissfully unaware of our absence and let rip again.

"Ssommerfaartplaan," he chuckled, in a ghastly caricature of a Danish accent. "That's really funny isn't it Liz..." his voice tailed off as he turned and saw his spectator staring in disbelief at his backside. We were speechless with mirth as Peter looked around inquiringly, as though trying to blame it on somebody else – she wasn't taken in.

We continued our stroll with Peter rather more subdued and walked along a lovely promenade by the water's edge. Substantial houses had their own private jetties and views across to the island of Bjorne – some folk have it made. We were in bed by 10 p.m. and fell asleep for the best night so far, listening to the drumming of rain again. Thank God we were inside.

The next day dawned bright and cheerful, and for those interested in the weather, I can divulge that it didn't rain again until we were camping in Budapest two months later – there would be times, however, when we wished it had. Cereal breakfast followed by packing up and off to the harbour to catch the ferry – this proved to be a tiny ship with room for about ten cars and us.

The crossing was delightful, with a flat calm sea, deep blue sky and lots of little islands to keep us interested – we could have been in Greece. After about an hour we berthed at the little fishing port of Soby at the western edge of the island. The berthing process itself was interesting, as we went in backwards, the ship being controlled by an officer in a little wheelhouse over the stern. He had obviously done this thousands of times and with a grubby white cap pushed well to the back of his head, he even had time to grin at the children as we edged in.

As soon as we were ashore, we headed towards a small supermarket to stock up for lunch and then to a cake shop for elevenses. The first one was the size of a pizza, gooey with layers of moist pastry and caramelised apple. The second was more doughy, with cinnamon and currants – both were delicious, and thus fortified we set off to cycle to the Eastern town of Marstal. What a glorious island it was. Fields of poppies, lavender and rapeseed fell away to a calm blue shallow sea that looked more like a placid lake. We cycled through peaceful thatched villages, and passed isolated houses whose gardens were ablaze with colour. A man wearing a white Panama hat sat in front of his cottage in the sunshine reading a book – I've often wondered what it was. He was so absorbed in it that he hardly noticed us.

The island was so narrow that the sea was never far away and we stopped at a pretty inlet just before the main town of Aeroskobing for our lunch. A lot of our clothes and towels were still wet, so these were spread over the marram grass to dry, while the children paddled about in the warm water. It was incredibly shallow and Alexander waded out at least two hundred yards before it was over his knees. Well what he actually did was to start shouting and screaming "I'm drowning," accompanied by horrible gurgling noises, with only his head showing above water far out in the bay. Peter was already charging through the water by the time he stood up and waved – that's our son; a complete idiot.

We ate sitting on a bench, put there no doubt for the perfect view. By this stage in our travels, our offspring had discovered Nutella Chocolate Spread, and would accept nothing else. This stuff had the consistency of the mastic that builders use to seal window frames – it probably would have worked just as well – and soon covered everything in sight. If not wiped immediately from faces and fingers, it set hard and simply wouldn't budge.

Aeroskobing is a gem of a place. It has a perfectly preserved eighteenth-century urban layout, and its colour-washed timber-framed houses, some leaning dangerously, face each other across cobbled streets which lead downhill to the old harbour. We spent a happy afternoon there, wandering around and trying to peer through the cottage windows. One cottage used to be the home of 'Bottle Peter' and inside could be seen hundreds of old model ships in bottles, including the ones that he made. Another housed the town museum and Peter was especially thrilled to see a collection of Danish Neolithic Axes. Danish Axes are superior to those found in any other culture, their great beauty resulting from the colour of the flint as well as the fine workmanship and high polish.

Finding ourselves in the harbour, we sat on the wall and sucked ices while the boys dropped stones on a huge shoal of jellyfish. These were extraordinary animals, pulsating and propelling themselves around in an apparently aimless fashion, sometimes diving and sometimes rising to the surface. What does a jellyfish think about all day? Does it object to having a large boulder dropped on it? Does it ever dream of leaving Aeroskobing harbour? Does it know it's Danish? Weighty questions indeed and ones which gave us pause for thought as we climbed the hill back to our bikes.

The remaining miles to Marstal followed the coast by the side of a limpid sea. It was so still that you could see the reflections of clouds – not even the wake of a boat disturbed it. The little red triangle on this occasion proved to be a huge field next to the sea just outside the town. I have a picture of the tents pitched here with the sleeping bags draped over them drying in the evening sun, with bikes and trailer in the background and the blue sea beyond. We all look relaxed and happy and so we were – it had been a day to treasure.

We slept well and by early morning were waiting at the harbour for the ferry to Langeland. The only disheartening note was sounded by the campsite owner, who on hearing of our plans to travel across

East Germany regaled us with dire stories of impossible and impassable roads. While waiting for the ferry, Krister found a shop selling stickers, so we bought one showing the red and white Danish flag and proudly applied it to the side of the trailer. Let's hope others would follow. A small crowd began to gather at the quayside as we waited for the boat in the sunshine. Some pushed bicycles and others had empty bags, presumably for their intended shopping trip to Rudkobing. All knew each other and were talking and laughing without an apparent care in the world. The sad thing was that I found this so unusual – here was a real community. Right on time there were three hoots and the ferry steamed into view round a small headland. It left again in under ten minutes and in this short time unloading and loading of cars, passengers and bicycles was accomplished with cheerful shouts and waves.

Drinking frothy, milky coffee out on deck we paid for our tickets and studied the map of Langeland. I was impressed to see that we were already on sheet number three but it has to be said that most of this and the preceding one were taken up with the turquoise blue of the Baltic, with dotted lines showing the ferry routes.

"Well I think taking these little ferries is jolly pleasant," said Peter defensively. "After all this is supposed to be a holiday as well. No point in killing ourselves."

We certainly weren't doing that and Denmark so far had been delightful. Langeland was so narrow that we could cross it in less than two hours – if there was a connection on the other side, we could be on the next island of Lolland by late afternoon. Creeping slowly into the harbour at Rudkobing, we were able to see the long and elegant arched bridge linking Funen and Langeland. I love bridges, particularly as they are very striking to photograph and this one had lovely shadows on the uprights contrasting well with the almost white concrete. As soon as we had disembarked I was off with my camera bag and Peter knowing from bitter experience that "I won't be a minute," could mean anything up to half an hour, struck up a conversation with a Swedish couple en route to Narvik.

The back of their car was bulging with camping equipment and when told of our destination, they looked with undisguised horror at the now rather grubby bikes and trailer. In fact, they were far more vulnerable on their travels than we were, a fact not immediately apparent but true nevertheless. Far from being secure havens, cars are complicated liabilities waiting to go wrong and we witnessed this deep in Czechoslovakia, where we found another Swedish couple stranded it seemed indefinitely, as they attempted to sort out their defunct, immovable piece of scrap metal with the aid of a disinterested insurance company and the Czech telephone system. We moved slowly but at least we moved and with the help of an old margarine pot full of essential tools could sort out the majority of problems.

Cyclists are great 'bodgers' and are endlessly swapping tips designed to keep you going – for example, one solution to a flat tyre is simply to stuff it with grass!

The short isthmus across Langeland consisted of a series of undulating poppy fields and we stopped for lunch in the largest of these for some 'Monet' style family photos. I have never seen poppies like these. A sea of waving red stretched away into the distance and on the skyline could be seen a series of prehistoric burial mounds for which the island is famous. No wonder ancient man populated these islands so prolifically all those years ago. The climate is mild, the land rich and easy to farm, and the sea a source of sustenance as well as a means of travel.

The ferry from Spodsberg on Langeland to Tars on Lolland crosses the wide Langelandsbaelt, which looked to us as wide as the English Channel and unusually for Denmark, was devoid of any smaller islands. The journey was somewhat enlivened halfway across by the realisation that Krister had left his helmet behind on a café table. Poor little chap, he really had a dressing down. The most difficult part of our journey still lay ahead, and he would have no protection at all. It was also bright orange and made him highly conspicuous.

"You're HOPELESS, you're ALL HOPELESS," I fumed, widening the target of my wrath. "Didn't anyone see it? Alexander don't you ever see anything?"

"Sorry," sighed Alexander resignedly, "sorry for losing Krister's hat; it's all my fault. Everything's always my fault, it's never anyone else's. Just blame me for everything."

'Grumbleweed' was our pet name for Alexander and how appropriate it was as he mumbled on in a similar vein for several minutes. Oliver stared moodily at the table while Anna, in the face of the first family tiff so far, seemed to have a resurrected desire to go home.

"God this is awful," she proclaimed in dramatic tones. "I don't think I can stand much more of this."

Peter, as usual, was trying to make the best of things and at that moment was adjusting the straps on MY hat to see if it fitted Krister.

"Well that's a bit of luck," he exclaimed as he made some final alterations. "That'll do him nicely – what do you think?"

You can well imagine what I thought, but let's leave it at that. What I did was to speak to a very nice lady in the ship's cafeteria who quickly managed to contact Spodsberg on the radio telephone.

"Yes they had found the hat and yes they would send it over on the next boat – delighted to, no problem."

Honestly, what would my family do without me? The enforced wait for the 'hat' was quite pleasant – we weren't in any rush – and spent the time watching the ships come and go over a shimmering sea. As the ramp came down on the third one to arrive, a pretty blonde waitress complete with pinafore emerged waving Krister's hat and he went up rather sheepishly to retrieve it. Perhaps we had over-reacted after all – on the scale of disasters it was barely worth a rating.

The main road from Tars to Nakskov was noticeable for its complete lack of traffic, until we realised that this was due to the sporadic nature of the ferry timetable. Our campsite was on the far side of the town near the sea and the tents were sited under the low, sweeping branches of a large willow tree. I had bought two tins of minced steak in gravy and these with fresh peppers, onions and tomatoes cooked on our petrol stove made the basis of a very tasty stew which we ate with rice from the supply in Alexander's panniers. Strawberries for dessert from a little man who came round the site with a basketful – who could want more?

After supper, our statutory evening walk brought us to a bathing pontoon which, because of the shallowness of the water, must have been at least three hundred yards long. All along it were graphic signs portraying the perils of diving – a very wise precaution in the circumstances. At the end of the pontoon, surrounded by water and marsh birds of all descriptions, we watched yet another glorious sunset.

Stopping by the harbour in Nakskov the next day, I went off to do our usual shopping while Peter looked after the bikes. To his horror, I returned carrying, as well as bread, bottles of fizz and fruit, a plastic washing up bowl and a large plastic sieve.

"You must be mad," he moaned "We can't possibly carry those – what on earth do you want them for?"

To be honest I didn't know, I just had a hunch that they would come in useful and since everyone else refused to have them, I strapped them to the back of my bike thus enhancing my appearance as a travelling tinker.

Passing the tall spire of St Nicholas Church, where a Swedish cannonball fired in 1659 is still lodged, we followed a long, flat, straight road towards Maribo. It was only twenty miles and soon we were cycling past the pastel-coloured cottages of this delightful little town set on the northern edge of a large freshwater lake. Our campsite was also on the lake and since it was another baking hot day, we were soon swimming among the reeds looking across at Maribo's fifteenth-century red-brick cathedral.

It was still early, so leaving Anna washing her hair and Krister collecting fossils, the rest of us set off with the intention of cycling around the lake.

We, or rather Peter, misjudged this, not only the distance, which turned out to be nearly thirty miles, but also the track, which after a promising start, deteriorated to a boggy footpath. I don't know what it is about Peter, but unless he finds mud in large quantities on our various expeditions, he's simply not fulfilled. I think he would have persisted on this occasion had he not disturbed a Danish bird watcher who complete with bobble hat, anorak (it must have been 35 degrees) and binoculars was trying to quietly observe the shoreline.

"Excuse me, can we get round this way?" shouted Peter, disturbing a large flock of wading birds in the process, either because of his voice or the lurid nature of his cycling clothes.

"We're a bit lost," he added by way of explanation.

With great self control and betraying hardly any evidence of his true feelings towards us, the kindly Dane directed us back to the road, occasionally peering at the sky in the forlorn hope that some feathered activity might return. Funny people, bird-watchers – odd, but predictably so as if they are adhering to some sort of formula. They all wear glasses as well – must be the strain.

Unable to continue around the lake we explored the town with its half-timbered buildings and striking cathedral before returning home to our tents and another simple supper made memorable by a bottle of ice-cold Riesling from the camp fridge for us and beer for the elder two. It seemed incredible, but tomorrow should see us in Gedser and the end of the Danish stage after only eleven days of very relaxed cycling.

Saturday, 9th July and we cycled the thirty-seven miles from Maribo to Gedser along cyclepaths and quiet country roads under a cloudy sky. Alexander gave us all a nasty shock in the morning by falling badly off his bike for no apparent reason. I think he just lost concentration, but of course would never admit it. Apart from grazes he was unscathed, but his panniers had gaping holes torn in them where tins of chicken and ham had made contact with the road. It was a reminder not to get complacent – a broken wrist or worse would ruin everything. Shortly afterwards we stopped to savour the last of a succession of Danish pastries which had sustained us on our travels. It was definitely the most sticky and tasty of them all. We would miss them over the coming weeks.

At Nykobing, as we were negotiating our way through the town, Peter suddenly stopped us just after we had turned right at a set of traffic lights and in a very serious voice informed us that,

"We have been travelling east for the past eleven days. At this junction we have turned south and will be travelling almost due south for the next eight hundred miles until we reach the Danube."

This took some time to sink in; here we were on the pavement of a busy road in Denmark and Peter was talking about the Danube as though it was around the next bend. Even more surprising, however, was the unanimous feeling that we could do it – it would take time but we could do it. We might just be on bicycles, but given time, great distances are attainable.

As we pedalled down the long peninsula of Falster island towards Gedser, the traffic slowly changed to include a high proportion of German registered cars all with a large 'D' stuck on the back. Perhaps it was an optical illusion but most of the 'D's looked much bigger than the 'DK's we were used to, or any other national sticker come to think of it.

Wherever we looked, there seemed to be huge generators with their propellers swishing round just slowly enough to see, making the most of the prevailing winds which must sweep across this narrow neck of land almost constantly. Alexander, in his never-ending search for the perfect torture, suggested strapping your enemy on to one of these blades for a few hours. The thought of this nearly made Peter sick as he hates any sort of fairground ride.

Nearing Gedser itself, we couldn't help noticing the most appalling smell. It really was indescribably awful and we even noticed the local schoolchildren, who appeared an otherwise hardy breed, wrapping handkerchiefs around their faces as they chattered to each other on the way home. This was odd, since apart from the hankies they seemed to be ignoring it – unlike ours who were going through the usual routine of blaming one another. It wasn't Danish pigs, it wasn't manure and the intensity rose and fell leaving an unpleasant tingling in your nose and throat.

Baffled for the moment, we tried to find our site and for the first time so far our triangle let us down. There was a site yes, but not the spotless rural type we were accustomed to. Daneland, as the huge sign proudly proclaimed, was Denmark's most southerly leisure complex with chalets, shops, restaurants, swimming pool, crazy golf, camping and yes that appalling smell which seemed stronger here than ever. There was an air of dilapidation with peeling paint everywhere and not a hint of grass or flowers on the bare patch of dried earth that served as the camping area.

"This is ghastly," Alexander groaned in a voice made adenoidal by the fact that he was pinching his nose.

"Well, there isn't anywhere else," said Peter wincing as another waft passed over. "I'll go and book in and ask if their sewers need attention."

At reception, the pong was only slightly diminished and again we were surprised that the inevitable blonde beauty manning the word processor didn't seem to notice it, let alone explain it. Peter and Anna put up the tents while the boys made good use of the indoor pool and I wrote up the diary noting that we had so far cycled 263 miles and tomorrow we would be in the old East Germany.

We were faintly depressed in Gedser – partly because of the gloomy nature of the place, partly because we were anxious as to what lay ahead and partly because we had completed what we knew would be the easiest part of the trip. To cheer ourselves up, we went over to Daneland's restaurant at about 6:30 p.m. for our supper. This was decorated in exceedingly bad taste, served nothing but pizzas and was completely deserted.

"Well I think we'll all have pizzas," Peter announced to the young waiter, closing the menu with a flourish. Despite the lack of ambience, it was nice to be sitting at a table and after a few glasses of wine we were feeling positively mellow.

As we were finishing off our meal, a group of young men came in and started to fiddle with the electrical equipment near our table. It didn't take many "Testing 1, 2, 3, 4..."s accompanied by a horrible electrical whine, for us to realise that live music was about to be unleashed. What were we to do? Sneaking out at this stage would be rather obvious but staying put might be even worse. The lead singer, clearly reading our minds, came over and introduced himself before we could effect our escape and discovering we were English, asked for a request.

They were a talented group and played Beatles songs, folk music and the latest Danish pop hits, stopping for a little chat with their sole audience between each one. We applauded enthusiastically and since there was no prospect of anyone else eating, the cook and waiter came out to join us as well. The group called themselves 'The Big Attraction' and only played together in the summer for a week as they all had full time jobs during the rest of the year.

"I'm sorry we're such a small audience," I said during one of their pauses for beer refills.

"Oh don't worry," replied the singer. "You've been marvellous. It's been empty for two nights!"

A contract is a contract. They were paid to play at Daneland for a week and play they would. Before leaving these pleasant fellows, we managed to ascertain two important facts.

Firstly the roads in East Germany were indeed bad and they advised us to stay in Denmark! Secondly the smell still permeating the atmosphere was due to piles of rotting seaweed washed up on the windward side of the peninsula; if you stayed long enough you got used to it we were assured.

We weren't staying.

Chapter 6

Northern Germany

The ferry left at 9 a.m. so it was a bit of a scramble getting packed. Peter had been up making tea at 6:30 when a huge hare the size of a dog, lolloped past within a few feet of him apparently quite unconcerned. During the rush, Ollie announced that his swimming trunks were locked in the swimming pool. Blondy at reception was totally unhelpful so Peter pushed him through a small open window and a few minutes later he emerged triumphantly waving them in the air – sucks to Daneland.

There was already a queue for the boat to Rostock and we started talking to a Danish cyclist with the most clapped-out bike I've ever seen. Everything seemed to be held together with bits of string and his helmet was perched at a peculiar angle at the back of his head exposing a wide expanse of forehead. Panniers that had seen better days bulged with old plastic bags but the final touch was an orange bath towel draped over his saddle drying in the early breeze. He was a harmless, rather lonely chap who was planning a tour of the German Baltic coast before returning to Denmark via Bornholme.

When our turn eventually came at the ticket booth, we were confronted with one of the most unhelpful people I have ever met. She was fiftyish, with blue rinsed hair and glasses – a bit like Dame Edna – and glared at us before we had even opened our mouths. When we asked for six one way tickets to Rostock with bicycles, the glare deepened and she started waving her arms around and muttering in a peculiar combination of German and Danish pointing at her large and very detailed ticket book. With some translation help from our fellow cyclist it became clear that she didn't have the time to write out six individual tickets in the triplicate required by the system.

Any thinking man's solution would be to change the system but no, we were entering the Communist World and had just met one of the Dinosaurs. With a loud:

"Tack sa mycket for din hjalp," to Dame Edna – thank you so much for all your help – accompanied by cheery waves, we pushed the bikes over to the railway station where the tickets were provided with no fuss at all by a helpful Danish girl.

The embarkation area was criss-crossed with railway lines and it appeared that they extended from the quayside on to the car deck.

"Be extremely careful getting the bikes on," warned Peter. "And if I were you, I wouldn't ride."

I wish he had conveyed this piece of advice to the other chap who at this very moment was pedalling his rickety heap down the loading ramp. He must have got his front wheel stuck firmly in the lines to explain the graceful arc his body described in the brief few seconds before regaining contact with the earth, followed shortly afterwards by his bath towel which fluttered down like a parachute. He lay there, unable to move, with his legs entwined in the frame, while the cars behind him edged forward judging whether they could get past without running him over. I don't think they would have cared either way – our opinion of car drivers, not high to start with, was rapidly reaching new depths. Leaving my bike, and glaring at the cars, I ran over to help.

Amazingly he hadn't broken anything and like all true cycle tourists, his first concern was for his machine which he inspected with an expert eye. His mudguard had come adrift, but producing yet another piece of string from his pocket, this was soon repaired and we continued our process of embarkation with Peter having to manhandle the trailer through the ruts. Hardly had we completed this, than the reason for them became apparent as an entire passenger train clanked onboard marked "Copenhagen-Chemnitz" – giving a new meaning to the expression Boat-Train.

The ship itself was rather spartan, quite different from the cross channel ferries we knew so well, and appeared to be run by an East German company. We were intrigued by the other passengers, most of whom seemed to come from Poland or Russia and even further east and whose sole *raison d'être* was to load as much beer as possible into a bizarre array of bags. Some had even gone to the trouble of bringing luggage trolleys and one pot-bellied individual was taking large gulps from an open can as he attempted to secure the remainder with elastic straps. He was helped in his labours by his enormous wife and podgy son who appeared to be just as enthusiastic and even suggested buying another crate to add to the already tottering pile. This proved impossible, so they had no option but to sit out on deck and drink it, belching loudly in the process. They weren't alone in this and it was obvious that the Sunday ferry to Gedser provided the inhabitants of Rostock with a perfect day out.

The crossing was sunny and calm taking about two hours. We bought bars of chocolate and a small scale map of Europe from the shop, and spent the voyage tracing out our route so far and gauging what was to come. All the seats were occupied with determined drinkers so Peter nipped down to the car deck and returned with our foam rolls. Having an overview proved to be very useful and every evening for the remainder of our journey we would ritually place a dot on this map indicating the day's travel. This was usually only 1-2cms from the last dot but even so it was quite amazing how rapidly the line joining them up moved along showing our progress. 'The Map' is now framed and has pride of place in our dining room where it is in a perfect position to impress our guests!

Large navigational buoys appeared on the port side and soon the cranes and derricks of Rostock were visible on the horizon. Rostock lies some way up a river, and to avoid cycling through it we disembarked at Warnemunde on the coast. There are many 'mundes' (mouths of rivers) on the Baltic coast, the most famous being Peenemunde where Hitler's V2 rocket factory was situated before being destroyed by the RAF. The port was run down and tatty, with weeds growing through the paving slabs and railway lines going in every conceivable direction. Expecting the 'third degree' we had our passports ready, but to our surprise walked straight out of the main gates without being stopped – only a few years previously this would have been unthinkable.

The traffic was awful, with the ubiquitous Trabant car sounding like a lawn mower and producing clouds of smoke from its exhaust. Carefully avoiding the potholes and making sure we were all ready, Peter launched us into the maelstrom following the signs to Bad Doberan. There weren't many and the few shiny black and yellow ones we did see had obviously been put there since reunification. By heading west however, we found the coast road which was thronged with holiday makers wearing bathing suits designed circa 1950 – the sandy beaches of the Baltic coast, along with those of the Black Sea, constituted the Communist playground for fifty years and old habits were dying hard.

The main evidence of Westernisation were hundreds of 'Coke' signs – there was hardly a shop or even a building without one. This held true in Czechoslovakia and Hungary as well. All the hopes and aspirations of the Iron Curtain peoples were now expressed in a dark fizzy drink that apparently rotted teeth – well most teeth around here seemed to be rotted anyway so perhaps it didn't matter. We stopped to fill our water bottles at a garage notable for the fact that every one of its brand new double glazed windows was smashed and swastikas were daubed on the doors. Oh dear oh dear. We had heard that Rostock was a neo-nazi stronghold and here was the evidence. So far we weren't too impressed with East Germany and it wasn't long before Anna was voicing what we were all beginning to think.

"This is ghastly – why don't we turn round and go back to Denmark?"

Denmark had indeed been easy and there was so much of it that we hadn't seen. We could take the ferry back to Gedser and cycle to Copenhagen and then down the whole length of Jutland back to Esbjerg – it even sorted out how we were going to get home. There is a ghastly American saying, "No pain, no gain," which on this occasion summed up the situation nicely. If we had simply wanted an easy time, we could have found a beach in Denmark and stayed there, but the whole point of this journey would have been lost.

We were unanimous in our determination to press on as we turned west once again and continued our journey.

Bad Doberan was formerly the summer residence of the Dukes of Mecklenburg and still retained an air of faded grandeur. In the centre of this neo-classical town we found a lovely landscaped park complete with two Chinese pavilions built in 1810. Our bicycles attracted considerable attention and we kept a close eye on them as we sprawled on the grass eating lunch. The spirit of free enterprise was much in evidence with many stalls selling anything from vegetables to computer games which Alexander gleefully informed us "were ancient". Leaving the children to look after everything, Peter and I went shopping for supper. We couldn't find a single food shop, or any other shops for that matter, so we returned to try and get something from the free enterprisers.

We had noticed 'tramlines' in the road but were quite unprepared for the sight which greeted us around the next bend. Puffing incongruously up the middle of the high street, with little Trabants dodging about it like pilot fish, was an enormous steam locomotive complete with tender and carriages. Nobody else gave it a second glance, but we were left rubbing our eyes in disbelief as it disappeared up the hill. Back at the park, we noticed some mouth-watering chickens roasting on a spit for six marks, but decided with regret that we had no room, so settled for fresh salad vegetables instead.

A long uphill drag from the town led to quiet rolling countryside and we made good time. Most place names ended in 'OW' – Gorow, Bolkow, Luckow – all small villages where nothing appeared to have changed since the war. Farmers still used carts pulled by horses and there were no signs of any shops, let alone Chinese takeaways. In Luckow we stopped in the grounds of a beautiful Schloss, and wondered who had once lived there. A VW Golf was parked outside the elegant portico – was this a descendant of the Count come to claim his inheritance, or was it the new owner from the west having bought it for a song?

The roads initially weren't too bad, but deteriorated as the day wore on. The main problem lay in the fact that over many years the tar had migrated to the edges where it was tucked up in petrified waves of asphalt. Since this was precisely where we wanted to cycle, life became bumpy, slow and tiring. It had been a long thirty-five miles by the time we arrived at Butzow looking forward to a pleasant campsite and hot showers. Unfortunately there was neither. The town was practically deserted with the odd spire sticking up here and there and entirely cobbled like something out of The Brothers Grimm. No camping signs and very few shops – just the odd cat wandering around. Two farm workers appeared and Peter went over to ask for help.

"Camping Platz bitte?" was rewarded by a "Nein," accompanied by a shake of the head. The little red triangle on our map lay just to the north of the church, so to make absolutely sure there was nothing here, Peter unhitched the trailer and shot off on his bike to search more thoroughly, his wheels juddering on the cobbles as he went. Unbelievably he found it, tucked behind the town on a lake with only one small hand-written sign announcing its presence and our faith in the maps restored, we followed him there through a succession of medieval side streets.

Camping Butzow was a patch of grass by the side of a beautiful lake. Nobody else was here and the caretaker, who also looked after the adjacent sports field, looked surprised to see us. He spoke not a word of English, which wasn't his fault, but Peter only had four words of German, three of which have appeared above. The fourth was "Dusche?" or better still "Varm Dusche?" to which our friend excitedly said "Ja Ja," and beckoned us over to the fence.

A long length of garden hose lay coiled many times on the top of an oil drum in the sun and ended in a sprinkler attachment nailed to a fence post. "Varm Dusche, Ja ja," he repeated several times accompanied by vigorous washing movements. Well, it had the merit of simplicity and at least it didn't need a token – the problem was that it didn't have a door or any walls for that matter. Oh well, who cares and I was filthy, so when he disappeared I stripped off completely and managed a tepid wash in the fresh air, peering around furtively to see if anyone was looking. I couldn't persuade anybody else, so I started making our supper of tinned ham and the salad purchased earlier. I also hard-boiled an egg each and with a packet of buttered crispbread and tinned fruit for dessert, we did rather well.

Right on cue our friend reappeared when we had finished and started off with his "Varm Dusche" routine again, but this time pointing at a building on the other side of the playing field. After a mime involving igniting something with matches, tracing an hour on his watch followed by the his now familiar washing movements, we gathered that he was going to light the boiler in the sports pavilion so we could have proper showers. He was genuinely trying to help and we were touched that he cared about us. Off he went and a few minutes later clouds of black smoke came pouring out of the chimney signalling success with the boiler.

An hour later we trudged across the playing field carrying our towels, soap and shampoo, dreaming of luxurious tiled shower cubicles, gleaming taps, bright fluorescent lighting and a never ending supply of hot water. The hot water we had, but the rest...! It had been built at least sixty years ago and nothing had changed. A dark corridor lined with sports trophies of ages past and faded musty photographs led to 'the shower room'. This had a stone floor, stone sinks and a huge stone trough above which were suspended about twenty sprinkler heads each with its own chain to turn it on. Everything was dark and brown, although whether from dirt or simply age was hard to tell. Peter lent over and gave one of the chains a tentative pull – nothing happened, so he tried fiddling with an impressive array of valves and taps sticking out of the mass of pipework on the wall. It looked rather like the engine room of a ship and I half expected the command "full ahead both" to come booming down a voice pipe, as water began to hiss and leak and rattle.

After much trial and error, we got most of the sprinklers working, stripped off and gingerly stepped into the spray which was gurgling away down a drain the size of a manhole. For an instant, seeing us all standing naked beneath these huge shower heads in this dark gloomy place, gave me a ghastly vision of what the gas chambers must have been like. It was so vivid and the odd thing was that Peter felt exactly the same – we had just seen the film *Schindler's List* so perhaps that explains it. Shaking these morbid thoughts away, we concentrated on getting the day's dirt out of our hair and then drying ourselves with the skimpy towels we had brought without dropping our clothes on the floor. Somehow the steam and heat had improved the depressing atmosphere and we were much more cheerful getting dressed. I think being really clean lifts your spirits anyway.

The lake and surrounding reed beds were bathed in a limpid, golden evening light by the time we returned to the tents and we spent the dusk watching the bird life returning to the water whilst we sipped hot mugs of coffee.

Six a.m. and we were awoken by the sound of a metallic hammering, just outside the tent flap. Poking sleepy heads out, the source was identified as a man marking out the playing field into running lanes. He was joined shortly afterwards by others carrying tables, numbers, javelins and all the other necessary paraphernalia of a major athletics meeting. By 7 a.m. competition had commenced and most of the town's schoolchildren seemed to be participating. What was surprising, apart from the early hour, was the intense enthusiasm shown by everyone – children, teachers, judges, spectators were giving their all and having the time of their lives. No wonder that East Germany's record of achievement in the Olympics is so high.

Word about us soon spread and it wasn't long before a man with a group of younger children came over to talk. He was the English master and was delighted to be able to converse with the first English people he had ever met. He had never been to our country but his accent and grammar were excellent, picked up no doubt mainly from illicit radio and television programmes. He was fascinated with our trip and explained everything to his class, who looked at us and the trailer with wide-eyed astonishment. None of them it appeared, had ever been abroad. In return, he told us about life under the

Communists and how it had altered since reunification. The main change it seemed, was unemployment – originally non-existent, but which now had increased alarmingly as 'market forces' took over.

"Mainly it is the officials and soldiers," he said with a smile. "Whilst wearing a uniform we thought they were so important, but now without it we can see how ordinary they are."

He was very pro-West and optimistic about the future, perhaps because of his job. Others we met were much more cautious about the impact of capitalism and as we waved our goodbyes I secretly wondered for how many more years the friendly citizens of Butzow would be holding their annual sports day with such a sense of communal fun.

The bumpy cobbled streets of the town made it impossible to cycle, especially with the trailer which lurched alarmingly from side to side, so we walked to the shops passing what must once have been a beautiful church but which now was almost derelict. We saw this time and time again in East Germany – a lasting legacy of a system that virtually outlawed religion. There must be thousands of churches awaiting restoration – it's bad enough back home without the persecution. Loaded with bread and yet more chocolate spread, we followed the road and railway which lay beside the river Warnow towards the town of the same name, since our preferred route south, according to our friendly schoolmaster, was blocked. Road quality was rapidly assuming great importance and Peter would often shout from the front,

"Looks okay for the next mile," or "Mind that pothole," or worst of all, "Patch of cobbles ahead."

Cobbles came in two sorts; big and small. Big cobbles were impossible to ride on since their size allowed the bicycle wheel to follow every undulation, shaking machine and rider into a jibbering wreck. Small cobbles were better, since the wheel was too big to fit between them and if taken slowly were just bearable. Virtually all the towns and villages we passed through were cobbled, while the roads connecting them had an ancient tar surface of a quality varying from poor to awful.

Going through the village of Lubzin we came across a gang of road workers trying to patch a particularly bad stretch. The odd thing was that they were all women and wet with perspiration they leant on their pickaxes and shovels gazing at us as we passed. They obviously hadn't been very successful in their endeavours since shortly afterwards the road became so bad that we had to get off and push. Large uneven cobbles with great depressions here and there, bordered by an overgrown hedge, extended as far as the eye could see. Oliver, initially trying to ride, shook loose our precious bottle of 7 UP from his rack and it crashed to the ground splitting open, spraying us all with the sticky fluid.

One after the other we plodded along, praying for a piece of tarmac and meanwhile being attacked by every horsefly in Germany, presumably attracted by a mixture of sweat and sugar. The heat was unbearable and every so often a truck, seemingly unaffected by the road surface, would roar past leaving a thick pall of dust behind it which quickly found its way into our eyes and mouths. Alexander was leading the way with Peter some way behind the rest of us, manhandling the trailer over the worst of the bumps. This lasted for nearly an hour, and when Alexander suddenly shouted "I can see a proper road!", we all experienced the sort of emotion that Columbus' crew must have felt when discovering the New World.

We were now entering the Mecklenburg Lake District and from here to Berlin would pass a succession of small lakes and ponds lying in a generally flat, sandy landscape, separated by forests and fields. We had been told not to expect too much from the North German plain but in fact it was very pretty with the glint of bright light on water wherever you looked. The evening sunsets were often spectacular with lovely colours reflected in the still surface of whichever lake we happened to be camping beside.

After thirty tortuous miles which seemed more like sixty, we arrived at Golberg finding the lakeside site without difficulty and immediately consumed bottle after bottle of deliciously cold water from the nearest tap. Peter poured a couple over his head and beamed with pleasure as the water soaked his shirt and shorts. Clothes bags from the trailer were quickly unloaded, bathing trunks found and the boys were soon running to the bathing jetty already festooned with local children. A drab grey concrete building near the lake served as the town's bathing centre and through an open window at one end an old lady was selling a limited range of sweets and ice creams. Again, we couldn't help feeling that it looked all rather 1930s in its simplicity – the Dutch had yet to find this place, but give them time.

The water was warm but rather cloudy with the stirred up silt from the bottom swirling around making it impossible to see your feet; a feeling I have never liked in case of lurking evils. The children seemed unaffected by such thoughts and spent a happy few hours swimming and diving in waters untroubled by the usual hordes of windsurfers and jet-skis to be found in the west. However, the site was obviously preparing for a tourist invasion, for it had installed a new green Portakabin complete with toilet, hot shower and basin which originated from a firm in Munich. Plumbed into local water, electricity and drainage this provided a welcome change from the usual facilities in this part of the world and also enabled me to do some washing in my little red bowl which, even Peter was forced to admit, had proved invaluable.

Just as dusk was gathering and our thoughts were turning to bed, a large BMW motorcycle growled down the track in front of our tents, its headlight wavering, coming to a halt just opposite them. On it were a young couple dressed in identical black leather suits with matching boots and black mirrored helmets, looking as if they were about to audition for a part in *Knightrider* (if you haven't seen it, don't bother). We didn't need to look at their number plate to know they were Swiss. The wealthy youth of Switzerland spend the summer roaring all over Europe on expensive, gleaming, brand new machines with enormous back tyres, often in groups and always with the finest camping equipment.

We sat on our mats and watched with interest as the girl peeled herself out of her suit (Peter was especially enthralled) before unclipping the beautifully made rigid panniers and extracting a tiny tent from one of them. Her 'other half' put this up while she sorted out the clothes and sleeping bags in the other one. Peter was delighted to see that their stove and mats were the same as ours but had to admit defeat with everything else. Our pitch looked like a shanty town in comparison with theirs, but then I suppose there were six of us.

Lying in the tent that night we asked each other what we missed most of all. For Anna it was her friends, for Alexander his pet lizards, for Krister our cat Whisky and for Ollie his rabbit Thumper. For Mum and Dad there was no doubt it was a decent pillow – strange how children have yet to develop this kind of sensible attitude, putting ridiculous things like friends and pets above everything else.

We had to pack up in the shade of a tree the following day, since it was blisteringly hot by 9 a.m. When we were moving it wasn't too bad, as a cooling breeze would be generated by our speed, but standing still was purgatory. A family conference before we departed unanimously voted for sticking to main roads in an attempt to avoid cobbles and potholes, so keeping the Goldberger Sea on our left, we headed east towards Karow and Mirow.

The surface on the initial stretch of road had only just been laid, the jet black tarmac contrasting with the brilliant white paint of the markings. It was wonderful and we purred along through sandy soiled pine forests managing an average 11mph. Unfortunately the accompanying traffic was managing an average 60mph and being overtaken by a huge heavy goods lorry towing a similar sized trailer was a frightening experience. Imagining what would happen if we were hit by one of these monsters was made easier by the profusion of dead animals lying by the side of the road, precisely where we were cycling. Dogs, cats, badgers and innumerable hedgehogs stared up at us with lifeless eyes out of a gory mess of a body.

"Zander. ZAAANDS. Did you see that Zands?" Ollie would shout, turning round to Alexander as he spoke and wobbling in the process. "That was GROSS, that was really YUCK you could see all its GUTS hanging out. Ugh."

We had to be careful of the hedgehogs as Peter was sure we'd get a puncture if we ran over them, but his warnings in this regard fell on deaf ears as far as the boys were concerned who proceeded to run over every hedgehog spine they could find. The animal carnage on roads has to be seen to be believed and the hundreds of corpses we saw during the remainder of our journey strongly reinforced our growing aversion to the internal combustion engine. Cars and lorries are ruining the environment and it made us especially depressed to see how possession of a large, usually West German, car was considered to be the most important symbol of prosperity. Outside rundown, scruffy looking houses or flats, would be parked shining new Audis or even Mercedes and if the owner was really well off (or more likely a crook) there might be a satellite dish perched on the roof, its saucer sucking in the detritus of Western civilisation.

I suppose that being starved of such essentials for fifty years alters one's judgement, but nevertheless I didn't envy these people the materialistic future that awaited them, targets of every multi-national company in existence. Isn't it incredible how Britain's economic success or lack of it is gauged by how many hundreds of thousands of cars it can sell, despite their terrible impact on our lives.

It became a little quieter after the medieval walled town of Plau where we stopped for some well-earned ice-creams in the local petrol station. Continuing eastward we spent the hottest part of the day having lunch in the shade of a copse of trees and it wasn't until late that afternoon that we crossed the Rostock-Berlin autobahn, thrilled to see our first sign to Germany's capital 120km away.

After fifty-three miles, a record for the entire trip, we wearily pedalled into a campsite just to the north of Mirow to find it full of hippies and weirdoes drinking copious amounts of beer. Peter needed no further persuasion on this occasion and led the retreat through the deep, soft sand to the road. An hour later we were desperately tired and losing our collective sense of humour, as he led us along mile after mile of cobbled roads looking for another elusive campsite. We gave up at one point and tried to get a room in an expensive hotel, but it was run by a close relative of Dame Edna from Gedser (it rhymes) and we were soon sent packing with,

"Nicht zimmer, nicht zimmer," ringing in our ears.

Eventually I hit upon the brilliant idea of asking someone – Peter will only rarely do this, as to him it is an admission of complete failure in his map-reading abilities and results in that Oriental disaster 'loss of face'. Five minutes later we were putting up our tents on the deserted municipal 'zelt platz', by the side of yet another lovely lake.

Unfortunately, it didn't stay deserted for very long, as a huge party of schoolchildren complete with canoes and rowing eights proceeded to pitch their tents all around us until we resembled a Bedouin encampment. I had noticed a restaurant built of the ubiquitous grey 1930s concrete close to the site, the only sign of decoration being some jolly umbrellas shading the dining tables on a balcony overlooking the lake, and too tired to contemplate cooking, we had a quick wash and went over for our first meal out in Germany. The menu was extensive but not surprisingly was written in German and we were unable to understand a word. The waitress and the adjoining table of young couples tried to help, but since until four years ago the official second language in Mirow was Russian, they had to resort to miming various animal noises in an effort to describe the meat dishes. For Anna, a near vegetarian, this was too much and watching our neighbour in the middle of his second pig impersonation with a look of acute distaste on her face she announced,

"I can't possibly eat any meat – eating meat is DISGUSTING."

Finding a meatless dish in Germany is like asking a bunch of cannibals to dine off rice pudding – the Germans love meat and seem to relish any part of any animal. The bits not immediately consumed are simply turned into a vast array of lurid sausages which consist largely of blood and gristle.

"What about some fish?" Peter suggested. "There's something here called Fiske – I bet that's a fish."

Sinuous movements of the waitress's hand confirmed that this indeed was the case and Anna, probably visualising cod in a crispy batter with golden chips, agreed to give it a try. The rest of us settling for a mixture of schnitzels and steaks, leant back in our chairs, drank our beer and watched the fattest man we had ever seen diving into the lake from the little jetty just below the balcony.

To say he was ungainly would have been a compliment – his run started some distance from the water and he would then hurl himself into the air, arms and legs outstretched like a free-fall parachutist, before landing abdomen first in a huge plume of spray. It looked decidedly painful, but completely unaffected he would clamber out like some prehistoric reptile before repeating the process.

Eventually our meals arrived and we reluctantly had to tear ourselves away from this entertainment to console Anna, whose supper consisted of a huge fish lying on its side with a baleful eye staring up at her. It looked as though it had been just caught, garnished with a few lettuce leaves and put on a plate, rather like those still-life arrangements so beloved of eighteenth-century oil painters. Anna's colour drained while the boys chortled and pointed:

"Are you going to eat the eye first or save it?", "Didn't it move just then?"

Poor Anna; we were all starving after the long day but even I, who love fish, couldn't have managed this. Peter came to the rescue by removing the offending object and taking all the fish off the bone while we all made contributions to her plate with potatoes and vegetables – team spirit was still strong.

Amends were made with the biggest ice-creams we had ever seen, stuffed with fresh fruit and covered in chocolate, followed by strong coffee made the Turkish way with the dregs still at the bottom.

The night that followed this pleasant interlude however could only be described as 'disturbed'. It started at 11 p.m. when Peter realised that Anna still hadn't returned from cleaning her teeth an hour ago. Putting his jacket on over his pyjamas, he got out of the tent to investigate, eventually finding her 'getting to know' a young German boy behind the showers, all memories of supper having obviously disappeared. It must be hard trying to form relationships when your Dad suddenly appears in his pyjamas shouting:

"WILL YOU GET INTO BED?!"

I really do sympathise. I also sympathise with anybody who has ever had to put up with an enforced 'sing-a-long' which on this occasion meant us. The sound of a guitar tuning up depresses me enormously – the longer the tuning the worse is the playing and tonight's tuning took a very long time indeed.

The opening number 'Michael Row the Boat Ashore' had me reaching for the cotton wool – I've never liked it and the moronic nature of the words seemed to be accentuated by the guitarist who could only play two chords. The assembled chorus however, sitting around a blazing campfire in the best boyscout tradition, thought they were marvellous and after a bout of self-congratulatory applause, sang it all the way through again. So it went on until 3 or 4 a.m. with mainly 1960s pop songs repeated at least twice and sometimes more, accompanied by those two chords... plunk plunk plunk, plonk plonk plonk, plunk plunk plunk.

The fact that Peter and I knew most of them made it worse, since we found ourselves lying on our backs, staring up at the roof of the tent, mouthing each line as it came. It was simply impossible to ignore it all as 'background noise' so with aching, twitching legs we endured it stoically until their repertoire had been exhausted.

The next morning, our vocalists were up early, loading their boats with tents and provisions prior to the next stage of their journey through the myriad of interconnecting lakes and waterways which are a feature of this part of Germany. We wondered where they would find their next hapless audience. Actually I'm being rather unfair – they were having a simple, healthy, open air holiday and enjoying it with innocent, youthful high spirits. They weren't fighting each other, or being sick, or terrorising the locals as I suspect our compatriots were doing at that very moment in Spain and Greece – another triumph of capitalism I don't think.

The clear blue skies with rising temperatures promised another blistering day and partly because of our bad night and partly because we had been cycling for ten days, we decided to stay in this very pleasant spot for at least another twenty-four hours. The children of course had slept like logs and lost no time in leaping into the warm, clear waters of the lake while Peter and I went shopping in Mirow. We were running short of money but had to cycle up and down the main street several times before spotting the bank, which appeared to have no distinguishing features whatsoever.

Inside, we waited with some trepidation to see which form of currency, if any, this particular branch would agree to change. Throughout our travels this remained a problem – we had brought Traveller's cheques, Eurocheques, Eurocards and Visa, but there seemed to be no reliable way of predicting which would be acceptable. As on previous occasions I got them all out and fanning them like a pack of cards, offered them for inspection to the girl sitting behind a computer screen – yes they had arrived here as well, like the cars and satellite dishes.

Traveller's cheques got the thumbs up but only £100 worth were allowed after several telephone calls to head office – at the present rate of expenditure this would last only two days. We returned to the tents laden with fresh brown bread, ham, cheese, fruit, yoghurts and plenty to drink and spent the rest of the day lazing, eating, reading, swimming and sleeping in a patch of shade – luxury. The site was now nearly deserted apart from the odd canoeist, one of whom fascinated us by dismantling his craft and packing it away in a small bag. The canvas skin was held taut by an ingenious wooden frame which came apart in convenient hinged sections. When finished he simply shouldered his rucksack, picked up his canoe bag and walked away.

Another meal at the restaurant (minus the 'fiske') followed by a much better night's sleep and we were ready, dare I say eager, to be on our way. I certainly was, since my back seemed to be stiffening up alarmingly and I was hopeful that a bit of exercise would do the trick.

Our route now lay south again but it took nearly an hour to get out of Mirow since over a mile of cobbles was in the process of being dug up and we had to push. We were back on minor roads again heading towards Rheinsberg and only a few miles away from the chilling railway junction of Ravensbruck, site of a notorious concentration camp just to the north of Berlin.

Crossing the Muritz-Havel Canal, Peter could hardly believe his eyes when the road to Canow became a track of soft sand, some 2ft deep in places and absolutely impossible to cycle on. It was certainly the correct way, with signposts and even the odd car skidding and lurching from side to side, but to call it a road stretched even our credulity. The sand had the consistency of flour and pushing laden bicycles through it was an absolute nightmare, particularly since we were now approaching midday and the heat was stifling. Plod plod plod pause, plod plod plod pause and so on – if you've ever seen the film *Ice Cold in Alex*, you'll get the general idea. I don't think any one of us would have been surprised to see a camel or two.

Oliver, covered in bleeding bites and looking as though he'd been savaged by a rabid dog, finally lost all his stoicism and wailed pitifully. Peter of course had disappeared with the others in his search for civilisation, so I joined Ollie on his mound of sand and wondered, not for the first time, what on earth had possessed us to do this.

We emerged eventually into the oasis of Canow where, just as in the film, we found the nearest bar and ordered long cool drinks – never has a beer tasted so good. Our troubles were far from over, however, for although we were now on a better road, it was so hot that the tar was beginning to melt. It was Alexander who first noticed a peculiar crackling sound coming from his tyres when he ran over certain shiny patches of tar and being Alexander he soon had both his brothers 'crackling' for all they were worth as they searched for the most satisfying bits. The noise was actually caused by tiny bubbles popping in a thin layer of tar as it softened, but by late afternoon our tyres were sticking to the road with a noise like tearing velcro, making progress painful to say the least.

At one point, exhausted by this feeling of cycling through treacle, we stopped for a drink only to find ourselves literally sinking into a black, smelly goo. Too late did we realise that only our broad tyres rotating had kept us 'afloat' and putting our feet down trapped us like flies on flypaper. I'm glad to say that our sense of humour hadn't completely deserted us and for a few minutes we were convulsed with the sight of various members of the family vainly trying to escape, trailing long strands of tar behind them. In a shady spot, we had to wait for it to cool before Peter attempted to clean it all off with the aid of a lethal looking knife which he kept strapped to his crossbar "in case of emergencies" as he put it – he wasn't very successful.

After the hardest day so far we crawled into Lindow and booked into a very busy site by the side of yet another lake. The Berliner's holidays had obviously started and this area of forests and lakes was a traditional and popular destination. Swims were followed by the best showers yet – instead of tokens you paid for the entire shower head on the end of a piece of hosepipe, which entitled you to hot water for as long as you wanted it. You could even book the shower head at a particular time rather like a squash court, so you could be certain of a wash – amazing what a bit of lateral thinking will do to an almost universal problem. The site owners were very helpful and even tried to book us into a Youth Hostel in Potsdam which we hoped would be our next stop. Unfortunately, although it had eight hundred beds, it was solidly booked up for the entire summer – no doubt by well-off, middle-aged tourists travelling by car.

Thank God the next day dawned cloudy, for even though we were all now as brown as berries, the combination of bad roads and intense heat was truly exhausting. However, we made good time on reasonably good surfaces and our spirits were lifted near Kremmen by seeing the first GB plate since leaving Esbjerg seventeen days before. The driver turned out to be Welsh and from his haircut we guessed he was in the Army – the trailer had a large CWM on the back and a Welsh Dragon on the front so he was delighted. Also near Kremmen we saw a huge Red Army War Memorial with its five pointed red star perched on the top but showing signs of neglect with peeling paint and weeds growing through – I wonder if it will still be there in a few years, somehow I doubt it. The countryside looked so peaceful now that it was hard to visualise the desperate fighting that must have occurred in 1945 as the Russians advanced from the east.

Our plan was to avoid the centre of Berlin and loop around to the west aiming for Potsdam. This unfortunately meant using a major and very busy ring road to Nauen, which went for mile after mile through dense pine forests. By 5 p.m. we had already travelled over forty miles and tired of the dense traffic, gave up all hope of making Potsdam that evening and instead headed for Ketzin where a campsite was marked on our map. This took nearly an hour to find, as it was situated at the end of an inevitable sandy lane, and there wasn't a single signpost to advertise its presence. The site was spacious and nearly empty but even so, the Warden insisted on escorting us to our pitch which turned out to be a few square yards of sand next to the play area. My back was playing up again and this probably explains my entry in the diary that evening.

"Is this a holiday I ask myself? I think it's sheer, bloody, hard, work!"

It proved to be a prophetic remark, for on waking the next morning I found that my back had seized up completely and I was totally unable to move. My lower back had been fused with steel screws twenty years previously because of a congenital problem and the constant jolting on bad roads over the past few days had sent it into spasm. This was very bad news indeed as two previous episodes had seen me in hospital on traction for at least two weeks followed by a few months in a plaster jacket.

It seemed that our GREAT IDEA had come to an abrupt and premature end.

Chapter 7

Potsdam, Berlin and Southern Germany

I'm not normally a religious person but the help we received that July morning could only have been sent from Heaven itself. As I lay in terrible pain, unable even to stand up, Peter busied himself with packing up and sorting out the tents, trying to believe I'm sure that this wasn't really happening to him. A hefty dose of Brufen got me into a sitting position but walking, let alone riding a bicycle was out of the question.

"Why oh why can't I have a healthy wife?" moaned Peter, who knew only too well what the implications were – he had spent many a happy hour in hospital with me.

"Well at least we're near Berlin," he continued in an effort to make me feel guilty. "The medical facilities are really good here and it's so convenient for getting a flight home."

The children had sensed all was not well and drifted off to await developments – Anna I think was secretly hoping that this might provide a rapid return to her one and only Duncan and appeared cheerful for the first time in several days.

While sitting in that awkward position so typical of back sufferers – legs out straight, buttocks turned to one side and my weight supported on my hands – a middle aged lady came across from a nearby caravan and although she spoke virtually no English, seemed to understand my problem instantly. Presently she was joined by her husband and after much discussion in rapid German gave me a box containing six tablets indicating that I should take one in a glass of water. Walter and Lieselotte Wulfrath were from Cologne and like us, visiting Potsdam and Berlin for the first time. Walter had a back problem and so they never travelled without his pills, but since Peter had tried every painkiller known to man over the years in an effort to sort me out (failing miserably in the process) he wasn't particularly optimistic.

"I've never heard of Piroxicam before," he confided, "but give it a go if you think it'll make these two happy – they might even leave us alone then."

Happily for me they did not leave us alone, but continued whispering to each other and giving me sympathetic glances from time to time.

"Vi tink zat is not possible to go bicycle," announced Walter. "You must go mit us in Auto."

They simply took over and before long I had been helped into the back of a large Mercedes which had my bicycle strapped to its roof while Peter and Walter, with the help of a map, arranged to meet at the Sanssoucci Palace in Potsdam. Off we went, with Peter and the children cycling behind and Walter taking it slowly so as not to jar my back. Potsdam was about fifteen miles away and every so often Walter would stop to make sure the cyclists were still behind. On one occasion he got very excited and pointed out a pair of Storks nesting on the top of a telegraph pole, which he insisted on showing to the children.

It was marvellous to be driven along in luxury and what was more, I believed that I could feel my back slowly beginning to relax with the pain subtly ebbing away. Far from dropping me off in the town centre, this lovely couple insisted on finding us a cheap hotel where I could rest and recover. This took some doing in what was probably the busiest week of the year, but of course they managed it and by midday Walter was shepherding the family into the car park of the Hotel Herberge in Neu Fahrland just to the North of the Sanssoucci Palace. Only when they had explained our problem to a very helpful hotel manager, made sure of our rooms and established that we were happy with the total daily cost were our saviours prepared to leave us. We had wrecked most of their day but this was waved aside with smiles and the comment,

"Vi haf a boy in England – vi hope if he has need, zen some person vill help him."

I know what he meant, but somehow I didn't feel quite the same optimism as he did, knowing how most people in the UK regarded foreigners. We waved and waved as they drove off and I half wondered if these 'good fairies' of ours would simply disappear around the next bend and vanish into thin air.

The manager, clearly briefed in his task by Walter, saw us up to two very large, basic but clean rooms and then with Peter's help manhandled the bicycles and trailer into an unused ground floor washroom, covering himself with oil in the process.

It was sheer bliss to have so much living space to ourselves after living in tents for so long and the hotel was very quiet, occupying a lovely position on the side of the Wannsee with views of sailing boats, trees and shimmering water. We had lunch on the hotel's patio, after which I took another of Willem's magic pills and lay down for a little while. The boys went off exploring, Anna shaved her legs (a favourite pastime taking at least three hours) and Peter took his back wheel apart in an attempt to replace a spoke broken by the terrible roads of the past few days.

By late afternoon I had improved to an extent I would not have believed possible and not wanting to waste any more time, we set off on the bikes to cycle the four miles to the Sanssoucci Palace. Potsdam was developed in the early 18th century as a garrison town but under Frederick I and II (the 'Great') Royal palaces were built and it became the centre of the Prussian Court. It reminded me of Bath and as we pedalled along, we passed ornamental stone buildings, statues and fountains, now rather grimy with age but giving us a wonderful idea of the grandeur that once had been.

We couldn't have picked a better time to look at the palace since the crowds had gone and the sun was low in the sky, bathing the whole structure in a wonderful light which reflected off the tall elegant windows and the dazzling gilded decoration. It is set on a plateau with beautiful gardens dropping away in a series of terraces linked by a broad but shallow central stone stairway, at the bottom of which are fountains surrounded by busts set on marble pedestals at least twenty feet high. Tree lined avenues leading from the fountains frame distant vistas of yet more palaces in a way that pleases the eye with a marvellous sense of proportion.

We posed by the fountain for a photograph, drinking in these splendid surroundings and absolutely thrilled that we had come five hundred miles to be standing here. The fact that we had done it ourselves somehow heightened our appreciation of this lovely place and set us apart from the other evening visitors. Deciding to return for a more thorough exploration the following day, we left the park with the intention of finding somewhere for supper.

This was harder than it sounds, for Potsdam fell into the eastern zone and outside the palace, which had been restored to its former glory with grants from the west, there was a maze of dilapidated streets lined with once glorious baroque buildings, now sadly crumbling away. Incredibly, more by luck than judgement, in the courtyard of one of these faded mansions we found that an enterprising young couple had set up a restaurant complete with bright decor and an open range, on which the male half of the business was busy creating delicious-looking pizzas. His attractive partner took the orders and within fifteen minutes we were tucking in to a really scrummy meal – our incredible luck seemed to be continuing. But then perhaps it wasn't luck, perhaps it was the fact that with our simple lifestyle we appreciated things that others took for granted.

Unfortunately we couldn't linger as we didn't have any cycle lights and as it was, we had to pedal the last mile back to the hotel through inky blackness hoping that the cars would see us in their headlights – not very clever.

What a wonderful night we had and what luxury to have a pillow again – the first since Faborg. Breakfast was rather stale, in keeping with the hotel's tired and forlorn atmosphere, but the coffee was strong and hot, served in brightly coloured pink and yellow mugs. The morning was spent back at the Sanssoucci walking around the extensive grounds, now crowded with Sunday promenaders and enjoying the various entertainments. These varied from an excellent mime artist dressed in a gold Regency costume and moving like an automaton to the music of Boccherini, to live recitals given by professional instrumentalists.

Meandering slowly along the pink gravelled paths we came across flautists, violinists and even a string trio, all playing beautiful music appropriate to the period of Frederick and often dressed in brocaded coats, breeches and in one case a powdered wig. They certainly evoked an atmosphere of elegance, gaiety and perhaps intrigue, both political and amorous, for no doubt these shaded walks could have told many a tale. Particularly beautiful was the gilded Chinese Teahouse, built when interest in the art of the far East became suddenly fashionable – it looks slightly incongruous now and one can but imagine the impact it made in 1750.

We lunched outside at a pavement café on deep-fried Camembert cheese, salad and fried potatoes (a combination we became especially fond of) before walking through the quaint Dutch quarter with its gabled red brick houses on our way to the Cecilienhof Castle. This famous setting for the Potsdam conference in 1945 is situated in the attractive parkland of the Neuer Garten and was built in 1914 in the style of an English country house with a mock Tudor facade. Even though Churchill and Roosevelt must have felt more at home here than Stalin, they were destined not to stay long and this probably affected the disastrous outcome of the conference, which set the scene for the division of post-war Europe into east and west and the start of the Cold War. Churchill lost the 1945 General Election and was replaced by the ineffectual Attlee, while the ailing Roosevelt died, being replaced by Truman.

The huge conference table is still there, together with the bedrooms and briefing rooms used by the Allied leaders. Perhaps the West's fate had been sealed before the conference even began, for greeting Churchill and Roosevelt as they arrived in July 1945 was a huge circular flower bed planted with the Red Star of Bolshevism – a symbol that was to dominate Potsdam and thousands of other cities trapped behind the Iron Curtain for the next forty-four years. It is still there today.

Walking back through the park, we stopped for ice creams at a little kiosk but quenching our thirst proved expensive when Peter realised that we had been overcharged by six marks (about £2.75). After an argument, the money was reluctantly refunded but it was a warning to be vigilant as we travelled deeper into areas of economic deprivation. Cycling back along the long tree-lined road leading to the hotel, we were amused to see an ancient three-wheeled car passing us being driven by a tiny little man who was sitting next to his enormous wife. Such was the disparity in weight, that the car listed alarmingly to one side as it puttered along emitting clouds of black smoke.

"That looks jolly dangerous," Peter remarked. "Let's hope he goes slowly around the next bend."

Unfortunately, the little man could not hear this piece of advice for on turning the corner, we came across the car on its side in a ditch with the mountainous woman trying to climb out through a window. Neither of them was hurt and it was obvious that this was a fairly frequent occurrence judging by the expert way the "trike" was righted and pushed back on to the road, before puttering off again. Back at the hotel, the manager listened to our day's activities with a friendly smile and laughed when the tricycle tale was retold – these vehicles were apparently once commonplace and indeed, many a working family would dream of owning one.

We had hoped to visit Berlin on the following day and were delighted to be told that a bus went every hour from right outside the front gate – what a convenient spot.

So it was at 9 a.m., that we stood waiting for the bus to Spandau wondering whether or not to take our jackets since the sky was decidedly overcast.

"It will never rain," promised the manager. "It never rains in July."

We of course didn't believe him and spent the rest of the day lugging those wretched coats all over Berlin in temperatures akin to Death Valley.

The journey into Spandau took thirty minutes and we travelled through a succession of fairly drab suburbs before suddenly bursting into 'tinsel town', with expensive shops, advertisements on hoardings and thousands of cars – we had arrived in West Berlin which at first sight appeared indistinguishable from any other European capital. A U-Bahn (underground) station at the bus terminus seemed a better alternative than walking, so we descended into the spotless depths and for no better reason than recognising the name, bought six tickets to Potsdamer Platz.

It couldn't have been a more fortuitous choice, because after a smooth and rapid ride we emerged into what had once been No Man's Land around Check-Point Charlie. It was an absolute wasteland but is destined, I am assured, to become the new political and administrative centre of a united Germany. There, not twenty yards away, stood the 'L' shaped sections of the Berlin Wall still covered with their psychedelic graffiti and looking anything but threatening. Peter gave the children a little discourse on why the city was divided and how the wall was toppled, pointing to the drab East German tenement blocks behind us and the smart West German offices in front.

Krister, being a great collector, immediately wanted to acquire a piece of this history and spent ages poking around in disgusting corners for 'bits of real wall'. These he would bring to Peter with a hopeful look on his face for authentication and in order not to disappoint, approximately half of these were eventually 'passed' as genuine. The poor little chap consequently lugged about two pounds of rubble around with him for the rest of the holiday in his handlebar bag, but the constant bumping reduced them to a fine powder which was eventually lost through a hole in the bottom.

Drinks at a disgusting hamburger stall incongruously situated in the middle of all this had produced in all of us the intense desire to have a pee. Where to go? Peter solved the problem by finding a broad set of steps leading about thirty feet underground and ending in a massive steel door. He was excited because his guidebook gave Potsdamer Platz as the site of Hitler's Bunker and this was obviously part of the recently rediscovered system. Thus it was that the entire Hilton family were able to express their true feelings towards the mighty 3rd Reich in a way that is universally understood. I gather that Churchill, Montgomery and Eisenhower did the same to the Siegfried Line after D Day.

We walked up the old line of the Wall towards the Reichstag and Brandenburg Gate noticing an extraordinary Hippie colony on our right. This was built out of logs in the style of an American Cavalry Fort and had a huge set of entrance gates with towers at each side. It really was most impressive and obviously home to Berlin's growing population of weirdos.

The Brandenburg Gate, forever associated with images of stormtroopers and torchlight processions, was in fact built in 1790 and is surmounted by a huge statue of Victory driving her chariot towards the East, an aspiration not realised since this part of Berlin was just inside the Russian zone. It marks the beginning of the most famous avenue in Germany – the Unter den Linden (under the limes) although none of these trees remain. Clustered around the Gate were little stalls selling the souvenirs of a disintegrating Communist system – Russian Army hats, Naval cap tallies, rank badges, uniforms and the usual nests of dolls – while a brightly dressed Mongolian woman turned the handle of a barrel organ which produced lively Slavonic folk music. Resisting these wares we walked down the Unter den Linden towards the Marx Engels Platz admiring the grand architecture of the public buildings including an ancient underground lavatory where Anna, for some reason, insisted on going into the men's.

Spying a sign declaring "Wurst mit Pommes/Brod – Dm 4.00," Peter joined a short queue, while we sat down at one of the tables and waited for lunch – and waited, and waited.

The kiosk was manned by an enthusiastic but painfully inexperienced mass caterer. He would listen carefully to each order and repeat it constantly to himself as he set about preparing it as though he had never done it before.

"Eine mit brod, zwei mit pommes," he would mutter as he looked around as if deciding where to start. "Eine mit brod, zwei mit pommes," he would repeat before slowly putting three sausages on to an otherwise empty grill; the thought of putting on sufficient to satisfy the ever lengthening queue apparently did not occur to him. "Eine mit brod, ZWEI mit pommes," with emphasis, as a small portion of frozen chips was removed from a freezer and carefully lowered into hot fat.

So it went on until after about fifteen minutes three paper plates would be presented with a flourish to the astonished customer who had been watching the chef's antics like a spectator at a tennis match.

"Ach so, vi haben eine mit brod und zwei mit pommes – danke und auf wiedersehen."

Clutching his meals, the lucky recipient would scurry away while the next hapless person shuffled forward to give his order. Peter was looking more and more agitated, partly because of the wait, but partly at the prospect of ordering "sechs mit pommes", and enduring the hostility of those still waiting behind him.

After an eternity, the food arrived and was demolished in less than five minutes – Alexander even had the nerve to ask for a second helping but one look from Peter was enough.

We continued our stroll towards the 1200ft high television tower which deliberately dominates the skyline of East Berlin. A spectacular eighteenth-century facade on our right, proved on closer examination to consist of a huge painted canvas stretched over scaffolding, thus concealing in a highly original way the construction work going on behind.

Crossing Museum Island we ended up in the spacious Alexanderplatz made oddly claustrophobic by the surrounding unimaginative office buildings. In one corner was the famous World clock made from two enormous horizontal concrete discs supported on a pedestal about fifteen foot high. On one disc were engraved the world's capital cities with a strong bias towards places such as Havana and Kabul, while the other disc rotated above and showed the relative time with large bronze Roman numerals. It was apparently popular as a rendezvous point during the dark days of the Cold War, but it now seemed rather forlorn, without a spy or lover in sight.

Failing miserably to extract any cash from a row of brand new Eurocheque cash dispensers, we bypassed the enormous queue waiting to ascend the television tower and went into a nearby S-Bahn (overground) station to avoid the long walk back to West Berlin. Public Transport in eastern Europe is excellent and for all practical purposes is free – well, you're supposed to buy a ticket but they're jolly hard to find and nobody seems to bother anyway. Peter had tremendous ethical difficulties with this and would spend ages fruitlessly searching for a ticket machine or kiosk. He never found one and consequently would spend the whole journey in a state of nervous tension waiting to be caught – it never bothered me but then nothing like that ever does.

Alighting at 'Tiergarten' we spent an hour or so wandering through these famous gardens, enjoying the flowers and sunshine before sitting down outside a most attractive thatched café for ices and coffees. We could have been in the heart of the countryside and the children watched in fascination as two elderly Fräuleins, complete with feathered Tyrolean hats, fed scores of sparrows with the crumbs from their cakes. There were so many that occasionally they had to shoo them away with a wave of their wrinkled hands. I wondered how long they had been coming here for afternoon tea and what terrible experiences they must have been through when Berlin was just a pile of rubble.

My back was beginning to complain again so we walked slowly towards the commercial centre of West Berlin passing the impressive Victory column and zoological gardens on the way. By this stage I had to sit down again but a round of drinks in the shadow of the Kurfurstendamn church, left in its ruined state as a memorial to World War II, cost us £15 – a sort of memorial to the level of prices we thought we'd left behind. On the way back to Spandau and our bus back to the hotel, Peter managed to persuade a Pharmacy to sell him a box of Walter's magic pills by showing his passport. I now had enough to see me through the rest of Germany and felt much more confident about our chances of finishing this trip despite my back. We had survived the first major hurdle albeit with some help and were all keen to get going again after our enforced but very pleasant rest.

Our washing was clean, the bikes were mended, the trailer was packed and we were in the process of saying goodbye to our friendly, smiling manager who seemed genuinely concerned at the prospect of our launching into the unknown again.

"But ver vill you sleep this nacht?" he asked with a worried look at the children. "I perhaps can find hotel?"

It was difficult to explain that we weren't exactly sure where we were going, let alone how far we would get – booking ahead simply spoilt this freedom and made us worry unnecessarily. He couldn't understand this and we saw him waving after us for a long time as we cycled away towards the centre of Potsdam.

Despite the heavy traffic we negotiated this fairly easily using cycle paths and by mid-morning were well on the way to Treuenbrietzen. The road was long, straight and lined for mile after mile with trees. It was good to be moving again and pleasant, even therapeutic, to let your thoughts drift as your legs moved round mechanically accompanied by the whirring of chain and cogs. The edge of the road on our right, normally marked by a white line, would speed past at about 10mph and as long as you avoided running into the person in front it was possible to almost daydream. When a good pace was set up on a quiet, well-surfaced road, it was incredibly relaxing and nothing would be said for perhaps an hour.

Lunch was taken deep in a still forest with the light filtering through the trees. Foam rolls would be spread out over the pine needles and a large bag of crisps opened to satisfy the children while I started to slice up the large fresh loaf of dark brown bread. This would be buttered and eaten with ham, Marmite, peanut butter or chocolate spread depending on preference. Dessert consisted of fruit and biscuits and perhaps a few sweets if they were lucky. Occasionally we would find cakes but they were nowhere near as good as the Danish ones. The whole lot would be washed down with a two litre bottle of 7-UP and the dirty plates and knives would be packed away into the trailer with the rubbish in a plastic bag under the net, to await the first available bin.

At Treuenbrietzen we turned left towards Juterbog and made use of the longest cycle path encountered so far, extending for at least twenty miles. It would have been absolute bliss, but unfortunately we soon discovered that it was covered with masses of broken glass which littered the path every fifty yards or so. Peter gave up shouting "watch out – glass!" and we simply ploughed through, hoping that our tyres would stand up to it. Not for the first time, we were relieved to have brought mountain bikes with fairly wide wheels – thin touring tyres wouldn't have lasted five minutes in Germany. We never did find out the reason for all this glass but it was a common feature of cycle paths in Eastern Europe. I can only assume that beer drinking car and lorry drivers simply threw their empty bottles on to the paths in gleeful anticipation of the havoc that would ensue. However, I am glad to report that we did not suffer a single puncture due to glass.

It was also on this path that we sustained our first prang, when a little girl, hardly in control of her brand new bicycle, collided with Anna and fell off. I have to say that it was partly Anna's fault, as she had a habit of riding in a daydream in the middle of the road paying no attention whatsoever to the world around her.

At Altes Lager, after thirty-eight miles, we passed an attractive little Gasthof entitled Zum Strammer Max and Peter went in to see if there were any rooms free. Max, who owned this establishment was a larger than life character with a florid red moustache who literally threw himself into the task of making sure our needs were taken care of. Within ten minutes of arriving we had two nice three bedded rooms with hot showers, the bikes were locked in a garage and we were making ourselves coffee from the tray provided – all for £10 each including breakfast.

Surrounding Max's pleasant haven were dilapidated houses that looked almost derelict with broken windows and peeling paint. From the TV aerials sprouting from the roofs we assumed that they were still occupied and indeed I thought I saw a scruffy individual peering out of a window at us. To have a well-maintained, freshly-decorated building in the midst of near squalor was quite a common sight and I suppose represented the triumph of the individual dragging himself up by sheer hard work, while the rest had yet to wake up to the fact that Communism had disappeared and they had to get off their backsides or starve.

Max took our order for dinner in his little bar which as a feature had an enormous artificial tree in one corner, complete with fairy lights and model birds sitting in the branches. He went to enormous lengths to make sure we understood everything and then shot off into the kitchen to help his wife prepare it. Needless to say it was delicious – I'm sure Max will be a millionaire in five years.

It amazes me writing this how often we went for evening walks after hours of cycling – perhaps we just couldn't keep our legs still. This evening was no exception and after dinner we strolled behind the Pension into an area of woodland and open heath. We weren't particularly surprised when we came across a large derelict building with all its windows broken, but our curiosity grew as we found one after the other lining what must have been a big road. Further on, as the trees gave way to sandy heathland there were yet more, but this time they were the size of large hotels.

It was a lost city with doors creaking in the evening breeze and weeds, or even small trees, growing in profusion everywhere seeming to signify the return of nature to this once thriving community. They hadn't just been abandoned but systematically wrecked with every single window broken in an orgy of violence. The answer to our puzzle was provided by a small white stencilled notice low down on the front of one of the barracks – for that is what they were – almost covered with grass. We couldn't read it, for it was in the Cyrillic lettering of Russia but that said it all. We had stumbled on the barracks of the largest Russian Tank Regiment in East Germany, for tank tracks could be seen criss-crossing the flat heathland to the north and dark brown patches in the sandy soil signified where sumps had been drained of their oil.

Krister, poking around for souvenirs as usual, found a Russian Officer's fur hat complete with ear flaps and stood proudly holding it for a photograph, although it was too filthy to contemplate taking with us. Oliver, not to be outdone, found a child's swing made from tubular steel painted with black stipples to look like silver birch bark, no doubt to remind them of home and the shimmering trees of the Russian Steppe rather than the gloomy German Pine forests. The Russians had apparently made no attempt to integrate into the local community which they treated with disdain – so much for the global Communist brotherhood – and it was not surprising that the barracks of this occupying power were wrecked in such a vengeful way. I have to say that American attitudes in the NATO sector are almost as bad, with airforce and army bases self-sufficient with hamburger bars and cinemas etc., ensuring virtually no contact with the local community at all.

Crossing over the road from Max's after breakfast the next day, we rejoined the cycle path and completed the last few miles to Juterbog, stopping at a supermarket to stock up for lunch. It was shortly after this that disaster nearly struck, as we were labouring along a tree-lined road into a stiff headwind, strung out in our usual cycling order. A car behind, thinking he could just overtake us and nip in before the oncoming traffic, miscalculated and on braking heavily lost control. Tyres screaming, he slewed towards Alexander and Ollie missing them by a few inches before overcorrecting and hurtling towards a tree on the other side of the road before coming back towards us. The amplitude of these oscillations finally diminished and he sped off to his next date with death leaving us severely shaken.

Peter later told me that he nearly abandoned the trip at this point rather than subject us to any more risks – getting killed was certainly not the general plan but herein lies the heart of the problem. It was inherent in a journey of this sort that there would be risks as well as gains – the difficult question to answer was whether or not the balance of risk versus gain was acceptable. I suppose you can only tell in retrospect but I'm certain that without some risk there is never any gain. Rather subdued, we leaned ever closer to the gutter and continued towards Herzberg.

Krister sustained our first puncture of the trip shortly afterwards which was due, we thought, to him cycling into the gutter. Unfortunately, he had a puncture thereafter every single day for the next twenty-one days, an occurrence for which he was severely berated until Peter at last tracked down the cause to a tiny piece of wire protruding from the inside of his tyre. I kept telling him to change the tyre but when it comes to bikes he always knows best. Anyway I think he probably quite enjoyed the tube changing ritual, which by the time we reached the Danube was down to about forty five seconds with the aid of a bright orange tyre remover of which he was immensely proud.

By late afternoon it was very hot, we were some way from our chosen campsite and we had already covered forty miles. Crowding round the map we spotted the sign for a Youth Hostel only a few miles from the main road at Uebigau and since another night in a bed might help my healing back, we decided to see if we could find it. We had barely covered half the distance when we were flagged down by a young man in a car and he came up to us talking rapidly in German. At first we thought he was asking the way, but it soon became clear that he was a newspaper reporter interested in the strange sight of an English family cycling along a country road. He became positively excited when told of our route and scribbled away in his notebook before asking if he could take a group photograph for publication with the story. We never did see the final result but it must have appeared, for over the next few days people would wave and cars toot their horns in recognition.

Although we saw a solitary, ageing sign with the Youth Hostel triangle on it, pointing vaguely down the road, we couldn't find it and had to ask in the town.

"Jugendherberge bitte?"

The inevitable two old men nodded and repeated, "Schloss, Schloss," several times. We thought they had misunderstood, but the Youth Hostel when we found it did indeed turn out to be a lovely old manor house set in its own grounds on the outskirts of the town. It must have once been the elegant family seat of a local Count before the war swept everything aside and Communist doctrine made sure that it could be freely used by the masses. The masses certainly hadn't looked after it very well and its once magnificent gold and white stucco facade was crumbling away, although some of it still managed to gleam in the low evening sun. A drive leading to the sweeping front steps encircled a flower bed in the middle of which, rather incongruously, was a grave, with the inscription 'Ernest Hirschfeld 1920-1944'. Was this an itinerant soldier just buried here for convenience, or was it the Count's son killed on some distant battlefield and brought home to the gardens he must have known so well as a child during earlier and happier times?

Inside the echoing entrance hall with its fine carved wooden staircase, there was no sign of life and we began to wonder if it was open. Eventually a rotund housekeeper with a pinafore around her ample middle appeared from the kitchens in the basement where she had been preparing the evening meal. At first she wasn't too sure if there were any vacant rooms, which rather surprised us since apart from her the building appeared to be completely deserted, but eventually she beckoned us to follow and carrying an enormous bunch of keys, led the way up several flights of stairs to the attics, where at the end of a narrow corridor were two sparsely furnished rooms complete with military style steel bunks. We of course were delighted, but remember that the alternative was sleeping on the ground – everything is relative.

The bikes and trailer were locked away in a garage and we laboured up and down the stairs ferrying clothes and panniers to our rooms, which being so close to the roof, were stiflingly hot. Just as we were finishing, an orderly crocodile of children aged from eight to about sixteen, came marching across the gardens at the rear of the Schloss and came towards us, singing and laughing. They were a ballet school from East Berlin and had come to Uebigau for two weeks of intensive training and rehearsals. Their ballet master was a charming man of about thirty, who spoke some English and when hearing of our exploits insisted on acting as general information service and translator for the remainder of our stay. No wonder the hostel had trouble finding us rooms. A tidal wave of children burst through it running and shouting while our new-found friend attempted to restore order with a few crisp instructions and a good-natured indulgent smile – he obviously loved them all.

"We are having our meal in ten minutes," he informed us. "Would you like to join us?"

In the once elegant dining room of the house, tables and chairs were arranged on the bare wooden floor with one set aside for us. Almost immediately, huge bowls of a steaming goulash were put on our table along with a gigantic jug containing a murky brown liquid. All eyes were on us as we passed the food around and tentatively poured some of the liquid into thick china cups. Sensing our hesitation, the ballet master was quickly to hand.

"It's cold sweetened lemon tea," he informed us. "We find it most refreshing."

It was absolutely delicious and the children were soon holding out their mugs for top ups. The goulash was filling as well as tasty and unbelievably, considering the size of the portions, we managed to finish it all. The whole meal was over in fifteen minutes and then cleared away with everyone lending a hand – they certainly didn't hang about here. Following supper the ballet children trooped downstairs for showers following which we were told, they would have an hour to themselves before bed. Most of them spent this time queuing patiently at a little 'shop' which cook had set up in the hall selling chocolate and fizzy drinks, or playing card games. Anna and I went to have a shower and were bombarded with the children's voices outside the bathroom window asking our names and wanting desperately to hear us speak in English.

By 9 p.m. all was quiet. We couldn't help but reflect on the fact that these happy, healthy children were enjoying their holiday together almost as an extended family in a very simple way, without the need for any entertainment other than that which they could provide for themselves. It was charming, old-fashioned and almost certainly doomed not to last for many more years as the dubious pleasures of Western teenage life were discovered. Are these countries going to gain as much as they lose? I was beginning to doubt it.

As I lay awake that night watching the bats flitting around outside our window, I marvelled again at how totally different each day was and what kind, caring people we had met. Tomorrow should see us in Dresden and from there it was only another day to Czechoslovakia. There was no rush though; perhaps we would rest for a few days, perhaps not. It didn't matter; we seemed to be drifting slowly through central Europe as if carried along by a great sluggish river; the scenery changed but you were never too far away from where you had started and never too far away from where you were going. At no time did we feel alarmed or isolated at having travelled so far – everywhere we stopped was somebody's home and for that night it was our home as well.

The dancers said their farewells as we were packing up the bikes next morning and they disappeared through the trees in the park, singing until we could no longer hear them. Our feelings of idyllic rural contentment were somewhat shattered on receiving our bill for 178 Dm (about £75) from the Hostel – prices in this part of Germany appeared to have rapidly caught up although facilities obviously hadn't. Still we'd had a good meal and plenty of memories so perhaps it was worth it.

We spent most of the morning pottering around the town and after some difficulties with envelopes etc., managed to post seven films home to Brian. The first ten miles were delightful on quiet roads through farming country just east of Torgau, where American and Russian troops first met on opposite banks of the Elbe in 1945. Thereafter it was busier and blisteringly hot, so when we reached Elster-Werda at 1 p.m. we were more than ready to stop at an inviting kebab kiosk set up in the car park of a supermarket – there is a big Turkish population in Germany so kebabs are fairly popular. These were enormous with masses of lamb, salad and spicy dressing stuffed into a huge piece of hot pitta bread and they made a most welcome change from our usual picnic fare.

It was just as well that we'd had a substantial lunch, for the afternoon proved to be hard work, with real hills appearing for the first time. I remember one particularly vicious one leading up to the village of Grobdobritz which seemed to be high in the sky surrounded by almost alpine pastureland. There was no easy way of doing this – it was simply a matter of selecting a lowish gear and pedalling in a slow rhythmical fashion trying to distract yourself from the increasing pain in your thighs, calves and back. Walking was even worse. At least you are sitting down on a bicycle. The road would creep past at anywhere between 2-5mph according to our speedos, while the sweat ran into your eyes and dripped off your nose. Standing on the pedals, a favourite method of racing cyclists, is almost impossible with panniers and completely impossible with a trailer. Poor old Peter – whatever problems we might be having, he was really struggling, with his orange flag lurching around alarmingly with each pedal stroke. I even used to overtake him with a smug look and an occasional, "Come on slow coach," which he could never reply because of the gasping nature of his breathing. It was only when the trailer was finally weighed at Budapest for customs clearance home, that we realised he had been towing over 70kgs for nearly three months – well, it was his idea.

Of course what goes up must come down and after long swigs from our bottles we would freewheel down the other side at increasing speeds as our confidence increased. Well actually Krister's confidence never increased and staring fixedly at his computer with a look of intense concern he would descend at precisely 11mph while the others zoomed down shouting out their speeds to each other.

"Twenny, twenny two, twenny five... Zands, ZANDS wha-av-uu got on yours?... Twenny seven, twenny NINE, THIRTY... ZANDS I DID THIRTY!" and so on until the road flattened out and they would stop to compare recorded maximums on their computers while waiting for the others.

Peter tried to put a stop to this rivalry since it was only a matter of time before a horrible accident occurred, but if he went down slowly they would simply wait for a few minutes for him to get well out of the way and then race down as before.

After a long stretch through pretty woodland and several enforced rests due to punctures and misplaced chains, we eventually stopped at Friedewald just to the north-west of Dresden having covered forty-six miles.

It would have been harder to have found a nicer or more convenient spot even if we had planned it, which we hadn't. A small quiet campsite on the edge of a beautiful lake was guarded by an immense woman dressed in a garish floral-patterned swimsuit. She took our details and heaving herself to her feet, waddled with a terrible limp over to the spot where our tents should be pitched. She talked and gesticulated constantly but in an uncanny way managed to make herself perfectly understood.

Just as we had finished the tents, facing them west into what promised to be a lovely sunset, we were somewhat startled to see a completely naked couple rise up out of the long grass about twenty yards away as if from a trapdoor and start embracing and hugging each other, turning their bodies this way and that to catch the now golden afternoon light. They seemed completely oblivious to our presence and even when Ollie started pointing and sniggering continued to pose and posture. It took another individual walking past with his 'undercarriage down' to realise that we were in a nudist camp. Anna being at that sort of age, turned a bright shade of crimson and staring at the ground muttered repeatedly:

"I don't believe this, I don't believe this," like some sort of Buddhist mantra.

It wasn't as bad as it seemed. The caressing couple had three lovely little girls and being very discreet about their feelings for each other soon disappeared back into the grass where all you could see was the odd arm or foot. Anyway, what on earth was all the fuss about – anybody would think we were prudish or something – being British does have its drawbacks. It reminded Peter of the one and only skiing holiday we'd had some years before. Fancying a sauna, he had charged into the little wooden hut only to find it full of naked woman displaying their wares in the most uninhibited fashion – why do German women have hairy armpits? Instead of taking off his bathing trunks and asking them to move up, he made a theatrical pretence of examining the basket of glowing coals before clearing his throat a few times and leaving – honestly, we are a hopeless nation.

Hardly had we come to terms with our lot, than the multi-coloured whale reappeared bearing an armful of pamphlets talking nineteen to the dozen.

"Ach is goot, goot – so interessant" she wheezed grabbing one book and opening it to show us pictures of the surrounding countryside.

"Moritzburg is so schon, Dresden is so schon, Meissen is so schon."

We were getting the message that it was pretty schon around here and were desperately trying to think of ways of getting rid of her when an ear splitting whistle rent the air.

"Ah der dampf zug," she exclaimed. "Kommen sich ansehen der dampf zug," and with that she grabbed Peter's arm and dragged him over to the fence.

There puffing gently at a small country station was a beautiful steam train, which as we looked gave another shrill whistle and emitting clouds of black smoke, slowly moved towards us. It passed just behind the campsite and then to our surprise seemed to head out over the lake pulling a long chain of carriages behind it until it disappeared, hooting into the distance. Closer examination revealed that the railway track was built on stone piles only about 6ft above the surface of the water, which were invisible from where we stood. Peter made the fateful mistake of expressing interest in this train and within a few minutes his new-found girlfriend was back bearing yet more booklets and photographs.

"Der dampf zug is so schon. Der dampf zug…"

I quietly slipped away at this point leaving Peter to smile and nod like an imbecile as she slowly turned the pages.

Dresden lay sprawled along the Elbe between us and Czechoslovakia so we decided to stay at this tranquil spot for a few days to gather our strength, rather than risk getting stuck in the middle of a big city. It was just as well that we did, for on the following day we cycled into Dresden leaving the tents behind and went through mile after mile of ugly industrialised suburbs which had no apparent end. I almost despaired of reaching anything interesting but we persevered and at last Peter recognised the spire of Dresden cathedral in the distance from his guide book. Pushing the bikes over a horrendously busy bridge complete with clanking trams, we reached the relative peace of the old city and the Zwinger Palace.

This is described as Dresden's main tourist attraction and as far as I am concerned is the only one. Leaving our bikes conveniently locked up in the shade of the Palace wall we spent the remainder of yet another baking day exploring the sights. Actually, this part of Dresden was delightful and gave a rather poignant reminder of what the rest of the city must have been like prior to the immense destruction wrought by the RAF in February 1945. Saving the actual palace until the afternoon, we first explored the Theaterplatz, one of Germany's finest squares, dominated by the opera house, the cathedral, and a fine equestrian statue. A broad flight of steps led from the square to the Bruhlsche Terrasse or 'Balcony of Europe' an elegant promenade from which there were fine views of the Elbe with its many bridges and fleet of pleasure craft, as well as further imposing statues and expensive restaurants.

Returning to the shade of a lovely Renaissance doorway, near a most impressive medieval style mural made entirely out of Meissen tiles, we sat on a wall and enjoyed delicious Italian multi-coloured ice creams purchased from a small van and made with loving care by a tubby little man who seemed perfectly content with his job – a far cry from the inevitably tattooed and ear-ringed surly yob we were used to in the ice-cream vans of Wales.

On the other side of the square just behind the opera house, was a graceful landscaped park with a single jet of water erupting at least fifty feet from the centre of a small lake before cascading back again in droplets and spray. An exclusive looking hotel had a dining terrace overlooking this tranquil scene and weary of economising all the time, we settled ourselves at a comfortable umbrella-shaded table conscious of the rather disdainful looks directed our way from the incumbent clientele.

This consisted mainly of elderly women wearing sunglasses, from whose wrinkled arms a mass of trinkets glittered in the dazzling light and the occasional bored looking white-haired old man, who seemed to be considering whether his lone survival amongst these complaining old crones was such a good thing after all. For they complained almost endlessly, picking away at one thing after another – weather, food, waitresses and probably us. Being well off does appear to have its disadvantages, since expectations are always so much higher and disappointment invariably follows – we were just grateful to be sitting down.

After the interminable bread and spread, a hot lunch in these lovely surroundings, accompanied by a couple of beers was real luxury. Peter enjoyed himself so much that he left his cycling glasses behind and despite going back later was unable to find them.

Almost as if wanting to savour the moment when we would finally enter the Zwinger, we walked around to the rear and after lazing on the banks of the moat watching the ducks for nearly an hour, at last crossed the bridge and passed through a wonderfully Baroque gateway topped by an enormous Royal Crown. Inside lay a huge courtyard surrounded on all sides by various wings of the palace and containing within it four ornate fountains each sending their single plume of water high into the sky. Because the palace was only one or two storeys high, a huge amount of sky was visible, giving an impression of light and space somehow complimented by the extraordinary complexity of the architecture.

The best way of describing it would be to compare it to an oversized version of Cinderella's coach – glass, crowns, gilding and a green painted copper roof, with hardly a space free from decoration. As in Potsdam, musicians complimented the eighteenth-century atmosphere by playing appropriate music on flutes and violins, accompanied by the constant sound of running water – it was easy to imagine those tranquil, cultured days of Mozart and Haydn before the Napoleonic Wars and all that followed that brought misery to Europe.

It was so hot that we resorted to actually drinking from one of the many fountains – too late did we realise that a dog had had the same idea, but he was swimming in it as well. However, despite imbibing some pretty suspect fluid, including regularly filling our bottles from taps in lavatories, we were only ill once and that was almost certainly due to food eaten in an expensive Austrian Restaurant.

We didn't leave the Zwinger Palace until after 5 p.m. – it had made our day – and braving the Dresden rush hour retraced our route through the awful suburbs, stopping only to stock up for supper, to our peaceful little campsite. Well, peaceful for me but Peter was immediately set upon by his girlfriend bearing yet more books and pamphlets. "Der dampf zug," she started, but he was already disappearing towards the lake in an effort to escape, miming swimming motions with his hands. To our amusement and his horror she waddled after him in hot pursuit and was last seen pursuing him through the water like some kind of over-inflated beach toy.

When he eventually managed to shake her off, we brewed up some tea and considered the best way of crossing the Czech border. The most direct route to Prague lay due south but this involved sinuous twists of the road suggesting mountains of some considerable height. A much flatter road followed the Elbe in a lazy curve to the east before swinging south at Bad Schandau and crossing the border at Decin. We had been travelling for long enough now to realise that hills should be avoided wherever possible, even if the alternative was longer, but how could we possibly negotiate the whole length of Dresden complete with baggage and trailer? Despite peering intently at the map there was no way around this city and the best we could come up with was postponing our journey until Sunday, when hopefully the traffic would be lighter. Tomorrow was Saturday and what better way of spending it than having a ride on "der dampf zug", which at this very moment was hooting and belching out clouds of black smoke, which drifted away in a light breeze over the trees, before commencing its surreal journey across the lake.

I love steam trains and this one was a classic, evoking romantic memories of *Dr Zhivago* and *The Railway Children*. It pulled into our station at 11 a.m. the next day hissing and clanking with water dripping out of every pipe and coupling. It was a living entity and it was clear from the way the brass gleamed that the railway staff loved looking after it. The journey to Radeburg took only twenty minutes passing through a peaceful landscape of lakes and farms with a top speed of about 20mph. Briefly we glimpsed the turrets of Schloss Moritzburg through the trees at the edge of the track, as well as a peculiar building rather like a lighthouse standing by itself in the middle of the lake. Perhaps it was just a folly, or Rapunzel's prison, as it was hard to visualise anything bigger than a rowing boat moving across the lily covered waters. Every time we crossed a road, the driver would hoot and vigorously ring a large bell, as there were no barriers or lights to warn the traffic of our approach. We jolted and swayed in a peculiarly soothing fashion and if we ventured outside to the little platform next to each coupling, we were soon covered in black specks from the funnel.

Radeburg was a fine old town but to our surprise was practically deserted (perhaps it was a holiday) and after wandering around the spacious square and peering into the windows of firmly closed shops, we made our way back to the little railway station hotel for refreshments prior to catching the 2 p.m. back to our campsite.

After lunch, only Alexander wanted to come to Moritzburg, so we left the others swimming and reading while we set off pushing our bikes along the railway track. This sounds ridiculous, but others were doing it and the next train wasn't due for thirty minutes – besides, it appeared to take at least three miles off the journey. I was alright until I reached the bit where the tracks spanned the water but as Peter and Alex plodded into the distance carrying their machines over their shoulders and stepping gingerly from sleeper to sleeper, I found myself paralysed with fright and unable to move.

While wondering if I was either destined to drown or be run over by a train and quietly cursing my men for abandoning me, one of those rare things happened which could only have been preordained. From the bushes at the side of the track emerged a double for Arnold Schwarzenegger clad in the briefest of swimming costumes and pausing only to look down on me with eyes of the deepest blue, picked me up effortlessly in his arms and carried me across what had become in my imagination a flimsy suspension bridge over a crocodile infested river before setting me down lightly on the other side. Returning for my bike he gave me another piercing gaze before disappearing back into the jungle while I swooned like a sixteen year old – I almost followed him but couldn't find a convenient creeper.

"WILL YOU GET A MOVE ON?" broke into my reverie and I came back to earth to find a rather disgruntled husband peering suspiciously into the trees...

"And who was HE anyway? – you only had to ask and I would have helped."

After another one hundred yards there was a footpath leading away from the tracks and since "der dampf zug" was due any minute, we followed this hoping to get on to the road.

"I think it's down here," shouted Peter pedalling into a large clearing amongst the trees. It took a few moments to adjust our eyes to the gloom after the bright light on the water but when we did so it was obvious that we were not alone. Spread around this glade in every conceivable attitude were about fifteen stark naked couples – men lay on women, women lay on men, two were half way up a tree while others were just standing in various poses, the dappled light dancing over their rather white bodies. They weren't actually doing anything – this was a ritualistic Germanic communing with the spirits of the forest and we had clearly broken the spell.

"Excuse me," said Peter in a voice loud enough to dispel any forest spirits and in an accent akin to Basil Fawlty. "Can somebody show me the way out?"

Nobody seemed inclined to help but after an embarrassing silence, a man lying on his back with his head and shoulders propped up by the buttocks of a dark-haired girl who appeared to be staring intently at the roots of a tree, languidly raised an arm and without uttering a word pointed at a barely discernible track.

"Thanks very much," said Peter and then somewhat unnecessarily to us in view of the still pointing finger, "HE SAYS IT'S THIS WAY."

Carefully avoiding where we stepped, we made our escape with Peter nodding and smiling to each body as we passed it; "Thanks again everyone," until we thankfully made it to the road.

Moritzburg is probably the most beautiful château I have ever seen. Set on an island in the middle of a lake it was built as a hunting lodge in 1542 and added to over the years reaching its zenith in 1730 under Augustus the Strong. A tree-lined causeway over the lake led to a gently sloping carriage ramp, which itself led to the broad stone terrace, which completely surrounded the building. The facade was painted in the ochre and white of Saxon Baroque and the gently curving roof lines were studded with pretty little dormer windows. Behind this fairy-tale building lay a formal garden with box hedges and pink gravelled paths leading to the one hundred acre game park still stocked with deer and wild pigs. Most of the crowds had gone and we were able to cycle around the empty grounds stopping every now and then to take photographs.

What a fine last memory of East Germany which had been a mixture of heat, hard work and interesting sights. The people, although noisy by nature, had been very kind and willing to help despite our almost complete lack of language.

Tomorrow should see us in Czechoslovakia and apart from anything else much more mountainous country – we were now all brown and fit after over six hundred miles of mainly flat terrain but most importantly felt confident that we could cope and indeed were eager to get over the border.

Chapter 8

Northern Bohemia

Another blistering day made packing up a sweaty chore before we had even got going. Our friend still in her swimsuit – did she ever wear anything else? – was almost tearful to see us leave and hobbled down to the road to wave us off. To our intense relief, Dresden was almost deserted and Peter slowly led us through, shouting exaggerated instructions at every junction.

"I'm going RIGHT, I repeat RIGHT. I'm stopping. I'm going to turn LEFT. OLIVER will you stop mucking about and listen. Can you hear me at the back?" and so on until we crossed the Elbe and found the main road to Pima.

This road would have been hell on any other day, despite a cycle path running along most of it, but we managed without difficulty and by lunchtime were labouring up a horrible hill outside Pima while the river made a detour to the north.

We were now entering a beautiful area known as Saxon Switzerland where the Elbe leaves Czechoslovakia through a series of sandstone gorges, and peculiar rock formations tower high above the river valley. The walled fortress of Konigstein sprawls over the summit of the largest of these, dominating the town nestling at its foot and commanding the river as it has done for four hundred years. Rejoining the Elbe at Bad Schandau, a famous spa town just before the border at Schmilka where the river turns South eventually joining the river Vltava North of Prague, we found ourselves at the bottom of a steep gorge with the railway on one side of the river and the road on the other.

Traffic was light, the surface good and our spirits high as we pedalled towards the border post in the distance. Borders are confusing things and it was only after we went through a second customs post some miles from the first – having previously stopped for celebratory photographs – that we realised we were finally in Czechoslovakia. The rock formations here were quite spectacular and they dwarfed the hotels and shops making up this small border town, looming over them like great lumps of plasticine.

Lining the road for perhaps a mile from the border were little wooden kiosks all selling Western fizzy drinks and cartons of cigarettes – Marlboro, Camel, Winston – with a swarthy, shifty individual sitting outside each one on a chair. Nobody seemed to be stopping and they appeared to make no effort to sell their monotonous wares – even if you did want to buy something how on earth would you decide which one to go to? Perhaps an ugly scene would follow with the ones not chosen clamouring for your custom and shouting,

"Why him, why not me, that's not fair!" leading to a general melee with cigarettes strewn all over the road.

One has to ask why cigarette companies are flooding Eastern Europe with their odious products anyway – presumably it's because sales are falling at home and these poor people are made to see smoking as a passport to happiness.

It was now 5 p.m. and we were tired and perhaps suffering from a feeling of anti-climax after imagining the border to be our goal. The road snaked along the side of a steep valley through dense woods of oak and beech with hardly any traffic to worry about. Our destination was Decin but in our weary state it took well over an hour to cover the eight miles from the border. The Northern outskirts were gloomy and industrial with a mass of derelict factories and railway sidings. There wasn't a hotel or campsite anywhere and I began to feel distinctly uneasy about the prospects of us finding somewhere to sleep. Eventually we found a 'Zimmer Frei' sign pointing up a side road and so with a faint rising of spirits, we set off to investigate. The river valley here was precipitously steep and after about fifty yards of a 1:4 we all ground to a halt panting and gasping.

"This is ridiculous!" I wheezed. "Why don't Daddy and Alexander leave us here and come back if they find something?"

This practical piece of advice was greeted rather unenthusiastically by the group leader since it involved unhitching the trailer and leaving it precariously wedged against the kerb to prevent it from running away. We were left in a forlorn huddle while our two scouts bent low over the handlebars and inched slowly up the dizzy incline, their legs spinning furiously as for the first time so far, the lowest of twenty-one available gears was selected. Had there been low cloud they would surely have disappeared into it, but it was a lovely bright evening and we were able to follow them in a manner akin to climbers going up the Matterhorn.

Nearly half an hour passed before they returned, preceded by a brand new car driven at about 6mph by a dark-haired young man dressed in shorts, T-shirt and flip flops. He spoke absolutely no English and no German, but Peter assured me that he owned a hotel not far away with enough room for us all and would lead us there in a few minutes. How on earth he had understood all this bewildered me and when pressed he seemed unable to elucidate, so it was with some misgivings that we set off after our new found protector rather like infantry behind a tank.

In such a fashion we passed right through the centre of Decin, passing at least ten very acceptable looking hotels in the process, crossed the Elbe for the third time that day and turning off the main road, started meandering through suburbs which looked as though they had been recently bombed. Thoughts of robbery and murder passed rapidly across my mind but my shouts were ignored by Peter whose front wheel seemed glued to the bumper of our 'guide' like some sort of bizarre time-trialist.

After what seemed like an eternity, we stopped in front of a white painted building which appeared to be about ten feet wide and five storeys high sandwiched between two completely derelict tenements, the ground floors of which were full of rubble and rubbish. A large vertical neon sign over the door announced "Pension Xarcon" and still feeling slightly apprehensive we followed him inside to an entrance hall so narrow that it was only just possible for two people to pass. A wizened old lady, presumably the resident caretaker, was sitting behind a sliding glass window and after a rapid and incomprehensible exchange, keys were handed over and we followed our host up about seven flights of stairs to our rooms.

It was fine – two large rooms with showers and enough beds for us all if Krister slept on a sofa – and only £6 each including breakfast. He was genuine after all and proved it beyond all doubt by manhandling the bikes plus trailer into the boiler room before allowing us to do all our washing in the hotel machine for nothing – I felt guilty at being so mistrustful.

Lovely showers, clean clothes and not for the first time we experienced what was becoming an almost familiar transformation from destitute weariness to blissful contentment at the prospect of hot food and a comfortable bed. By 8:30 p.m. after a pleasant evening promenade we had found an old restaurant on the banks of the Elbe and sat outside in the warm twilight trying vainly to work out what was on the menu. The young waitress helped as much as she could by pointing out a few popular dishes and the food when it came was absolutely delicious. The view from our terrace over the river was glorious as on a bluff opposite stood a magnificent floodlit castle which we had failed to notice on the way into the town. By choosing this particular route we were following the traditional way into Bohemia from Saxony and here was a major fortification guarding this strategic crossing.

Fruit laden ice-creams and strong Turkish coffee inevitably completed our meal which came to £15 for all six of us including drinks and beers – something told me that we were going to enjoy Czechoslovakia. Walking back to our rooms, we passed a small circus tent in the process of being set up with the help of light from a generator. Trailers containing various animals were parked at the fringes of the light so we wandered over to have a peep. Crammed into an assortment of small cages were horses, llamas, zebras and even a camel waiting for the next performance. One of the horses was obviously disturbed and turned around and around in the tiny space endlessly following its tail, completely oblivious of our presence. The children thought this was terrible and there followed a lively discussion as to whether animals could comfortably be kept in cages – Krister had set his heart on a gerbil when he returned home and kept asking whether it would mind living in a cage. Funny how children think their parents know everything – it's rather touching.

We slept like logs and breakfasted well on rolls and ham with delicious coffee. A quick look round the town in daylight failed to reveal any food shops but we managed to draw some money out of a bank noticeable for the armed guards at every door and found a bike shop where we bought Ollie some new handlebar grips and Krister a new water bottle.

Thus provisioned, we set off, now well used to being the object of stares and the odd wave, heading south along the flat road running along the west bank of the Elbe. Although it was another scorcher at 33°C, the surface was good and traffic light so we made excellent time bowling along at 12mph. To either side rose impressive hills and we congratulated ourselves on our policy of sticking to rivers wherever possible – they are nature's motorways. Huge barges occasionally passed us and near Borek we passed a 'barge yard' where the monsters were being built; one was poised to be launched sideways into the water.

By midday we were frazzled and gratefully stopped at a roadside restaurant for lunch, schnitzel, salad and chips plus – yes those ice-creams – for £12. Picnics were clearly going to be a thing of the past. At Usti the traffic had become heavier and in an effort to escape this we crossed to the east bank, pushing the bikes over a big suspension bridge. This proved to be a good choice and we had a splendid afternoon's cycling through rural Bohemia.

The mountainous terrain was beginning to flatten off, being replaced by rolling meadows interspersed with small hills which looked like miniature volcanoes. At one point the road left the river for some inexplicable reason and we toiled upwards into the hills for nearly an hour before a breathtaking freewheel, during which all records were broken, took us back to the valley floor. We had planned to stop at Litomerice but couldn't find the promised campsite and so crossed back over the river to Terezin.

The small town was surrounded by massive red brick fortifications and deep moats in the shape of a star, within which were elegant houses, squares and boulevards. It should have been beautiful but it wasn't. An air of gloom and sadness pervaded the near empty streets and the buildings showed the now familiar signs of crumbling neglect. After some difficulty we found a tiny campsite next to the football ground and eventually finding the manager in a filthy bar, showed him a card written thoughtfully in Czech by one of Peter's friends informing the reader that:

"We are an English family cycling 2000km across Europe. We need somewhere to put our two tents and six bicycles for the night and also some water – thank you."

With bleary eyes he slowly traced the words with a dirty finger before passing the card round his drinking chums for their opinion. Much nodding and whistling through teeth followed, with Ollie being singled out for special attention as they looked at his skinny little legs and then back at the card. With a grin showing appalling decay, the manager waved expansively at his crummy site indicating we could go where we liked and returned to his beer, his head shaking in bewilderment that anybody would choose to do this.

We pitched the tents next to the low wire fence separating us from the sports ground and this made a convenient washing line and bike stand as well as allowing us a nice view. Within fifteen minutes we were sorted out with tea brewing on our wonderful stove – this was now our territory and our home, at least until tomorrow. Watching us with interest was a Swedish couple sitting outside their caravan and it wasn't long before Peter was greeting them with:

"Hej, hur mar du?" (Hello, how are you).

"We're fine thanks very much," they replied in perfect idiomatic English, establishing a linguistic dominance so complete that not a further Swedish word passed my husband's lips.

Actually they weren't that fine, since this was the couple mentioned earlier who had become stranded as a result of a broken-down car. They had been in this depressing place for nearly a week and seemed no further forward in replacing their broken alternator, but they had at least been able to explore the area fairly thoroughly and were able to pass on some advice, the most important of which not surprisingly was not to eat in the camp café.

Terezin or Theresienstadt to give it its German name, was built in 1780 to block Prussia's way Southward into Austria, being named after Empress Maria Theresa. The Serb Gavrilo Princip, who assassinated Archduke Ferdinand and thus started the First World War, was imprisoned here but its most infamous period was under the Nazis when the town, having been turned into a ghetto, acted as a collection point for the Jews of Czechoslovakia, Hungary and Romania prior to their onward transportation to the Polish death camps. Thousands also perished in Terezin itself and being sent there was a near certain death sentence; a name to chill and terrify. No wonder we had felt such an oppressive atmosphere.

We had been told by our Swedish friends that the Hotel Park in the centre of the town had a restaurant, so after cold showers in a grotty toilet block we walked into town to find it. A large, high-ceilinged room painted a uniform shade of brown, had tables and chairs strewn around in a haphazard fashion and the only other customers were a crowd of youngsters playing pool or occasionally putting money into the solitary fruit machine. It reminded me of a transport café circa 1964 – only the juke box was missing.

A tired looking waitress took our orders for more monotonous schnitzels as every other suggestion was greeted with a shrug of the shoulders. We also ordered some salads in an attempt to liven things up but these were brought instantly out of a nearby fridge and presented to us as starters. Czech salads are rather interesting since they consist of only one item e.g.: tomato or cucumber, chopped finely and suspended in about a pint of watery fluid. Not quite knowing whether we should drink it or eat it, we sat stirring up the contents of our glasses and picking out the odd large bit until the main meal came. It was unmemorable but it was food and at least it was cheap.

Peter in fact spent as much making a phone call to his mother, for today was 25th July and it was her birthday. This was no easy task and involved being taken to an antiquated phone in the caretaker's grimy little office on the first floor. He lived, slept and cooked here and appeared doubtful that an international call was possible – he was nearly right, since it took at least ten dialling attempts to get through, but it made Enid's day and made us realise how far away we were.

Walking back in the dark, we passed the Museum Ghetta or Ghetto Museum and made a note to see it before leaving. We also passed a bronze bust dedicated to a Doctor who had lived and worked here during the dark days of the War and had saved many lives before dying himself. To my shame, I can't remember his name.

Coffee back at the tents and for the first time we lit some small candles we had brought, perhaps in an effort to cheer ourselves up, watching them flicker in the darkness as we drank from our plastic mugs.

I don't want to wallow in this place, but it did leave a lasting and moving impression on us. In particular, the Museum, which we visited the following day, contained hundreds of framed drawings and paintings which had been produced in the ghetto art school during the war and smuggled to safety or hidden. Especially heart-rending was the fact that they were all made by children who had not survived and beneath each one was a name and date – Elizabeth Rosenthal 1933-1941, Jacob Kleinhoff 1936-1943 – and so on in an endless array.

Each picture could have been drawn yesterday, the wax crayon colours still bright, the pencil lines still sharp. Some showed camp life with soldiers and death but others, probably the majority, showed life outside with trees, birds, smiling suns and smiling faces. The children, usually full of questions, were very quiet as for perhaps the first time they could identify with the horrors of man.

Time to leave this place of gloom and sadness, but not before we tried to buy some food in the one and only 'supermarket'. We were pleased to find it, but this feeling soon changed on going inside, for the rows and rows of shelves were almost completely bare apart from a few tins of peaches and bottles of gherkins. Two check out girls sat expectantly next to their tills but since the place was almost completely deserted and there was nothing to buy anyway, this seemed excessively enthusiastic.

We had hoped to reach Prague today but it was nearly the end of me as temperatures crept towards 40°C and our water became almost too hot to drink. I just couldn't force my legs to go round and found myself dropping behind within a few minutes after each fresh start. Shade was scarce and I would peer down the road trying to work out if I could make it to the next tree. Nobody else seemed to be as badly affected and the boys especially were as skittish as ever, darting into every available lay-by and parking area, thereby adding miles to their route.

I suppose in retrospect I was suffering from heat-stroke and since I was the only one not wearing a cycle hat, it was hardly surprising. I could not get cool and several times during the day had to lie down and sleep, making progress painfully slow. We drank litres and there were some awful moments when our bottles ran out several miles from the next tap. Every petrol station – and there weren't many – was greeted like an oasis as we knew we could get water and shade. We didn't worry about food and we existed on a few packets of biscuits packed away in the trailer.

We should have stopped, but Prague beckoned and we struggled on. At Podhorany we left the main road because of heavy traffic and tried to find a quieter way across country – this proved to be Peter's worst tactical mistake of the whole trip, as for an hour we laboured up and down hills trying to find the correct way, before giving up and returning to where we had started.

He was mortified, knowing how tired we all were, but we knew he had done his best and there was not a single complaint even from me – I must have been ill! Just as we were at our lowest ebb, a GB car passed us, waving and shouting encouragement – only the second so far – and with heads held high we tried to give an impression of British pluck.

Shortly afterwards, the worst of the traffic joined a motorway and we stopped beside a tiny lake, at the side of which families were swimming and picnicking. About thirty milliseconds later the boys were in the water and I was asleep again with the terrific heat gradually subsiding, since by now it was 5 p.m.

We were travelling south along the east side of the Vltava river and were still fifteen miles from Prague. After our rest, a long tree-lined road took us gently up to a rolling plateau high above the river valley. There were very few houses or even farms and it was hard to believe that we were so close to the capital. The sun was now very low and that familiar fear of being caught in the open without somewhere to stay began to take hold. We probably could have managed but camping 'au savage' I believe, is asking for trouble – we never tried.

Eventually a 'Zimmer' sign appeared, pointing west towards the river, so we turned off down a succession of small roads, slowly losing height, until we found it – unfortunately full. Sensing our disappointment, the owner pointed a finger towards the setting sun and repeated,

"Vltava, Vltava – Hotel, Hotel," several times.

Unsure as to whether this meant the river or a potential bed, we forced ourselves once more on to the bikes and headed off in the direction indicated. Peter was getting agitated by this time and as usual when he's like this, went on ahead to see if our salvation was around the next bend. He soon disappeared and it was with some surprise that we suddenly saw him shoot across the road ahead at right angles to the direction we were travelling, doing about 30mph – all I saw was a blur of orange as the flag whizzed past. The car in front of us was even more surprised at the apparition which missed his bumper by about six inches shouting, "Sorry!" as it did so.

"I was just scouting around and checking signs," Peter mumbled later by way of explanation. "And I thought it was my right of way."

We dropped deeper and deeper into the valley with steep hairpin bends going up the side of a gorge with no apparent habitation at the bottom.

"This can't be right," I wailed, nearly on the verge of tears. "And if you think I'm going back up this hill, you've got another think coming."

Eventually the small road flattened out and ran alongside the river with cliffs on either side – unfortunately it was heading north, away from Prague.

"I'll give it another mile," said a rather worried Peter, "and if there's nothing I'll go to the nearest house."

At exactly this distance, a long low building appeared on our left which to our intense relief proclaimed itself to be the 'Hotel Vltava'. There was nothing else there, but whoever was watching over us could not have led us to a more beautiful spot or a more comfortable, convenient and reasonable hotel. We had covered seven hundred and seventy miles and would stay here for the next four nights. My diary records:

"770 miles – still alive. Here starts our holiday in Prague."

Chapter 9

Prague

The manager spoke perfect English and worked out a very reasonable rate for our stay, giving us three double rooms with en suite bathrooms, breakfast and dinner for about £12 a night each. Five minutes after arriving we were sinking into wonderful hot baths and contemplating our good fortune – it really was extraordinary how quickly our luck had changed.

Changing into our best clothes – which meant a clean T shirt and shorts – we descended to the basement restaurant where our order was taken by a friendly young waiter with a hugely protruding lower jaw, awful teeth and the nasal voice of an untreated cleft palate. We wouldn't have been able to understand him even without these defects but it was sad that they hadn't been surgically corrected. Presumably that sort of expertise wasn't available here.

Peter tried to order a bottle of white wine so that we could properly celebrate our safe arrival, but despite trying to describe the colour white in every conceivable fashion, including picking up the starched tablecloth and waving it in front of the waiter's nose, it was a deep and lustrous crimson when poured into our glasses – I hate red wine. The meal however was superb – particularly the deep fried cheese which most of the children opted for, accompanied by a more solid salad than usual and good old fashioned chips. Peter and Alexander went for steaks which were served up with a fried egg appetisingly perched on the top.

Just to stagger upstairs to our rooms after the meal, to quietly write up my diary or read our Czech guide book before sinking into a comfortable bed, knowing that we were all fit and happy and that we could rest here for a few days, was the definition of happiness.

The next day, after a very adequate buffet breakfast, we asked the manager the best way to travel into Prague.

"It is no problem," he replied. "Just across the river is a railway station and trains run to the centre of Prague every hour."

This mine of information also agreed to do all our filthy washing and it was returned later that evening in neatly ironed piles for no charge whatsoever, as we were, as he called us, 'champion cyclists'.

On leaving the hotel for our day in the capital, we could appreciate for the first time in proper daylight, exactly where it was. It lay at the bottom of an isolated gorge, with high wooded cliffs towering above on each side of the wide river Vltava, giving the scene a faintly Swiss feeling. Its isolation made our discovery of it even more extraordinary than we had thought and one had to ask what a hotel was doing there in the first place. After a little prompting, the friendly manager let us into his secret – the hotel used to be the accommodation block for scientists working at what used to be Czechoslovakia's most top secret nuclear research institute. The ending of Communism had reduced the need for such a place and he had rented it from the Government in the spirit of free enterprise then prevailing, although the current high levels of bureaucracy and taxation were giving him second thoughts.

We crossed the river to a small railway station on the other side via a high footbridge which gave us a view of the now deserted nuclear institute a few hundred yards downstream. It was strange to think that standing here a few years previously would have earned us all stiff prison sentences as spies, but that now we were welcome guests bringing in much needed foreign exchange. At a little window sat the ubiquitous plump and scowling female ticket clerk who on this occasion seemed unable to issue us with return tickets, remaining unimpressed with Peter's elaborate pantomime of demonstrating our desire to come back, which included waving his arms repeatedly first towards Prague and then back to the hotel while mouthing the words "AND BACK AGAIN" rather like a backing group for a pop song.

Around the long river bend a train eventually came into sight and stopped with its doors at least 5ft above the platform. Getting on required not a little agility and we wondered how the elderly coped – perhaps they didn't travel much and indeed this train did appear to be full of soldiers and other young people.

The railway followed the Vltava into Prague through lightly populated suburbs and within twenty minutes we were alighting at the central station amid a hubbub of vendors and travellers. Outside trams, buses and thousands of cars made the atmosphere noisy, dirty and smelly, just like any other big city. This initially was a disappointment as for some reason we had hoped that Prague, with its wealth of history, would have had the atmosphere and peace of a fine arts museum.

The smells were no doubt worsened by continuing temperatures of over 33°C and seeking liquid refreshment, we dived into a dark but cool delicatessen in order to buy some cold drinks. Even though Czech restaurants and cafés were cheap, we still took great care not to waste money and tins of 7-UP bought from shops cost very little and in any case were consumed within minutes. A smiling young Irish woman obviously had the same idea and while waiting to be served, told us why she was in Prague. Her husband had recently died, leaving her with three small children and she was touring Czechoslovakia with them in a clapped out old Vauxhall, staying in cheap hostels and eating as simply as she could in order to extend their holiday for as long as possible. She was amazed at our journey but we were more impressed with hers – she had every right to be mooching around complaining about how unfair life was but no, she was getting on with things and giving her children a time to remember. Although we had experienced some bad days, the courage required to get through could hardly be described as enormous – her determination to carry on needed a strength of spirit on a different level altogether and we admired her for it.

Our thirsts quenched, we walked west towards the river and the Stare Mesto or Old Town, passing incredibly ornate and elegant buildings, some of which were decorated with 18th century painted frescos. One of these, the Stavovske divadlo, proved to be the very theatre where Mozart premiered Don Giovanni in 1787. A vast square surrounded by beautiful palaces and baroque town houses simply took our breath away. Everywhere there were tourists, street entertainers and young people handing out leaflets for forthcoming plays and operas, with a heavy emphasis on Mozart – his music also played from speakers outside a CD shop and it was no surprise to discover that he considered Prague his second home.

At one corner of this magnificent space, on the wall of the Old Town Hall, is a famous medieval astronomical clock with an hourly display of moving mechanical figures – unfortunately the face was so complicated with moons, stars and suns that we never could work out the time and despite rushing over every time a crowd gathered, never did manage to see it work. Another focal point of the square and of much Czech sentiment, is the astonishing, brooding Art Nouveau sculpture making up the Huss Monument, which is dominated by a gaunt, elongated and to my eye rather shapeless bronze man arising

114

from a writhing mass of other figures which merge like plastic with each other to form a massive base. It is certainly striking and presumably – although we were never sure – represents the suffering, anguish, but eventual triumph of the Czech nation. A much more difficult question to answer is whether or not it's in the right place – personally I'm rather partial to a fountain.

A short walk from this square brought us to another; much more famous but not nearly as beautiful. Vaclavske Namesti, 'Wenceslas Square', is the most famous place in Prague. In fact it is a long boulevard with a central pedestrian area that rises from the river to the imposing facade of the National Museum. It was here however that the drama of Czechoslovakia's recent transformation from subjugated Communist satellite to an independent and free Nation had been played out – it was from the balcony of the Museum, in front of huge demonstrations, that Vaclav Havel declared an end to fifty years of foreign domination in December 1989.

We walked slowly to the statue of Wenceslas on his charger, trying with some difficulty to recreate these stirring scenes as traffic whizzed past and a huge crane began to drive piles deep into the ground in front of the Museum with a rhythmic clanging sound. I think we expected a solemn silence broken only by massed choirs humming Dvorak's Slavonic Dances – but it was not to be. Instead, we were all very moved by a simple little memorial to Jan Palach who poured petrol over himself and blazed like a torch on this very spot in 1969, as a protest against the Russian invasion following the Prague Spring of Alexander Dubcek. A small cross next to some flowers in a glass jam jar already wilting in the intense midday heat, bore a photograph of a young smiling man and the date, 1969. On that day, Palach, self-selected from five friends by literally drawing the short straw and already full of morphine provided by a medical student, got out of the back of a car, walked the few yards to his chosen spot just below the statue of Czechoslovakia's saviour King, poured a tin of petrol over himself and lit a match, remaining upright in front of the horrified crowds until he died. This ultimate protest was followed a week later by another immolation of one of the remaining four, but it is Palach's name that survives and kept alive the flame of Czech resistance until the Russians finally left twenty years later.

Outside the museum was a banner advertising an exhibition of model dinosaurs, so Peter took the children in to see it while I wilted in the shade of the steps and watched the world go by. They were gone well over an hour and returned excitedly describing the life-size Tyrannosaurus and Stegosaurus moving and roaring, powered by an intricate system of compressed air pipes – the brainchild of a model-maker who had obviously outgrown plastic aeroplanes. There is a never-ending fascination with these animals – perhaps because they demonstrate conclusively that we weren't always the dominant species on this earth of ours. Wenceslas Square was now a seething mass of humanity and further refreshment being next on the agenda, we walked back towards the river looking for somewhere suitable to eat.

'Suitable' is a key word, for although there were numerous American fast food outlets with the inevitable discarded packaging strewn around outside on the pavement, they didn't meet my requirements for healthy sustenance and in any case were so full of Czechs deprived for so long of these delights, that getting served was out of the question. What a pity that one of the architectural jewels of Europe is being turned into an exact copy of Oxford Street. McDonald's epitomises what is wrong with Western Capitalism – the buildings are flashy and in bad taste, lacking character and individuality; the food is processed, cheap, full of fat and deeply unsatisfying; the staff are insultingly polite; you eat from plastic trays surrounded by hundreds of pale, podgy individuals doing likewise in a kind of feeding frenzy before rushing out again – no wonder America has the highest incidence of obesity in the world and yet this metabolic mayhem is being actively spread like a new religion.

The western market economy seems to be based on persuading people what they want through advertising, irrespective of need, desire or benefit so that huge profits can be made. This is all that ultimately matters, not the good of society or of the individual, not morality, not the environment, not the enrichment of our lives – just the God of profit. The question remains, why do we fall for it so consistently? Perhaps, in our strange 20th century lives, it comes down to needing instant gratification for our cravings, because long term contentment is such a rarity – hungry? – grab a hamburger, bored? – turn on the TV, go shopping? – get in the car, depressed? – grab a chocolate bar, stressed? – have a drink and so on.

All I know is that without a decent diet and a degree of physical fitness, life is miserable – in the west most people have neither. Leaving the good citizens of Prague to their gastronomic delights, we found a traditional fruit shop tucked up an alley and emerged several minutes later laden with grapes, peaches, bananas and a big carton of cold milk, all of which we consumed sitting outside on a bench in the brilliant midday sun.

We still had much to see, particularly the Hradcany with its cathedral, palace and gardens strung out along a high rocky spur on the opposite bank of the Vltava, forming the symbolic heart of the nation. To get there meant crossing the beautiful Charles Bridge built in 1357, whose sixteen Gothic arches carry it on a gently curving alignment from the bridgehead towers at either end, accompanied by a procession of theatrically gesticulating stone saints. Now given over to strollers and idlers and those trying to sell them something, it is difficult to imagine that until the 1950s it was the only crossing. I was captivated; never have I taken so long to get from one side of a river to the other. Stalls selling jewellery, musicians playing, artists drawing your portrait in seconds or hours depending on price, a puppeteer making a little old man play the guitar in time to his hidden tape recorder, wonderful old black and white photographs of Prague and last but not least, a smiling bearded young man dressed like Ali Baba holding a huge python.

"Pliz mista – yoo vant photo? Veery goot. Veery nice. NOoo bite – only ten Crown. Cum tutsh. Imm no bite," and so on until the boys, fascinated by this beast went over to stroke the dry, multicoloured skin.

Before you could say 'Forty Thieves', the snake was draped around their necks and Ali Baba was holding out his hand for his money – the photo never did come out.

Stopping for cartons of fresh orange juice on the far side, we wandered through meandering old alleyways – finding a bust of Churchill placed rather oddly on a wall – before climbing a long flight of steps to the palace gates. Standing guard over these, looking anything but fierce in their pale blue uniforms, were two soldiers who good-naturedly allowed Krister and Oliver to stand next to them for a picture. Walking through the courtyards with their soothing fountains, we quickly came to the magnificent cathedral of St Vitus with the main palace buildings beyond. This natural rock citadel developed slowly over the centuries into a complete cathedral town and in the cellars of the palace we found an exhibition with detailed models showing how the site had grown in size.

The adventure begins – Harwich docks.

Camping on Aero – Drying sleeping bags.

Suppertime.

Forest picnic near Dresden.

The Czech border.

Seeking shade in southern Bohemia.

Lunch at the Danube bend.

The Chain Bridge in Budapest.
Journey's end after 1500 miles.

The palace windows and balconies provided breathtaking views over the Mala Strana, or lesser town lying at the foot of the citadel and it came as no surprise to learn that falling foul of the State often meant falling out of a window, a process quaintly known as defenestration. The last to suffer such a fate was Jan Masaryk, son of the former President and sole surviving non-Communist member of Government, in 1948.

Finding a pretty café next to the palace, we temporarily broke our refreshment rule and made good use of our seats by writing rather atmospheric black and white postcards to friends and family at home. It was unbelievably pleasurable to write the following:

"Eight hundred miles completed. Temp. 33°C. Sitting outside the Hradcany Palace in Prague. Should be at the Danube in one week. All well and happy." Many had doubted us and this would be proof that we were on schedule and having the time of our lives.

Reluctantly leaving our table, we slowly descended the hillside passing the picturesque Golden Lane with its miniature medieval houses – once the homes of the King's goldsmiths – before strolling through the palace gardens set on a terrace high above the river and so back to the Charles Bridge. Our passage across it this time was, if anything, slower than before, since in the evening sunset everybody was promenading in an almost carnival atmosphere of musicians and entertainers. I watched an artist at work while Peter wandered off and listened to a classical guitarist giving a virtuoso performance of Bach and Albeniz.

We eventually got back to the railway station at 7 p.m. expecting to leap on a train and be 'home' for baths and supper by 7:30 p.m. – it was not to be. The problem essentially was that we had to choose from sixteen platforms, some empty, some with a train but all with incomprehensible lists of destinations written in Czech. We knew that our station was Rez, but this was too small to appear on any of the lists and we weren't even sure which route it lay on – oh dear.

"You lot wait here," said Peter, "and I'll –"

"SCOUT AROUND," we all chorused.

Alexander went with him for moral support and they returned after about twenty minutes looking rather perplexed.

"Well, which one is it?" I asked, barely managing to conceal the hidden message of, "and why the hell didn't you ask this morning?"

"It's a bit difficult really," he replied. "I've asked four people and they have all given slightly different answers. The ogre in the ticket office says the next one is at 8:30 p.m. from platform six, the guard at platform twelve thinks platform eight is going to Kralupy but isn't sure if it stops at Rez, a passenger at platform eight says it is definitely not going to Kralupy while the guard at platform eight says yes, it is definitely stopping at Rez but not at Kralupy and is leaving in five minutes."

Trusting the guard on platform eight we piled aboard and with a distinct feeling of unease about seeing our hotel again, we slowly pulled away from Prague. Peter spent the entire journey glued to the window and at virtually every stop had us all ready to leap off – it all looked remarkably unfamiliar but we were seeing it in reverse. His antics were viewed with interest by a German family of four sitting in our compartment and the trip was nearly over before the father in perfect English said.

"Don't worry, we are also staying at the Hotel Vltava – it is the next stop."

Sure enough, the train was running along the side of our 'Top Secret' gorge and within a few minutes we were walking back over the footbridge to the hotel and another evening of luxury.

Reading this now, I am amazed at our energy – so far we had spent only one day doing nothing by the lake at Mirow – we seemed unable to keep still and if not cycling, were walking miles sightseeing. Nobody had complained – so far – but with temperatures due for another record on the following day and with Prague radio giving regular warnings about over-exertion, we decided to try and find a swimming pool and just relax.

There was apparently one at Kralupy, a few stations up the line, but the manager had only vague recollections of where it was, which he tried to explain to Peter. Getting on the train after breakfast had the feeling of a trip to the seaside with bags full of swimming costumes and books to read but most importantly the expectation of doing absolutely nothing. The journey only took fifteen minutes and we found ourselves in a fairly large town spread over both sides of the Vltava with absolutely no evidence of a swimming pool whatsoever.

"He thought it was on the other side of the river," said Peter, already yards ahead in his continuing role as leader and pathfinder – however hard he tried, he was not really happy unless he had a map and we were all traipsing along behind him. The problem on this occasion however was that he didn't have a map and we didn't even know where the river was.

"Now Lizzy," he continued in one of his many futile attempts at teaching me basic navigation, "which side of the river are we on – west or east?"

"Er west," I hazarded a guess.

"Correct, absolutely right. And which side is our hotel on?"

"west again?" I continued hopefully, knowing as soon as I saw the exasperation in his face that I was wrong.

"NO NO NO – we started east, crossed to the west, came north and now we want to go east again – got it?"

No I didn't get it but there was no point telling him that, otherwise we'd be here all day.

"Now if we want to go east, which way do we go and most importantly HOW do we know it?"

Giving a passable impression of Shirley Temple with a finger in my mouth and my head on one side, I pondered for a few moments before coming up with my usual solution.

"Why don't we ask someone – there's a nice looking chap over there!"

"God you'll never learn," he fumed and pointing at the sun and muttering something about the northern hemisphere set off after a crowd of people along a footpath which brought us to the main bridge within a few minutes – some of this group were carrying fishing rods, so I wasn't that impressed.

On the far side, even Einstein seemed a bit perplexed, so under the pretext of buying a bottle of squash, I managed to find out the general direction from the helpful owner of a kiosk. Street after street of suburban houses led us eventually to our goal which was marked by hundreds of bicycles parked outside and excited voices from within. Entry was about 10p each, with tickets dispensed by yet another graduate from the Russian School of Interpersonal Relationships, but clanking through a turnstile we entered an attractive park surrounding three huge open air pools – this was going to be fun. The boys were off like rockets but Anna appeared rather reluctant to get changed.

"It's alright," she sighed. "I'll just read my book."

"But you haven't got a book," I replied. "And if you had you'd never read it."

A dripping Oliver and Alexander appeared at that moment rather spoiling the withering look now directed towards me.

"Gosh it's so lush – there's a diving board and they don't stop you and..."

"Just buzz off boys and give us a bit of peace," yawned Peter settling into the first chapter of *Crime and Punishment* for what must have been the fifth time since Esbjerg, "and Anna, go and get changed."

She needed a bit more persuasion, but eventually finding the male changing room – what is the matter with our daughter? – emerged wearing a horrible knitted black swimsuit three sizes too small with a hole in it. Flicking self conscious glances to left and right which made her even more obvious, she made her way back to us and sat down.

"Anna, where did you get it?" I said with astonishment. "I thought you had a lovely bikini?"

"I can't wear that," she replied in a voice meant to convey extreme patience with her stupid parents, "the top's too small and in any case I've always hated it. It makes me look too old."

How on earth any bikini can make a young girl look old is beyond me and she had chosen it after all; I for one could remember the hours spent rummaging through the entire stock of a French clothes shop the previous summer.

"Well that one makes you look about nine," sniggered Peter looking up from his book, "and make sure that hole doesn't get any bigger; I think the thread is beginning to unravel."

Casting an anxious glance at the bit of white skin now visible, Anna spent the next hour working out if this was indeed the case before eventually putting her hand over it and scuttling over to the pool. Peace at last; for the first time in over a month we were minus our kids and could please ourselves – it was unnervingly quiet however and I think we only held out for about ten minutes before going to see what they were up to.

Arriving at the main pool, we were just in time to watch a small child hurl himself off a diving board which must have been at least fifty feet high and free-fall for several seconds before landing inelegantly in the water in a huge plume of spray.

"Gosh that's dangerous," I exclaimed as we waited for the 'body' to come to the surface – this also took some time but the doggy-paddling red head who eventually did so needed no further introductions. "OLIVER!" I shouted. "What the hell d'you think you're doing?"

"Zands told me to," he panted, wiping the hair out of his eyes. "He's coming next," he added proudly, pointing at the sky from which Alexander soon plummeted with even less finesse than his brother.

I think he had attempted a somersault but all we saw was a tangle of arms and legs as he hit the water with the side of his head. Attempts to stop this activity were met with wails of protest and since there didn't appear to be any lifeguards about, Peter spent the next hour watching them from a poolside bench, several of which were dotted around the pool – in fact one of them was occupied by a girl in a horrible black swimsuit, who despite this disadvantage appeared to be surrounded by young boys. Perhaps they thought she was nine as well.

It was now midday and the park was filling up with a real cross-section of Czech society. Young girls giggled and chatted, pretending not to notice while boys with Elvis haircuts and microscopic swimsuits showed off in the pool trying to attract their attention; whale-like grannies fanning themselves in the heat waddled by the side of the smaller pool keeping a watchful eye on the maelstrom of waterwinged toddlers within; dark hairy-chested men with small gold pendants and large pot-bellies strutted like prize-fighters smoking incessantly; older children ran back and forth to the little shop, returning with an array of drinks and sweets while courting couples tried to get away from it all by lying on their towels next to the fence, hoping that nobody would notice their gradually entwining limbs.

There were no 'ghetto blasters', no alcohol, no litter, no yobbos playing football and no excessive noise apart from the sound of people enjoying themselves. This was their summer holiday and many would return day after day – no trips abroad for these children.

The only real problem in this otherwise very pleasant spot were the swarms of wasps which materialised whenever food or drink made an appearance. I have never seen wasps like these – they flew in formation like squadrons of MiG fighters and seemed to work in teams. One group would waver around your head in a hypnotic manner causing you to swat furiously with both hands, while the other would zero in on the now discarded food making a mouthful of wasp extremely likely when the next furtive bite was taken. To be honest they were welcome to our lunch which for the umpteenth time consisted of 'Parky' – solid Czech sausages served on a paper plate with a slice of black bread and a dollop of odious mustard – no wonder they were all so keen on a chickenburger from McDonald's. I think even I would have been converted eventually.

Alexander hit on the bright idea of leaving a nearly empty bottle of 7-UP a few yards away from us in the hope of distracting our tormentors, but they probably just called up reinforcements, for although hundreds crawled around and into the bottle, we didn't notice any difference. Every so often he would creep over with the cap in his hand and carefully judging his moment would quickly screw it down before shaking the bottle vigorously thus drowning the inhabitants in a sea of sticky, sugary fluid – they must have died happy. It certainly didn't deter their mates, however, for by the end of lunch the bottle was half full with wasps and Alexander had been stung twice as he held it about two inches from his nose in order to observe more closely the carnage he had created inside.

Learning yesterday's lesson about train times and not wanting to get back so late, we had worked out that the 5:30 p.m. from Kralupy to Rez would be the one of choice – the next was two hours later – and so by 5 p.m. we were ready to start the walk to the station – ready that is except Anna who despite searches could not be found. She eventually turned up at 5:15 p.m., soaking wet after a last minute swim "with this really nice boy", and as usual could not understand why her father was so upset.

"There's no time to change – just put your shoes on and GET A MOVE ON," he yelled, his voice at least an octave higher than usual, "We'll have to run all the way to stand any chance of catching it."

We must have presented an amusing sight that sunny evening in Kralupy as we ran the two miles in fourteen minutes and thirty seconds – Anna at the back still wearing the horrible black swimsuit which kept working its way ever higher as she ran and Peter in the lead taking hugely exaggerated steps like a scuba diver wearing flippers, because one of his sandal's soles had separated from the uppers and was flapping uselessly in the air.

We made it – just – but such was my exhaustion and relief that I left a bag containing my swimsuit on the train when we got off – I tried to blame the others but they wouldn't have it and insisted that I was carrying it. Crossing the bridge once again we were shocked to see a large GB registered jeep parked in front of the hotel – we had been away from our countrymen for so long that this almost felt like an intrusion. Our bicycles and sticker covered trailer were locked to a rack on the grass in front of the hotel and we wondered if the new arrivals had noticed them and when contact would be made.

It didn't take long, for as we were finishing our coffee that night they came over and introduced themselves.

"Eh lad, ah don't sippose you cud 'elp settle famluh argooment eh?" said the stout father addressing Peter in what we call a 'northern' accent – "Is them baahkes you'rn? – cos ma missus saiz – Jack she saiz – how in 'eck did those baahkes get o'er here anyroad?"

"Well actually," replied Peter in what he hoped was a nonchalant drawl, "well actually we um, we er, rode them here."

"Rode 'em 'ere! Eh Betty, did y'hear the laahke of it. They RODE 'em. Well ahl be…"

"We usually ride our bikes," continued Peter. "It's such a civilised way of travelling and it keeps you fit," he added with only a fractional glance at the man's pendulous abdomen.

"Well Ahh think it's bluddy fantastic – Eh lads [to his two large sons] Eh Betty don't you think it's bluddy fantastic. Y'all moost be right pleased at cuming t'end after all them miles from 'Amburg."

"Well, actually, we started in Denmark and will be finishing in Budapest," Peter answered – this was becoming embarrassing.

"BOODAPEST – that's bluddy fantastic. Eh Betty d'you 'ear that – they're riding them to Boodapest."

Betty and the boys gave us sickly smiles and in an effort to win a little dignity back she announced.

"Well atchully we came in our ISZOOZOO – it's atchully a brand new ISZOOZOO – it's a turbo diesel," she added with a look of triumph. "We've all got baahkes t'home as well but there's nowt room in ISZOOZOO t'bring em t'Prague."

"Ay lass that ISZOOZOO t'is bluddy fantastic," continued the Dad warming to the theme. "The boys luv it as well, don't ya lads?"

"Yes Dad," chorused the podges sensing their moment, "and Dad, don't forget t'tell 'im it's got four wheel drive."

We didn't talk much after this but we did observe them at dinner the following evening haranguing our friendly waiter because the eldest son's meal was incorrect and was sent back – I don't think we ever got exactly what we ordered at any time during our trip but we'd be the first to admit it was probably our fault and we were usually too hungry to care.

We had planned to leave on the following day but all of us felt that Prague deserved a second look so stayed the extra night – in any case we needed the rest and feeding up before heading for the Danube.

Our second day in the capital took on a much more leisurely air and for the first time we made great use of the extensive tram system to get around. The morning was spent exploring the Hradcany in much greater depth but on this occasion we approached it from the Powder Bridge to the north having first spent a pleasant hour wandering through the Italian gardens of the summer palace.

The high spot of the afternoon for Peter was finding, after some searching, the Orthodox Cathedral of Saints Cyril and Methodius – a rather unimpressive building situated on one of the main roads leading up from the river. It was here however on 18th June 1942, that the parachutists who were responsible for the attack on Reinhard Heydrich, one of the most feared men in the Third Reich, were discovered hiding in the crypt. Attempts were made to flood them out but rather than be taken alive they shot themselves – a story stirringly told in the film *Seven Men at Daybreak*. Heydrich died from his wounds on 4th June and a ferocious reign of terror was unleashed on the Czech people culminating in the destruction of Lidice on 10th June. The assassination had been carefully planned by the Czech Government in exile as a mark of revolt by a subjugated people and although the cost in human life was tremendous, it stood as an example to all the other occupied peoples of Europe. The Germans never felt safe again. Outside the Church we could see the bullet ridden ventilation shaft leading to the crypt through which the water was pumped and above it a memorial tablet listing the names of those who had perished – including the priests and Bishop Gorazd.

This Church together with Lidice comprise the two most sacred sites in Czechoslovakia and with any luck we would continue the Heydrich trail by cycling to Lidice on our way South. We have some lovely photographs of the children standing in front of this unusual memorial and we had to retell the story many times in response to their repeated demands. Krister said he would have tunnelled out in order to escape and incredibly when a friend of ours actually visited the crypt – it was closed when we were there – that's exactly what they had tried to do, with their crude tools and half finished tunnel preserved for posterity.

If this was Peter's high spot then mine was Mozart's house, which involved walking from the church to a bridge across the river, where we watched birds fishing in a weir, before meandering for two to three miles through rather depressing, dusty suburbs to an elegant eighteenth-century villa set behind high walls. Half way there, in temperatures again approaching 40°C, I am forced to confess that we stopped for a drink – in a McDonald's. It really wasn't my idea and I did make my protests, but expediency led us inside to a cool air-conditioned interior where my five children – Peter is included here – sat and slurped thick, creamy, ice-cold concoctions which no doubt were full of E numbers. I had a coffee.

I know that I've already described blindness once in this book but in an odd sort of way they are very matchable individuals – I suppose it gives you a chance to stare without appearing rude. A pretty young woman in her twenties, thankfully not wearing dark glasses but carrying the inevitable white stick, ordered something at the counter but then seemed rather uncertain as to where to go. To his credit, a paper hatted waiter materialised within seconds and escorted her to a seat just opposite us – what the American system lacks in food quality, it makes up for to some extent in courtesy and service – and when her mountainous chocolate sundae arrived, scores of eyes all around the restaurant were fixed on her, presumably wondering how she would manage to eat it. It was a joy to behold.

First she felt around the outside of the glass, a smile of delightful anticipation spreading over her face at the thought of the treat in store. Then with great care, she found the long handled spoon and bending her head low tentatively tried a little, the smile broadening as she tasted the melting chocolate. She ate slowly and carefully, her senses not distracted by anything else, as the mixture of ice-cream, fruit and whipped cream was explored and eaten little by little, with each new flavour causing a slight change in expression. Boy did she enjoy that ice-cream.

Mozart stayed in Prague on several separate occasions during his life and the villa he lived in has now been turned into a wonderful museum of memorabilia which graphically tells the story of his life – regular Mozart concerts are also held in the gardens. We browsed happily amongst Mozart's piano, Mozart's gloves – he had tiny hands – and even Mozart's hair before catching a tram back to the station.

We couldn't help but notice the myriad tram lines which were a feature of nearly every road in Prague – apart from contending with the traffic, how could we negotiate these deep ruts with our bicycles? We had already witnessed in Gedser what could happen if a wheel got stuck and there wasn't any traffic there – we would simply have to find another way through as we continued our journey south.

Chapter 10

Southern Bohemia

We were sorry to leave Hotel Vltava. It had been a real haven and they had been so kind. Peter spent a long time with the manager pouring over maps and trying to solve the problem of crossing the river without using the main Prague bridges. The footbridge near the hotel led only to the railway – there was no path or road on the other side and for a while it looked as if we would have to negotiate the tram lines after all.

"Perhaps you could see if the passenger ferry to Roztoky is working still," the manager finally suggested when all hope was fading – "it used to run some years ago but I haven't used it for a long time."

Like our friend in Potsdam he seemed slightly concerned about our future and standing on the hotel steps he waved furiously at us as we pedalled away. Our few days here had been almost perfect. A quiet country lane ran alongside the river and we passed several holiday cottages whose gardens were ablaze with colour and full of fluttering butterflies. Abruptly the tarmac ended and we tentatively picked our way through a moonscape of gravel and boulders which continued for over a mile. This was the quarry that we had been warned about.

"There is a NO ENTRY sign," he had said, "but just ignore it – everybody else does."

Despite this advice, we felt slightly guilty and hoped that further blasting operations weren't imminent in the scarred and gouged cliffs rearing skywards on our left. Trailing clouds of white dust behind us, we emerged at last from this man-made desert without being challenged and joined a proper road once again.

Scanning ahead hopefully for signs of the ferry, we eventually stopped for a drink at a small concrete slipway, deserted apart from an old boat tied up to a rickety post by a length of rusting chain. The boat was only slightly bigger than the sort of skiff you would take out on a boating lake but it did have a small inboard engine and the seats were covered with a canvas canopy supported on thin poles.

"D'you think this is it?" asked Alexander viewing the six inches of water slopping about in the bottom with an expression of acute distaste. "It doesn't look big enough to take all of us."

I found it hard to believe as well, but there was no other contender and after a while a man of indeterminate age, burned a deep brown by months of sunshine and wearing a filthy old cap and ragged trousers, emerged out of a little hut indicating that we should start loading. This took some time with three bikes on one side and three on the other – the trailer was heaved over the prow by Peter and Alexander each holding a wheel and lashed in place with a piece of rope. There was hardly any room left for us, let alone the captain who after clambering over our machines had to sit perched on the stern. From this uncomfortable position he cranked the ancient diesel into spluttering life and with the vessel tilting alarmingly to starboard, we cautiously backed away from the mooring before swinging around and heading for the opposite bank. It only took a few minutes and cost £1.50 but we were all delighted to have avoided the horrors of cycling through a busy city by this simple manoeuvre.

From Roztoky, a steep road hair-pinned its tortuous way up from the river valley to a quiet plateau from which we could make out the spires of Prague in the distance – the amount of industry or dense habitation around this city is negligible, which adds greatly to its attraction. It was a lovely morning and our spirits soared at being so free once again. Village followed village along lanes lined with small trees and flowering hedges as we made a great loop to the west in the general direction of Kladno.

Our immediate aim was Lidice and we arrived there at about midday with the sun beating down mercilessly out of a brilliant blue sky. Instead of following the road through the new, rebuilt village, Peter saw a path leading directly to a huge memorial cross in the distance and we pushed our bikes up the gentle incline noticing small lakes and meadows on either side – it must have been a beautiful spot. Nearing the cross, we could see the outlines of buildings protruding through the grass and in front of one of these was a tablet with the inscription, 'Horak's Farm'. It was in the cellar of this farm on 10th June 1942 that 199 men, the entire male population of the village, were kept before being brought out in groups of five and shot in front of a mattress covered wall as a reprisal for the death of Heydrich. The women and children were sent to the camps and only seventeen survived but they returned and formed the nucleus of a new Lidice which is there today as a symbol of peace and hope.

Next to these ruins is an impressive memorial, with colonnades, fountains and eternal flame, together with a museum where we spent some time. Such was our thirst that we had attempted to fill our bottles at the sacred fountain but the sweet old lady at the till beckoned us inside and promptly filled them all with ice-cold water from her tap. She was so nice and so keen for us, especially the children, to see everything and yet somehow so sad that we felt she must have been one of the original survivors herself. The same was true of the staff in the museum at Terezin. We had made it a rule not to buy any souvenirs because we simply couldn't carry them, but we made an exception here and gave the children a Lidice badge each – two of them still adorn my kitchen wall. Just as we were leaving, another elderly guide beckoned us down some stairs and ushered us into a small cinema where to our delight we saw a fifteen minute archive film in English, telling the story of Heydrich, his assassination and the destruction of Lidice with its rebirth after the war.

We felt like honoured guests, a feeling perhaps enhanced by the fact that we were the only ones there, but also as guests expected to never forget the sacrifices that had been made. I think that by teaching us to remember, they hoped that this would never happen again and so in a surprisingly optimistic frame of mind, we said our goodbyes and went out to find some lunch.

For the rest of that day we completed our great detour around Prague, travelling through idyllic countryside with hardly any traffic to spoil our enjoyment. At 4 p.m. we stopped at the village of Uhonice buying enormous red and golden peaches from a tiny little shop for virtually nothing – they were wonderfully sweet and full of refreshing juice which dribbled down our chins as we bit into them.

After thirty-eight very pleasant miles we followed the railway line into Beroun and found a campsite next to the Berounka river which ran through the town in a series of weirs. The site was busy and we had a glimpse of the dreaded yellow number plates as we waited to check in. This took some considerable time since several couples were in front of us and each appeared to be undergoing a lengthy interview in the warden's office, before finally leaving clutching a numbered metal plate which entitled them to a pitch.

"Let's just go and put the tents up," I sighed to Peter. "If they don't want our money that's their problem," and so saying, I wheeled my bike towards a distant field which seemed to be a little less crowded than the others.

Peter rather reluctantly came as well as he's not really happy unless the administration side is sorted out first – he just cannot relax. Anybody would think that we were going to be summarily shot judging by the anxious way he kept looking around. I frankly couldn't have cared less as I was too busy trying to work out where to put the tents. This was difficult. The centre of the field was taken up with a huge circle of Dutch caravans, lined up as though expecting an imminent Apache attack, with smoke rising from an open fire in the middle. A miniature Holland had been created here with its own extensive supplies of food and drink, organised games, television and even pets. Hardly anyone left the sanctuary of this enclave and I think we would have needed our passports to get in.

The hedges lining the field, usually a favourite spot, were all taken and this only left a patch of bare earth next to the river. The fact that this was the one spot chosen by the camp's dogs to relieve themselves eluded us initially and it was only after the tents had been pitched and the trailer unpacked that we noticed that unmistakable pong. Even without this, life would have been difficult, for a succession of Alsatians, Labradors and other mongrels trotted past us only to squat about four feet away with that peculiarly vacant expression dogs have when performing this ritual. Much sniffing would follow, including us and our baggage – which clearly didn't come up to the correct olfactory standards – before the hound sloped off, nose to the ground, occasionally giving our bikes a quick squirt as he left.

We would have to move before some of it found its unerring way into the deep grooves of my cycle shoes. I don't know what it is with me, but wherever there's a pile, I'll unknowingly find it and spread it generously around until somebody eventually notices. A few years previously, we had spent a morning looking at brand new campervans at a showroom in Carmarthen, admiring the gleaming fittings and luxurious carpets in their spacious interiors. I had noticed the salesman sniffing occasionally, head on one side, but it was not until we were on our way out from the sixth van that Peter nudged me and pointed at a trail of brown footprints leading across the pale cream Axminster and ending at my feet. We haven't dared go back.

Alexander, Krister and Ollie were already swimming in the river shouting gleefully from the opposite bank, so loosely throwing bags, kettles, towels and other paraphernalia into the trailer, the three of us pulled it over to the other side of the field before going back for the tents. Moving these was easier than we had imagined for after taking out a few pegs we simply lifted them up and carried them to their new resting place, the integral pole system maintaining rigidity and shape – in fact these tents were so well designed that unless a wind was blowing they didn't need to be pegged at all.

Thus settled and unable to stand the strain any longer, Peter disappeared in the direction of the office clutching the blue zipped wallet containing our passports and money – he was away some considerable time eventually returning with a numbered metal plate and an expression of acute exasperation. What normally took five minutes had become more like a searching cross-examination with a fat interrogator sitting behind a huge desk illuminated by a powerful lamp and covered with papers. Peter sat on a dilapidated sofa in front of this edifice but this appeared to lack any legs and having to squint upwards into the glare immediately put him at a tremendous psychological disadvantage. Ignoring Peter for a good few minutes – always unsettling – as he scribbled away, he at last put down his pen and taking off his gold rimmed spectacles leant back in his impressive chair and began in heavily accented English,

"Ach so," nodding slightly, "you vish to stay here at zis place – eh?"

"Er yes please," replied Peter, uncertain as to whether he was incriminating himself. A pause followed while fatty looked out of the window.

"Exactly pleez how long vil you remain?" he continued, bringing his gaze suddenly back to the victim as though searching for any weakness.

"Er just the one night," said Peter, shifting uncomfortably on the tatty sofa. "We're cycling you see."

"Ach so, zis is most interessant and vat exact number of persons pleez?"

"Well er actually there are six of us," Peter ventured timidly, as though not quite sure how it would be received. "We have four children," he added hurriedly, trying to create a good impression.

Replacing his glasses he seemed to ponder on the information given so far before once more picking up his pen and tapping his teeth with it.

"Vi must make the start I think, zer is much to be done," and so saying searched through the clutter on his desk before producing a registration form, which for some peculiar reason he read out loud, emphasising the various headings like some sort of Royal Proclamation.

Slowly and laboriously the form was completed, passports were handed over and examined minutely until at last, satisfied that all was in order, he rose from his chair and producing a large bunch of keys walked over to a locked cupboard. Opening this took some time, but eventually the sacred relic within was removed and reverently handed over – never again would a little metal tag take on such profound significance.

Time and time again we wondered how families could remain in places like this for the several weeks it must have taken for the long grass to grow up around their caravans and tents. It was crowded and the showers were icy cold but there was a bar/restaurant which appeared to be permanently full of teenagers buying beer and smoking cigarettes. Plenty of bicycles were in evidence but the furthest they were ridden was to the toilet block or the camp shop. After Denmark we had hardly seen other touring cyclists although many cars had roared past us with up to four bicycles hanging from a rack at the back or swaying precariously on the roof. Most of them would never be used outside the campsites but no doubt when comparing summer holidays with friends during the dark days of winter they would have 'cycled everywhere in Czechoslovakia', thus producing an envy which would be countered by some other fanciful exaggeration.

"Well our hotel was fabulous and the locals seemed so pleased to see us."

We've hardly discussed this journey since our return. We didn't really feel the need to and in any case there is nothing more boring than listening to the travels of others – I do hope though that reading about them is slightly more enjoyable!

We couldn't face the camp bar, so after freezing showers we walked into town to look for dinner. A high bridge crossed the river and from it we could see several fly-fishermen, up to their thighs in the fast-flowing water, casting with an intense concentration as dusk fell. Poor Alexander looked longingly at them for a while before joining us again.

"I'd love to have a go at fly-fishing Dad," he said pitifully for the umpteenth time. "I've always wanted to."

Peter, immediately guilt-ridden, tried unsuccessfully to defend his record on this issue, but it was no good – as a fishing father he was a failure. We had tried of course, but as in so many other things, initial enthusiasm had waned and Alexander's undersized rod plus oversized fishing bag lay untouched in his room. Initial attempts off the local pier had met with complete failure and after several chilly afternoons there – during one of which he managed to embed a spinner in my leg – we hit upon the bright idea of trying the local fish farm. This was the complete opposite. An artificial lake set in a gloomy landscape of mud and discarded pieces of agricultural machinery was stocked with thousands of permanently ravenous trout. Anything dropped into the water, including bare hooks, would be immediately seized thus ensuring complete satisfaction for any embryonic fisherman. It also proved rather expensive, as everything caught had to be paid for and taken home. For months afterwards our freezer was full of this tasteless fish which resisted all attempts to liven it up and in the end it was thrown out. This is the problem with fishing – the end product, unless you are absolutely crazy about it, is pretty unappetising. There must be thousands of fishermen's wives who secretly dread having to deal with the result of their husband's obsession.

"Hello honey, I'm back and I've caught three skate and two eels."

"Oh God," she must think, "not again."

Even when Alexander, in a rare moment of determination, went off all by himself and came back proudly holding the Scout's fishing trophy and the two pound flounder which won it, I was only able to extract a microscopic amount of edible, boneless, flesh from it which he chewed, however, with a look of triumph.

Flounder fortunately wasn't on the menu at the jolly little bistro we found on a corner of the main square and we were lucky to get the last table in a small alcove. The atmosphere was rather like an English pub, cosy and comfortable with soft lighting, and we spent the time while waiting for the food trying to work out the next stage. The Vltava river valley as we had discovered, was much steeper than our map had led us to believe and following it would mean continuously going up and down the sides of steep gorges. The only alternative was a road running beside a minor railway line but this crossed the Brdy Mountains with hills rising to 2500ft so whichever route we chose involved hard work. The terrain would rise inexorably to the Austrian border before dropping down to the Danube valley and flat cycling once again. Unfortunately it was two hundred miles away.

Oh well, let's have another beer and yes, here comes our waitress staggering under a tray piled high with steaks, schnitzels and a vegetarian goulash for Anna.

For some reason, we had probably one of the best nights so far and awoke with that lovely drunken feeling signifying complete rest. Peter cycled into town for some milk and as usual we breakfasted on various cereals eaten from our grey plastic bowls. Coco Pops was the most popular, since it turned the milk into something resembling a chocolate milkshake but we couldn't always get them and often had to make do with dubious muesli or generic cornflakes which bore absolutely no resemblance to the original. If we were lucky we could also have bread or crackers with some of the honey from Alexander's panniers and there would always be a plastic mug of coffee to finish. As with lunch and even supper on the occasions when we dined 'in' this would be eaten sitting on our foam rolls whilst enjoying the view and the feeling of being in the open air.

As we feared, the terrain after we turned south at Zdice became much more mountainous and even alpine in appearance, but in compensation it was really very beautiful with rushing streams and lush meadows on either side of a road which we had virtually to ourselves. In a particularly beautiful spot Oliver noticed a white memorial stone beneath a roadside tree and we all stopped to read it. It was inscribed to an eighteen year old boy who had been killed at this very spot – it didn't say how, but hoping that he hadn't been a cyclist we continued on our way rather subdued. This was not the first such inscription we had seen but they all seemed to relate to remarkably young people and many had fresh flowers in jam jars at their base. Our paranoia for safety, already high, would reach new levels after each one was passed.

Stopping at Jince for our picnic lunch was like stumbling on the film set for *A Fistful of Dollars* – the sun bored down out of a dazzling sky and bounced off the dusty main street adding to the already intense glare. Dust caked the trees and a door creaked to and fro while a solitary cat scuttled into a doorway. There was not a soul in sight nor any other sign of human life but then we had forgotten it was a Sunday – was it only a week ago that we were riding through a near deserted Dresden? It seemed like an eternity – so much had happened and there was so much more to look forward to. The town square was well shaded with tall trees, so we sat under these watching the shadows of the branches dance in the light breeze while we ate.

Just before Pribram we toiled up a crushing hill which saw Peter and Anna left far behind and our water stocks exhausted. The view from the top was worth it however, as we could see for miles over rolling Bohemian countryside full of yellow meadows, small lakes and tiny villages recognisable by the slender church spires. This is the country that inspired the folk-based music of Dvorak and Smetana with the lilting melodies on the violins giving just a hint of what was to come in Hungary.

An incongruously modern petrol station at Pribram saved our life and also amused the girl at the till as we came back three or four times for drinks, ices and packets of biscuits. While munching his third one, to our surprise Alexander suddenly leapt back on to his bike and started pedalling furiously up a nearby hill in hot pursuit of a car which had just filled up. I thought that the sun had got to him at last, but when he returned he was proudly holding a battered, but still unpunctured tin of drink which the driver had thoughtfully left on the car roof before driving off. Unfortunately it contained Whisky and Ginger and although he looked forward to sampling it for the rest of the afternoon, when eventually trying it he took one sip before throwing the rest away – he'll change.

Beyond Pribram, there was evidence of mining with huge spoil heaps rising up like hills and although we had intended stopping at Milin, it was such a perfect evening that we continued to Breznice. On the way there we passed through an apple orchard and the boys would load themselves up with the windfalls before choosing their moment to hurl them along the generally downhill road – it is a somewhat disconcerting experience to be overtaken by an apple doing 20mph and even worse to be overtaken by ten at the same time as they bounce and ricochet all around you.

Just before Breznice we passed an idyllic looking country house set in lovely grounds that had a Zimmer Frei sign. Why we didn't stop there is beyond me – we broke one of the first rules of cycle touring i.e.: stop if you see somewhere nice even if it's early – and we certainly paid for it. Breznice initially looked promising with a moated castle and medieval river bridge but once we pushed the bikes into the main street we realised our mistake. A fairground had been set up in the square and the place was thronged with people and booming with noise as the traders amplified rock music through enormous loud speakers in order to add an air of artificial excitement to their rather simple rides. Instead of taking their girlfriends on 'The Terminator' as they would at home in Swansea, the local spivs had to make do with sitting in plastic swans which went round and round monotonously accompanied by the thudding beat. Piles of litter lay everywhere and as we pushed our bikes through it, trying to avoid smears of dogs' mess and other suspicious wet patches, the inhabitants stared at us with glazed, bloodshot eyes while swaying unsteadily on their feet.

The only visible hotel was right opposite all of this, but it was packed with determined drinkers who spilled out of the bar and on to the street while a sweaty, harassed waiter attempted to keep them supplied with a perpetually laden tray, which for some reason he carried high above his head on one hand. Perhaps he would have been prematurely relieved of his burden had he brought it any lower. Peter of course thought this was ideal but I, expecting support from the others, put my foot down and refused to budge.

"I'm not going in there – it's noisy, dirty and next to that fair," I announced in what I hoped was a voice inviting no further discussion.

To my surprise, I was on my own and shortly afterwards found myself trudging up the hill trailing my family behind with a chorus of "Well you find somewhere then clever dick," still ringing in my ears.

I always like a challenge but after thirty minutes of fruitless meandering with a sullen family muttering mutiny amongst themselves, I was beginning to contemplate giving in. This of course would be unthinkable, so resorting to my well-tried method of asking someone, I began to look around for anybody remotely resembling Nigel Havers. The little old lady walking her dog could hardly be said to possess a perfect likeness to my hero but she would have to do and so producing my most appealing smile I slowly described in perfect English our desire to find a cheap, quiet but extremely comfortable hotel which also served appetising evening meals. Her lack of understanding was complete and absolute as she stared at me with a look of total bewilderment, but incredibly, instead of fleeing for her life she beckoned me to follow before turning back the way she had come.

There followed another of those many acts of kindness which sustained us throughout our travels. Knowing only that we were British and in need of some help, she led us to the home of the one person in Breznice who spoke some English as a result of working in a Coventry factory for seventeen years. Leading us back into the town, our new found friends stopped in front of a grimy building that we had previously thought was derelict. It had an arch in the centre rather like an 18th century coaching inn, which was not really surprising for this was precisely what it was, but unlike its English counterparts, no effort had been made to smarten it up at all.

Leaving the children outside, I followed the translator into a tap room that could have come straight out of a Hogarth print. Clouds of acrid smoke filled the air making me cough and peering through the gloomy haze I could just make out bare wooden tables covered with china tankards full of frothy ale surrounded by chairs and stools occupied by men in various states of intoxication. Some talked animatedly, others sang and shouted while yet more lay slumped on the tables sleeping peacefully amongst the din, their heads cradled in their folded arms. The only other woman in this drinker's den was the barmaid who in a spare few seconds between pulling pints strained to listen to our friend's request for lodging. Initially she shook her head but after a further few minutes of rapid Czech she relented and produced a bunch of keys from under the bar which she handed over to our two protectors.

Finding our rooms involved much unlocking of doors until we discovered them at last on an otherwise deserted first floor landing. They were small, threadbare, sparsely furnished and contained only two beds, each of which had a sagging depression in the middle. Nevertheless we could manage with two of the children sleeping on the floor and thanking our hosts, who both seemed embarrassed and apologetic at the standard of the accommodation, began to ferry our bags inside. The bicycles and trailer were stored in a downstairs room obviously used as an engineering class by the young boys of the neighbourhood, for lying around in various states of dissection were car and motorbike engines neatly labelled and displayed. No electronic ignition or power steering here – the engine design was pre-war and was probably inside the bonnet of all those Trabants we saw, which still appeared to be the commonest car on the road.

Alone at last, we inspected the primitive bathroom which was dominated by a huge cast iron bath standing on clawed feet and supplied with water from a gas boiler which was almost as big. Beneath the dripping outlet from the boiler was the most enormous brown stain on the enamel of the bath, which rather like a stalagmite in a cave must have been slowly growing for years and years. We all managed a wash of sorts with the children shrieking excitedly as they tried to avoid standing on "the stain" which in their minds had become a living entity. Anna of course made a huge fuss and declared it "the most disgusting place I have ever seen", and as if to emphasise the point found a brown mark on her sheet almost as big as the one in the bath.

This was paraded in front of our noses as we tried to explain that the otherwise starched material was just old, not dirty – look at the holes in it – but it was to no avail and in a dramatic voice she announced,

"Well YOU do what you like, I'm sleeping on the floor."

The floor, if anything, had more brown marks than the beds but there was no point in arguing.

We still hadn't eaten and since our inn did not serve food, we returned to the first hotel in search of supper. The noise had quietened down considerably by this time and they were in fact dismantling the fair prior to moving on. Our meal was much better than we thought it would be – well, what I mean is that the quality of the schnitzels, of which we were fast becoming experts, measured well against some of the curled up offerings we had seen and the salad had more solid in it than liquid, which was unusual. What Breznice did have, however, was a beautiful church, now lit up by the golden evening light, with its Sunday bells in the onion domed twin towers ringing like the Kremlin. Birds flew around the roof, silhouetted against the sky as they darted to and fro, calling constantly in a cacophony that merged pleasantly with the flatter sound of the bells. I took lots of photographs from different angles and we later walked over the bridge, complete with its statues of Saints, to the walled castle we had seen on first arriving.

We walked for over a mile in the dusk along a quiet road bordering the castle talking in groups of two or three about the trip, home, school, friends, future plans, in the relaxed way that folk have when they don't have a care in the world.

Our two friends came bright and early the next day, anxiously enquiring if we were alright. Of course we were; even Anna stretched out on her mat had managed a reasonable night's sleep – and we had another day stretching out ahead of us with no idea of what we would see or how it would end. Settling our immense bill of £12 – for all of us – we bought a huge loaf of crusty white bread, a packet of butter, a pot of jam and pedalled out of Breznice to find a convenient spot for breakfast. This didn't take long and by 9:30 we were sprawled on our mats in the sun, enjoying a gorgeous view in between mouthfuls of soft, doughy bread covered with sweet strawberry conserve – a breakfast fit for a King.

The countryside that morning was truly lovely, with gentle hills, forests and waving corn interspersed with small villages and even smaller lakes. It was one of those days when it felt good just to be alive and in a spirit of contentment we stopped at a little lake just to the North of Blatna for a few hours swimming and lazing, watching the few clouds motionless in an azure blue sky as we floated on our backs in the water. Blatna was a sleepy little town where we changed some money and lunched entirely on ice-creams in a smart new parlour where they were made on the premises. A huge banana long-boat in the middle of a blistering day can be thoroughly recommended as a fuel source for the afternoon.

The road to Pisek ran through extensive pine forests and undulated up and down for mile after mile with hardly any traffic. We passed an elaborate memorial to a battle long since fought with an inscription in German – it was certainly pre WWI but what exactly it referred to we never did manage to find out. Shortly after this, a car pulled up alongside and the middle-aged couple inside quizzed us in excellent English about our journey and destination. They lived in Bratislava, capital of Slovakia and almost implored us to visit them when we followed the Danube through into Hungary and Budapest, before reluctantly driving off, waving cheerfully out of the windows as they went.

Pisek was large, industrial and busy, the only redeeming feature being a small petrol station where the bearded, hippie like owner, sold us raspberry jollies and filled up our water bottles. We had planned to stop here but, with the exception of Anna who had spotted a sign to a luxury five star hotel, we voted to carry on in the hope of finding somewhere quieter, even though it was well past 5 p.m. We now appeared to be on an open plain again with the arrow-straight road disappearing into the horizon, seemingly narrowing as it did so. Mile followed mile and the white line sped past in a continuous blur, only occasionally interrupted by intersections or bus stops. Resting a few moments for a drink, we watched a plane climb and spin over a distant lake for some time before realising it was a model. This of course started Alexander off again, since radio-controlled aeroplanes come second only to fly-fishing in his list of unfulfilled dreams.

With thirty-eight miles completed, we turned left off the main road shortly after crossing a railway line and cycled into the town of Protivin finding the Hotel Blanice, a new building just off the main square, without difficulty. Like all smart places, this was expensive and a night here left us poorer by £90 – an incredible figure for rural Czechoslovakia. Perhaps I was becoming so used to campsites and threadbare Zimmers that I could no longer appreciate luxury but I do remember getting very cross that we were wasting all that money. Nobody else seemed to feel this way and within minutes they were sensibly enjoying the big clean rooms with their lovely sparkling en suite bathrooms, the large fridge full of cold Coca-Cola and most importantly the television which they had been denied for so long. Krister and Ollie stayed glued in front of Czech cartoons which they appeared to understand perfectly and I caught Peter avidly watching a gardening programme while he thought I was still in the bath.

Not surprisingly, at these prices we were the only guests and there was plenty of room in the lobby to store the bikes – I wish the trailer had been brought in as well but it was a quiet enough place so we left it locked to a drainpipe outside. This innocent action however led to a somewhat disturbed night, for at about 2 a.m., when we were deeply asleep, there came a fearful pounding on our door which when opened revealed the manager in a bit of a state. He seemed genuinely frightened and kept gesticulating for Peter to follow him stammering,

"Polizei, Polizei, Kom, Kom."

Why they needed two cars complete with flashing lights and five stern looking policemen complete with torches and guns to surround our little trailer has remained a mystery to us ever since, but there they were and they did not seem very happy. I watched this little scene from the safety of our open window while Peter tried to sort things out with a cheery "What's your problem matey?"

It was obvious they wanted it moved into the hotel for some inexplicable reason and they wanted it moved NOW, but their wrath was being vented on the manager who was clearly terrified. Peter didn't really help by deliberately taking an age to undo the combination lock for which purpose he borrowed a policeman's torch with an air of exaggerated gratitude. Almost crying with relief the manager helped him carry it into the hotel before locking the door with trembling hands and wiping the sweat from his brow with a paper hanky. They may have just been worried about the trailer being stolen and were simply ticking off the manager for not looking after us, but since he didn't know about it in the first place, it hardly seemed fair!

Due to this disturbance and the oppressive heat in our rooms, the rest of the night passed in a restless fashion with frequent trips to the bathroom for glasses of lukewarm water. Breakfast was served at a restaurant around the corner and consisted of the usual plates of cheese and salami with a basket of bread rolls. Our thirst was still unslaked and I remember asking the waitress for jug after jug of coffee and tea which she supplied with increasing amusement. The morning, unbelievably, was overcast for the first time in weeks and for a short while there was even a thin drizzle before the sun burst through, causing the roads to steam quietly.

The cycling continued to be easy along well surfaced roads with long, gradual inclines rather than the more exhausting steeper but shorter hills. We made good time and stopped for lunch in a meadow just beyond Cesnovice. At each stop, Peter would obsessively spin the trailer wheels looking carefully for any sign of deterioration in the buckle that had occurred in Denmark. His repair was holding up well however and the slight kink amazingly did not seem to be getting any worse. We didn't waste much time here, as only a few miles further on lay the capital of Southern Bohemia – Ceske Budejovice – where we wanted to spend the afternoon.

Not for the first time, we experienced the immense usefulness of bicycles as we gaily bypassed the stream of frustrated tourist traffic and coaches, aimlessly circling as they waited for a precious parking place to appear. We simply headed straight for the splendid main square via a mixture of medieval one-way streets and pedestrian-only areas and arrived in a matter of minutes, chaining our machines to a

142

convenient railing. Namesti Premylsa Otakara II is without doubt one
of the finest urban spaces in Europe, being laid out in the 13th
Century by King Ottokar II of Bohemia to mark the commercial
importance of the town, lying as it did on the salt route between
Austria and Prague. The square's sides are nearly 500ft long and are
lined with arcaded burgher's houses, many of which still have their
Renaissance facades. Cars are thankfully banned, the only visible
transport being horse-drawn carriages waiting for hire and the
impression of space is breathtaking. Fountains gurgled in the centre –
so much better than statues – and everywhere there were tubs of
purple azaleas lighting up the scene with splashes of intense colour.

Not having to worry about parking tickets, we took our time
wandering around and even relaxed in one of the many pavement
cafés to enjoy a glass of Budweiser which originated here several
hundred years ago. Leaving was just as easy and we pedalled away
south from this superb historic centre, through the busy industrialised
suburbs which had grown up around it, until we found the main road
to Cesky Krumlov, our planned stopover for the night.

We had rejoined the Vltava again and would now follow it nearly
to its source on the Austrian border. This, of course, meant climbing
and sure enough, before we had gone many miles the road began to
snake gently up towards the Sumava Mountains. Dark thunder clouds
cast shadows on tranquil meadows and conifer forests and I looked
nervously to see if our waterproofs were accessible. Ahead of us,
hills rose in a succession of waves, each one slightly higher than the
last and we began to wonder if our destination was attainable. We
still hadn't learnt the lesson that 1in on the map with hills in it would
take just as long to complete as 3ins without – mankind I think is an
essentially optimistic species.

"Not far now," Peter would say or, "It's downhill all the way," or
"No more hills after this," until we gave up believing anything he
said.

Oliver especially was deeply suspicious and would insist on being
shown exactly where we were on the map and where we were going.
Krister always wanted to know the precise distance left to be covered
and would then be glued to his computer until in the middle of
nowhere he would look up and smilingly announce:

"We're here Daddy," only to be given another approximation.
Alexander always wanted to go further than we intended and would

often be in a 'grump' at the end of a day at the prospect of stopping. Anna seemed oblivious to everything, pedalling in a world of her own while I would ask the most impossible questions.

"How long does this hill go on for?" "Is it going to be a nice campsite?" "What are we going to see in Cesky Krumlov?" To which Peter would answer, somewhat sarcastically in my view:

"Well the last time I was here there was idyllic camping to be found about half a mile away, with a delicious take away service and superb views."

I believed him the first time.

Our route criss-crossed over the river and verdant upland pastures interrupted the otherwise continuous cover of beech, spruce and fir. Settlements were few and far between and it was with some relief that we finally reached the top of a huge climb after a forty-six mile day and looked down on the red tiled roofs of Cesky Krumlov nestling in the valley below. Following last night's disturbances, we had planned on a campsite but with only one tiny sign stuck in a hedge three miles away as a guide, it took some time to find it – when we did, however, our spirits fell. Rather like Mirow, but much, much worse, a sea of tents and canoes filled every inch of the parched brown earth that constituted the site, which had an atmosphere like a rock festival. A lengthy queue indicated the position of the toilet block and we needed no imagination to predict what the inside would be like.

"Thank you but goodbye," summed up our general mood as we turned around resignedly and wondered what to do next. Providence as usual didn't keep us waiting long, for on the road back into town we passed a Zimmer that we had missed on the way up and yes, there was one room vacant. The pleasant middle aged man who owned the pretty Alpine Villa set well back off the road had no objection to us all cramming in, even though it would mean two or three of us sleeping on the floor and helped us to secure the bikes in the back garden before disappearing to find extra towels and pillows. The room was splendid with a big double bed that would sleep three, as well as another single bed, an en suite bathroom and a balcony which commanded a glorious view over the river valley to the mountains beyond.

We were soon at home, with the children fighting about who should bath first, who should sleep on the floor, who should have the single bed, who should have the biggest towel and who should change their shorts for a clean pair.

Because our ability to wash clothes was limited, we all tended to keep a set of clothes for the evening and wear our cycle clothes two or even three times – I didn't notice any smells from my position at the back so we can't have been too bad – unless of course I was as 'high' as the rest and couldn't detect it. Having a bath was too good an opportunity to miss though and when everybody had washed, it was filled with the contents of the dirty bag which were left to soak in water containing a cupful of my biological powder, while we went to look for supper.

The bistro we found just up the hill was crammed with youngsters from the campsite opposite, who had come to this canoeing Mecca for their summer holidays. They were a jolly crowd and even rearranged the seating so that we could all be together, cheerfully clearing a space at the end of a long trestle table crammed with friends talking non-stop. I had spotted plates of our favourite deep fried cheese on the way in and since by now we were all well and truly fed up with schnitzels, Peter was dispatched with a unanimous mandate to secure six plates of Camembert, pommes frites and salad. To make absolutely sure of the order he pointed to it on the menu and repeated "Kase, Kase", (cheese) several times to the waiter before dragging him by the arm to the table where I had seen this dish being eaten. It was still there and bending over the surprised diners, Peter encouraged the waiter to take a closer look before the "Kase, Kase", routine was repeated, this time with six fingers held up in front of his nose. The six schnitzels when they arrived weren't too bad but then the lighting was so dim as to make any objective analysis difficult. It was food and it was hot so why make a fuss.

Breakfast the next day was meticulously served by the helpful man who had booked us in and he was so concerned to make sure we had a substantial meal that he almost took it personally when some of the salami was left behind – he presumably had a wife but she didn't seem to do much.

Cesky Krumlov is, after Prague, an absolute must for anybody visiting the Czech Republic for the first time. Founded in the 13th century to command the important trade route to Austria, the town is crammed into a serpentine loop of the Vltava river and is dominated by an extraordinary fortress castle set on a rock high above. Even at this early hour visitors were arriving, but we cycled serenely into the exquisite main square – a smaller version of the one at Ceske Budejovice – before parking the bikes with the smiling permission of Krumlov's sole traffic warden.

What a jewel of a place, almost stuck in time, with streets dipping and twisting, forming a succession of continuously changing and intricate views. Drawn almost imperceptibly to the castle, we crossed a spacious forecourt lined with retainer's cottages before gazing at a family of brown bears living in and thus guarding the moat, as they had apparently done for hundreds of years. Steep ramps and arches led the way to a succession of courtyards, some of which were decorated with Renaissance perspective painting to give an impression of intricate stonework, while others had hunting murals and inscriptions in ancient German calligraphy.

The castle extended westward along a narrow ridge and in the process jumped a deep ravine by means of an extraordinary multi-tiered bridge, giving stomach churning views of the town and river below. Of particular interest was a sluice-gate, down which one canoeist after another shot at considerable speed on their way downstream. More than half capsized and of course this provided us and a large crowd gathered on the bank far below, with free entertainment for as long as we were prepared to watch. It was amusing to observe the various tactics used – some would stop and survey it warily, choosing the best line while others just bashed straight down shouting loudly as they did so to give them courage. Neither method appeared the more successful and the river downstream was littered with upturned boats and floating hats.

On the far side of the bridge lay ornate gardens set out with box hedges and flower beds in the middle of which we found a charming eighteenth-century summer villa with a balustraded stone staircase on each side leading to a central terrace. I describe this in some detail because the terrace and steps could be used as a stage with a semi-circular amphitheatre of seats positioned in front of the villa providing space for an audience. This ingenious seating was actually mounted on a huge turntable set into the ground and the whole structure could be rotated through 180° so the seats faced the gardens and parkland, literally leaving the villa behind. The performance that evening was *Giselle* and so the seating faced the gardens and trees – a play or

146

opera would have them facing the other way towards the villa. What
an original and clever idea.

Walking back through the courtyards and into the town once more,
we stopped at a riverside bar to watch the hilarious activity still
occurring on the water while drinking a most welcome beer. The
current flowed swiftly and strongly, carrying an extraordinary array of
craft rapidly downstream and explained why the campsite had been so
full – boating on the Vltava was obviously a national sport.

Anything that floated seemed to do and ranged from a solitary
truck inner tube containing a contented looking man wearing a white
hat and dark glasses, to an enormous raft with a wicker house in the
middle surrounded by potted plants and chairs on which the crew
lounged comfortably. The river makes a huge loop around the town
and practically meets itself again, the narrow isthmus between the two
waters making an easily defensible position fortified by a medieval
wall and ditch. Many intrepid explorers were simply hiring canoes
for the 'Krumlov Excursion' ending up only a few yards from where
they began about thirty minutes later.

The streets by now were crowded with visitors and the only table
we could find for lunch was perched on a narrow ground floor
balcony six feet above the water which gurgled merrily underneath.
There were already at least ten other people sitting down out there and
I began to seriously worry about the tensile strength of concrete and
cast iron. This was not a happy lunch, mainly because we didn't eat
anything; despite requests, nobody served us and we left hungry,
demonstrating perfectly in my view the offhand attitude that develops
when there is a never-ending supply of tourists. While waiting not to
be served, however, we were able to eavesdrop on the conversation
going on at the adjacent table.

Two young English women in their early twenties sat smoking
with the remains of their meal still uncleared in front of them, tapping
ash into the now empty coffee cups as they discussed the next stage of
their Grand Tour. They were accompanied by a pair of weedy
looking blokes who played no part in the conversation whatsoever and
remained sitting obediently with a rather bemused expression as their
future was decided.

"Well wot I fink is we jus' gotta go to Bratislaaaver cos this book
sez [as she tapped a large paperback guide] this book sez it's brill an'

it sez it's on this big river fing... oh yeah the Danoobe... so wot d'yoo fink Sharon?"

Sharon stopped playing with her hair for a few moments and kept it in position by pushing a pair of expensive sunglasses high up her forehead before carefully examining her brown well manicured hands on which bright gold bangles and rings glinted in the sunlight.

"Nah," she announced after a few moments. "It's flippin' miles that Bratis... Bratis... wat's iz name?"

"Bratislaaaver," prompted the other girl.

"Oh yeah Bratislaaaver – it's flippin' miles it is, an 'oo's interested in the bleeding Danoobe anyhow? Oi fink we shud go an see that Chesskey place wot has all that beer an everyfink."

With this pronouncement, Sharon settled back in her chair and turned her face up to the sun in order to consolidate the deepening tan. Her friend, undeterred by this dismissal of Plan A, thumbed through the book for a while before starting again.

"Wotsit called this Chesskey place anyhow? I fought we was already in a Chesskey place – Chesskey Crumb somefink."

"Chesskey Crumbloft?" Sharon suggested, her eyes still shut.

"Yeah that's it – well wot's this Chesskey called wiv all that beer then?"

These two girls were smart, well-off judging by their trinkets, as hard as nails, clever in a devious way but completely and utterly brainless – in other words a success. Thatcher's children personified. When they had eventually decided on their destination they got up, collected their bags and cigarettes and with:

"Settle the bill Kevin, there's a luv," to one of the dummy-like objects still sitting at the table, minced out to the car – it was probably a white Ford Escort XR3 Cabriolet, but I didn't look.

We spent the rest of the afternoon exploring the nooks and crannies of this delightful place that we hadn't yet seen and also, in response to repeated pleas from the children, tried to organise a canoe trip on the river. This proved impossible, as every boat seemed to be booked up for days ahead and we were advised that our only hope was to try further upstream where the demand would probably be less. We hadn't really planned on staying anyway, so even though it was late, we hitched up and pedalled out of the main square, the focus as usual of a thousand stares from the tourists still thronging the streets.

There followed a pretty seventeen mile cycle along the Vltava through forests and gorges but with the road always remaining close to the river so that any inclines were minimal. Parties of canoeists were still coming down and in places rapids, with rocks showing through the white water, added an extra thrill to the experience. No towns or villages spoilt the quiet, sparkling valley until we arrived at Rozmberk where on turning a corner we could see yet another imposing castle dominating the tiny town at its foot.

The one hotel was full but as usual – we were almost beginning to expect this by now – we weren't just abandoned but handed over to the care of an old man in blue serge trousers who after a short walk beckoned us to follow him into the main post office. Our initial surprise soon turned to gratitude, as we were shown into a large family room on the second floor in what appeared to be some kind of worker's hostel with communal kitchens and showers. Two would have to sleep on the floor again, but with our blow up mats this was no problem and often was more comfortable than the saggy beds. Most importantly, Peter returned after 'scouting around' to announce that he had managed to book up a pair of canoes for the following day – it looked as though we would have a trip on the water after all.

Breakfast of our favourite fresh bread, butter and jam from the Potraviny – Supermarket, eaten in the communal dining room under the rather unfriendly stares of the other inhabitants and we were ready for our expedition – unfortunately the canoes weren't. The 'boat hire' centre that Peter had so proudly told us about was a near derelict cottage on the river bank next to a roaring weir with a few bits of dirty old plastic lying about in the front garden. Closer inspection revealed that these were – or had been at some stage – canoes, but they had been so extensively repaired with pink fibreglass patches that little of the original material remained. The proprietor was a middle-aged gypsy with long black greasy hair, a filthy string vest and a pair of equally dirty trousers held up by a piece of string over which an enormous pot belly swung as he walked barefoot towards us.

"Nicht Boot, Nicht Boot," he announced pointing at the hulks lying on the grass.

That was obvious but sensing mounting disappointment among the troops, Peter persisted, somewhat unwisely in my view, in persuading this master mariner to provide us with alternative vessels. While waiting for these we wandered through Rozmberk which, apart from the brooding castle, consisted of only a few houses clustered at either end of a stone bridge adorned, like most bridges in Czechoslovakia, with a statue of St John Nepomuk – the patron Saint of bridges who was thrown from the Charles Bridge in Prague in 1393. Only fifteen miles separated us from the Austrian border which, if we survived shipwreck, we would cross the following day before a long downhill to the Danube valley and the longest cycle path in Europe.

Our canoes when we eventually clambered into them looked suspiciously like the ones we had seen earlier, but with even more pink patches which were so thin that the light shone through. Alexander and Krister came with me while Anna and Oliver went with Peter. Other voyagers we had seen were supplied with sturdy waterproof barrels to keep clothes, food and cameras dry, but all we had was an old plastic bag tied at the top with a bit of string. Arrangements were made to be picked up downstream at Zatan and we were off, pushed into the swirling current by his crafty looking sons who happily agreed to look after our valuables – we must be mad.

Peter's boat settled in mid-stream and with the odd skilful tweak of a paddle was effortlessly carried along at about five knots – ours did precisely the same but insisted on going backwards. Attempts to correct this made us twirl like a ballerina, but when the rotation stopped our direction of travel remained the same.

"Alexander," I shouted. "Stop mucking about and turn us around – you'll have us over."

The others of course were convulsed at the sight of me in a rage, my paddle flailing uselessly in all directions and shouted unhelpful comments as we continued to pirouette like a sycamore leaf.

"This is ghastly," I wailed. "Stop this wretched thing and I'll get out."

The fact that we couldn't stop added to everyone's merriment and the general mirth continued for some time before we realised what the problem was – we were sitting in it the wrong way round. Correcting this helped to some extent and we began to relax and enjoy the gentle lapping of the water and the slowly changing scenery on the banks. Nowhere was the water deeper than four feet which was just as well since we were soon capsizing in a series of rapids which boiled over rocks and large boulders with a roar we could hear some distance away. The canoes banged and grated against these, springing leaks where the patches had been applied and we began to wonder whether they would survive the journey intact. The second capsize of my canoe occurred in a deeper than usual section where the water was funnelled between two rocks in a smooth, glassy cascade. Before we knew it, we were up to our waists in fast flowing water and the canoe practically submerged – none of this mattered of course but our passports and money, sealed thank God in a plastic sandwich box, had completely disappeared.

Right on cue, not one but two Arnold Schwarzenegger lookalikes clad in their usual skimpy loincloths appeared on the bank and without hesitation dived into the piranha infested waters. Any hopes of practising their life-saving skills on me however were soon dispelled by my shouts of:

"GET MY PURSE," which by this time had finally surfaced about 100yds downstream and was now well on its way towards Prague.

They were marvellous and spent quite some time retrieving our baggage and emptying the canoe of water before waving us off again.

So passed a pleasant but exhausting day for although we were fit, muscle groups that had withered over the past weeks were now forced into life once more. Our destination at Zatan was marked by a shallow weir extending the full width of the river and one of the master mariner's sons wearing an orange baseball cap as a pre-arranged signal, was already there waving us in. The canoes were dragged to the side, emptied of water and loaded on to a trailer connected to the most battered car I have ever seen. The bonnet was pointing upwards due to a non-existent rear suspension, the paint was peeling off and the tyres were completely unblemished by any vestige of tread.

"Eine Person, Eine Person," announced the master mariner crossly – why did he repeat everything twice? – pointing at three apprehensive canoeists who had arrived just before us and were now sitting in the back making the bonnet point even higher.

Foolishly in retrospect, Anna was selected and expecting the rest of us to be picked up in under thirty minutes, we waved her off in a cloud of black smoke before returning to the weir, where we lounged in a torrent of cooling water as it poured over the concrete sill. Krister as usual pottered around looking for animal life and had soon found a fresh water leech and a water snake about six inches long which wriggled over the surface with its head held high like a miniature Loch Ness monster. As we crowded round to examine this latest find, Ollie suddenly said "WOW" and pointed his finger at another water snake which was big enough to be the first one's grandfather – it must have measured 4ft and swam confidently along, its evil head swaying from side to side in the air as it went. Withdrawing our feet hastily, we thought back to our earlier capsizes and wondered what other quaint lifeforms this river produced.

We had to wait over two hours for the 'car' to return and when it did we could get no sense out of the man at all. In response to "Where is our daughter?" and "Is she alright?" all we got in reply was,

"Nicht Auto, Nicht Auto," repeated at sporadic intervals.

Eventually Peter lost his temper, put us all in the back and shouting loudly in English told him to take us back to Rozmberk – linguists will have you believe that this is not the way to make yourself understood when abroad but take it from me, if accompanied by the correct sign language, it really works. There followed one of the most hair-raising rides of my life with the car plus trailer slewing all over the road, narrowly missing lorries and precipices as our driver turned around every few minutes to give us another blast of,

"Nicht Auto, Nicht Auto."

"What the hell is he talking about?" croaked an unnaturally pale Peter as another horn blast faded away behind us. "Of course he's got a car – I'm bloody well sitting in it!"

Thoughts of Anna kidnapped or murdered passed through our minds as this maniac at last screeched to a halt outside his house and we all rushed off to the Post Office with a final,

"Nicht Auto, Nicht Auto," ringing in our ears. Unfortunately it was locked and Anna had been given the key when she left us – shouting proved fruitless as did throwing stones up at the window and it was some time later that a familiar towelled head poked out of the window and looking down on us all said somewhat crossly:

"Can't a girl have ANY peace to shave her legs?"

Chapter 11

Austria

After another frosty breakfast – perhaps the residents didn't like our bikes parked in the hall – we stocked up with cheap Czech bread and ham for lunch, knowing how expensive Austria would be, before cycling to Vyssi Brod, the last town on this side of the border.

Like many frontier towns, this was full of souvenir shops selling products typical of the country concerned – in this case pottery, embroidery and walking sticks. Ethnic crafts must be identical throughout the world however, since these three items seem to be a prominent feature in every souvenir shop from Istanbul to Ireland.

We were expecting hills after Vyssi Brod and we were not disappointed; the quiet road looping ever higher until we could look back on an expanse of forested hills extending north into Czechoslovakia. There was hardly a car in sight as, nearing midday, we at last breasted a rise to find a checkpoint complete with barrier blocking our way. Having been fooled coming into Czechoslovakia, we didn't celebrate until reaching the Austrian side, but this was at least three miles away with an eerie stretch of uninhabited road between. This wide band of nothingness used to be an ultra-sensitive frontier between east and west with mine fields and electronic listening posts making it impregnable to any would-be escapee. Suddenly there it was; a neat custom's house and a typical Austrian chalet with geraniums in window boxes behind it. The guard was smart, polite and friendly as he inspected our passports saying laughingly:

"I'm afraid the road continues to go up for another 3kms but then it is downhill all the way to Linz."

We had somehow expected the crossing to be at the highest point, but in our excitement at having travelled right across the Czech Republic, this seemed a minor problem and after our usual photographs for posterity, continued labouring up the incline.

Even without going through the check-point we would have known immediately that we had entered a different country by the nature of the road, which stretched upwards like a smooth black river indicating tarmac of the highest quality. Road markings were painted in bright yellow and there was even a line in the middle – something we had not seen since Denmark. A neat fence ran along the side, on the other side of which lush pastures were dotted with grazing cattle. A farm came into view with orderly piles of chopped wood surrounding it and a gleaming new tractor was parked outside on the immaculate drive. It was perfect; almost too perfect. The quaint dereliction to which we had grown used over the past weeks would simply not be allowed to exist here – it would not be tolerated. Austria has one of the highest standards of living in the world and their rural 'perfection' is only achieved with a great deal of money and a great many rules. Who is right? – the sloppy east or the pristine west? – I truly didn't know.

Sure enough, after 3kms the road levelled out in a pine forest and as we emerged on the other side there was a panoramic view of fields and hills dropping gradually away to the flat plain of the Danube valley twenty miles distant and which was now shimmering a violet colour in the hazy light. The first town we passed through was Bad Leonfelden – as pretty and picturesque as an Alpine postcard with bright flowers adorning pots and baskets hanging in every conceivable place. A friendly local stared in disbelief at the stickers adorning our trailer and we chatted to him for several minutes explaining our destination.

"You English are all crazy," he smiled. "But in a nice way I think."

Starved of decent cakes for nearly a month I spent £12 on the most gooey and chocolaty that I could find before searching for a picnic spot. We found one by a tumbling stream under the shade of a copse of trees and with, of course, that lovely view. While eating, a stag broke cover nearby and sniffed the air before crossing the meadow to the trees on the other side – perhaps our clothes needed washing again.

Although, as the border guard had said, the road was generally downhill, we still had to contend with some ferocious climbs as it switch-backed into valleys before rising again. At last no further hills appeared to block our view and we free-wheeled for perhaps ten miles, stopping every few minutes to allow our rims to cool and to ease the cramps in our hands from constantly applying the brakes. I had to stay behind with Krister, as he still refused to go faster than 11mph, but the others shot on ahead managing 35mph past a surprised policeman holding a radar gun – I don't think bicycle trailers were on his list.

Passing castles and gorges we quickly came to the outskirts of Linz, Austria's second city, and were just wondering how to avoid the centre when an Austrian on a bicycle asked if he could help. Yet again, completely unsolicited kindness resulted in him leading us several miles to the Danube cycle path, where he shook our hands and wished us well before continuing with his afternoon.

There it was, glinting and rippling in the light breeze only 100yds away – the alluring dream that had pulled us ever southwards for so many weeks. It was a happy, emotional moment as we laid our bikes on the grass and had a communal 'hug' before scrambling down the few rocks to the water – extraordinarily our computers showed that we had travelled exactly one thousand miles.

The problem now was which way? Left or right? After Berlin and Prague we had decided to wait until the Danube before finally deciding – well we were here now so what was it to be?

"If we turn right," said Peter, "we could be in Salzburg or Munich in a few days and get a train or we could cycle through Bavaria to the Rhine."

I know what he meant. West was the completion of the circle, safe and predictable. We would be going ever closer to home and places that we knew. Also we had been travelling for over six weeks – this surely was sufficient achievement. It would however have been the wrong decision – an opportunity lost. We might regret it for years to come.

"I'm for going left," I said determinedly, certain for the first time in my life of the precise direction I wanted to go. "We'll never get another opportunity to see Vienna and Budapest on bicycles."

There was no dissent and Peter, I think, was relieved that I had said it and not him – it had been his idea and he didn't want to feel that we were unwilling ducklings trailing along behind him. Left it was and finding the first green sign on the "DONAU RADWEG" (Danube Cycle path) pointing towards "WIEN" we pedalled away with the setting sun behind us on a smooth, flat, traffic-free path which extended as far as the border with Hungary nearly 350 miles away.

Only a few miles had been covered before we saw camping signs and turned off the path towards a flooded gravel pit which had been turned into a large and attractive leisure park. A tiny area next to a restaurant had been fenced off for camping and the hard, dusty ground was already full of tents and bicycles belonging to the mainly young people who were either just beginning or finishing this marvellous cycle route. In the unlikely event that an appetite for cycle holidays has been stimulated by the story so far, the reader with limited time would be well advised to consider the Danube path as an ideal introduction. Starting at the Austro-German border at Passau it extends as far as the Austro-Hungarian border at Hainburg, passing through Vienna en route. Most of this route is on a dedicated path next to the river, but occasionally, deviations are made which take the rider through quiet villages and vineyards. There is a multitude of hotels, zimmers and campsites to choose from along the way, making the night stopovers very straightforward – most 'Radfahrer's (cyclists) divide the journey into seven or eight stages of forty to fifty miles a day making a most pleasant week's holiday.

Finding an unoccupied corner, we put up the tents, pushing the pegs into the baked ground with much huffing and puffing. By this stage of the journey, all our pegs were bent at peculiar angles, 'Sod's Law' dictating that a stone would always be lying just under the surface exactly where the peg was inserted. Because of the weight, we had also neglected to bring a hammer but in retrospect this is essential. We resorted to finding lumps of rock with which we would club away at the skewer rather like Neanderthal Man wielding a hand axe discovering, as no doubt our ancestors had, that the right tools make all the difference.

The lake was wonderful for swimming; clear, clean and warm with a steeply shelving shingle bottom. The boys discovered a slipway and found that the surface was so slippery that they could take a run before sliding all the way down on their feet and toppling into the deep water.

As we were preparing to walk over to the nearby restaurant for supper, a very friendly English couple, presumably noticing the large GB sign on the trailer, came over for a chat. They had driven from Hamburg and like us visited Prague before coming South via Cesky Krumlov and the Sumava Hills.

"We've driven nearly a thousand miles," said the wife. "We really want to go on to Budapest but it's much too far and my husband's got to be back in work next week."

156

"Well we've just cycled that far," I replied with a smile, "and we're definitely going to Budapest."

They were so interested in what we had done that they spent some time looking at our maps, tents and bicycles before taking their leave.

"I think that's marvellous," said her husband. "Next year we are definitely having a bicycle holiday. These two weeks have been such a rush that we haven't seen anything properly and sitting in our car in all that heat was a nightmare."

When I was being frazzled it didn't occur to me that sitting in a car would be worse but at least we generated a cooling breeze as we pedalled along. I remembered all the long drives we had made in the past through France with hot, bad-tempered children sitting in the back; they hadn't complained once this year – there hadn't been time.

Our meal, eaten outside on a balmy night under a carpet of stars was huge in portion, bland in taste, expensive in price and rich in bacterial contamination.

Krister awoke next morning with a temperature and stomach pains and we all fell ill at about twelve hour intervals thereafter. There was no point in staying put, however, so with the poor little chap stopping every ten minutes to be sick, we packed up and slowly continued our way east. The path ran flat and true, right next to the broad river as we cycled into the morning sun with a light breeze behind us ruffling the surface of the water. Enormous barges would occasionally pass, laden with coal or aggregate and often so low in the water that they appeared in imminent danger of foundering. Sometimes, several would be lashed together making two or even three abreast, the whole ungainly mass being pushed by a tug wedged in the stern.

We were not alone on the path and kept company with a mixture of cycle tourists, commuters and roller-bladers going in both directions – a sort of motorway for self-propulsion. The tourists were often elderly Americans easily identifiable by their Bermuda shorts, appalling cycle position (with knees hitting their chins at each stroke), white hair and expensive dental work who were partaking in organised daily stages of twenty to thirty miles. Each night would be spent in a luxury hotel with all baggage, apart from a small lunch box, taken on ahead by car and put in their rooms. We often passed these five star stopovers as we searched for a campsite with just a slight twinge of envy at the thought of hot baths, clean sheets and a wonderful meal accompanied by fine local wines – we could never afford it. Our laden trailer, however, was often a source of comment.

"Say Elmer, will you just look at that!" exclaimed a wrinkled old lady wearing a broad hat, sunglasses, bobbysocks and trainers. "It's so keyute the way all their luggage is'n that there little box on wheels."

"Weell Aah doo declare," Elmer would reply, "an' jus' take a look at those little ones having the time of their lives I'll bettcha."

This conversation could go on for some time but never involved us – we were simply part of the local colour provided for their interest and entertainment.

The path left the river for a short time just before 11 a.m. and passing a shady Gasthof we took the opportunity to have an early lunch. Other cyclists clearly had the same idea and many of the tables under a vine covered trellis were already full of lycra covered 'Radfahrer's tucking into succulent steaks and apple strudel. Prices however, were prohibitive, the cheapest thing on the menu being a toasted cheese and ham sandwich for £3 – six of these and lemonades set us back £25. Picnics were about to make a come back.

I always feel like a poor relation in comparison to the rest of Western Europe where living standards and prices seem to be so much higher than our own. Whenever we are abroad, I always have to carefully work out what we can afford and eating out is certainly a luxury. We are such a long way behind the other member states of the Common Market and the pound undergoes one devaluation after another – it is never strong and it went down relentlessly while we were away. The Austrians on the other hand, despite backing the wrong horse fifty years ago, have never had it so good and accept this good fortune with a smug condescension as though it is their natural due. Where have we gone wrong?

The toasties when they came were disgusting. Mother's Pride white sliced bread with one piece of processed cheese and one piece of slimy processed ham – yuck. To survive until the better value of Hungary we would have to be careful and cook for ourselves once more.

This break did nothing to improve Krister's tummy – nor anybody else's for that matter – so we pressed on through more immaculate villages and orchards until the town of Mauthausen, site of yet another infamous concentration camp. We saw no sign of this though but instead found a large municipal outdoor swimming pool where the children spent the afternoon swishing down water slides while Peter and I phoned Brian.

"You're going the wrong way!" a distant Brian shouted down the line. "I thought you were coming home – you're all MAD."

It was great to hear him again and to discover that our house was still standing. I don't know what we would have done without him and he came into the house at least once or even twice a day to check that all was well. We might have the lowest standard of living in Europe but there is no doubt that we also have the highest level of crime and we had left our home like Fort Knox with alarms and multiple locks on every door.

"I wouldn't do that if I was you Sir," a policeman had said on the last occasion we were burgled. "It just makes them angry and they'll smash 'em down."

Wonderful advice from our custodians of law and order.

After only twenty three miles we were forced to stop at a little site near Naarn since by this stage Ollie was doubled up with cramps and also had a temperature. I would love to have tucked him up in a cosy bed but the best we could manage was a mat and sleeping bag under a willow tree, where he lay looking very sorry for himself. Leaving Anna, Alexander and Krister to look after him, Peter and I cycled back a few miles with the now empty trailer to a supermarket we had passed to stock up for supper and breakfast. This arrangement proved excellent and within a short time were on our way back laden with goodies; I made a mental note to try this technique out next time I visited Sainsbury's, visualising the deprecating looks as I parked next to the usual selection of Range Rovers and BMWs. Ollie of course was charging around on our return but on seeing us winced and held his stomach until a little more sympathy was extracted.

It was a lovely little site next to a small lake and separated from the Danube by a high embankment. As the afternoon wore on, more cyclists arrived and we watched with interest the various techniques for setting up camp. Most travelled in pairs and carried their luggage in enormous panniers, the tent usually being a tiny igloo which needed thin flexible poles threaded through tunnels in the fabric before a fly sheet was pegged out to cover it. To our perverse delight this all took a very long time indeed. The tent closest to us was owned by two young lads from Budapest who were able to give us much useful information about the Hungarian part of the route, where there was no official path and low lying swampy country made a detour from the river necessary. In return, Peter tried to help with a noisy bottom bracket on one of their bikes, but his spanners were the wrong size to take it apart. Bicycle maintenance is absolutely infuriating, because nuts, screws, axles, chains and all the other important bits that make a bike work – especially bottom brackets – are never standard and require a huge range of tools to undo them. Manufacturers must take a macabre pleasure in making DIY repairs as complicated as possible.

No tools could repair the large bulging split that Peter had just noticed in the side of our trailer where the fibreglass had finally given in after weeks of jolting with too much weight. There was nothing we could do except wedge a stuff sack over it in the hope that nothing would fall out. We could only keep our fingers crossed that the worst of the terrain was behind us and that it wouldn't get any bigger, thereby obstructing the rotation of the wheels.

The following day was a Sunday and this had several implications. Firstly we had no money, having spent our last schilling at the supermarket and secondly we were asked by a fellow camper if we would like to attend a memorial service at Mauthausen Camp. To the latter we at first said yes but on reflection decided we had had enough of the Nazis at Teresin and Lidice so changed our mind – in any case it would have meant retracing our steps for ten miles and we wanted to press on.

Lack of 'readies' was much more of a problem, since we couldn't even afford the site fee of £15. Our selection of credit cards and cheques were turned down with a firm "Nein, Nein," but eyes lit up with a reverential smile when I managed to find some forgotten Deutschmarks hiding in my purse. "Ach so – goot, goot. Danker. Danker." Good old Sterling had already been given the thumbs down.

Hoping to find a cashpoint at one of the towns en route, we set off rather late since Ollie still wasn't quite right, climbing the embankment to the cycle path under an uncharacteristically cloudy sky. The river here was broad and wide, with the flat countryside extending to the horizon on each side interspersed with small villages and white steepled churches. Near the water, the vegetation was as lush as a tropical jungle with the flowering rhododendrons and eucalyptus trees arching over our heads alive with the cries of birds. Maize grew as tall and as thick as bamboo and I would not have been surprised to see a dark skinned Indian girl wearing a sarong carrying a water jug on her head. Mile followed restful mile with no sign of a town, so we stopped in a clearing on the riverbank for a leisurely picnic. Opposite us lay an island with a white shingle beach on which a family were spending the day, their little boat bobbing gently at anchor.

The current was tremendous and Alexander, strong swimmer though he is, could only just keep in one place with his front crawl and only dared go a few feet from the rocky bank on which we had spread ourselves. The occasional monster barge combination swept past doing about ten knots – it was incredible how these were steered, since the Captain would begin his rudder correction at least half a mile from any bend and I don't think they could stop. A luxurious passenger ferry marked 'Budapest' also went by, vividly demonstrating that this huge waterway, which rises in the Black Forest, links so many major European cities before emptying finally into the Black Sea 1500 miles away. It is the continent's major artery and was the route that our ancestors took as they gradually colonised Europe from their origins in the east. We could have stayed there all day.

At Grein, the character of the scenery changed with the river funnelled through an impressive gorge about five miles long. Medieval castles guarded the narrows and the path was forced to follow a main road wedged in between the water and steep cliffs. It was beautiful, rather like a Norwegian Fjord, with light dancing on the wavelets and shimmering from the water vapour trapped between the precipitous slopes. We found a wooden pontoon jutting out over the dark green depths as the current rushed past with even greater speed than before and sat there eating biscuits until the sun began to dip behind the high hills. At Persenbeug we at last found a cash machine accepting Visa, having failed miserably throughout the day to have our Eurocheque cards recognised by all the flashy computers bearing the EC sign that we had come across.

"What you need," whined the adolescent in our bank who had a badge on his blue pin stripe suit proclaiming him a 'Foreign Currency Consultant', "is a Eurocheque Card – this is recognised throughout the countries you propose to travel in and of course your personal identity number makes the transaction completely foolproof."

Yes, so foolproof that we never managed to extract a cent. Oh well, let's try this Visa one.

Insert card. Look, how clever, it's recognised me as English and is telling me what to do in my own language.

"ENTER PERSONAL NUMBER"
Personal number entered.

"PRESS CONFIRM"
Confirm pressed.

"ENTER AMOUNT IN SCHILLINGS"
Two thousand schillings entered.

"PRESS CONFIRM"
Confirm pressed.

"PLEASE WAIT A MOMENT"
Moment waited while mechanical whirrings occur. Then:

"INVALID. YOUR CARD HAS BEEN RETAINED FOR SECURITY REASONS"

Bloody marvellous – no money and no card. This country is beginning to irritate me. Taking courage in both hands we inserted Peter's card, knowing if that was eaten as well we would be in trouble – fortunately after some electronic ponderings it reluctantly spat out not only the card, but also £50 worth of schillings, which at the current rate of expenditure however would be gone by tomorrow.

Marbach, where we stopped for the night, is a name that will live in infamy in the annals of our family. No longer in a gorge, the river was broad and sluggish once again, a description which perfectly fitted the bad-tempered woman in the campsite reception. Sitting behind a counter, she was booking in another couple with much sighing and shaking of her head as if it was all too much trouble, when we all trooped inside.

"You must VAIT," she snarled at Peter, taking note of the passports in his hand. "Only VUN must VAIT," she added with a malevolent glance at the children.

The couple in front didn't seem to be faring any better, as each question they asked was greeted with either a shrug or shake of the head plus more sighs – perhaps it was just the way she breathed. Our turn at last.

"Hello," smiled Peter. "I wonder if you..."

"Number of perzons," interrupted fatty without looking up.

"Er well there are..."

"Paassports," she commanded still looking down but now holding her hand over the counter, the fingers twitching irritably.

These were inspected suspiciously and returned by the disembodied hand.

"Auto registration number?" as she scribbled away.

"Er well we haven't got one," said Peter apologetically.

"Nicht Auto!" (I'd heard that before somewhere). "NICHT AUTO!"

"No – er I mean yes. We have come mit fahrrad [with bicycles]," he explained with an ingratiating grin accompanied by pedalling motions of his hands.

More shaking of the head indicated that she was not about to enter into an enthusiastic discussion of gear ratios and we waited while she added up the amount due on a calculator.

"Drei hundert siebenundfunfzig schillings," she eventually announced after several minutes of muttering, thus wiping out half of our hard won capital at a stroke. Assuring us that we could go "Alles, Alles" with a dismissive wave of the hand, we thankfully picked up our bicycles and trudged over the gravel path to a vacant spot next to a hedge that separated the site from the main road.

We had just about sufficient time to pitch the tents and stack the bikes before fatty reappeared, waddling down the path carrying a mobile telephone like a policeman's radio. Our score for the inspection that followed was not a high one.

"Zis tent must NOT be zer," she fumed pointing at it with the aerial of her telephone. "An zese fahrrads must NOT be on ze tree, an zis truck," with a contemptuous glance at our trailer. "You zaid NOTHING of zis truck – you must pay extra vor zis truck."

By inspection number three we had satisfied all the major demands and were simply being picked up on details like our washing line and foam mats.

In an effort to escape Stalagluft 2 for a few hours, we sneaked out to find some supper despite our previous experience. Camping at the end of a long day is one thing, but cooking and especially washing up, was beginning to pall. Next to the site was a small marina, dug out of the river bank and full of yachts and motor cruisers. At one end, a Danube barge, permanently moored and well past its useful life, had been converted into a snack bar and was already full of raucous middle-aged Austrians doing their best to imitate a Munich Bier Kellar.

The men were loud, red faced and corpulent, dressed in short-sleeved, white, open-necked shirts and belted slacks over which the inevitable beer belly drooped as a sign of their masculinity. The hard-looking women, cigarettes in hand, were listening intently to their husbands, agreeing with whatever they were saying with an enthusiastic "Ja, Ja, Ja" whenever there was a momentary lull in the male-dominated conversation.

The remaining half of our reserves were squandered on almost inedible food, served on paper plates from a filthy kitchen in what had once been the barge's wheelhouse and any chance I might have had of escaping a tummy upset disappeared with this second load of salmonella.

I spent the rest of the night being violently sick into my plastic washing up bowl, which had proved itself to be a most useful purchase, while Peter snored peacefully in his sleeping bag outside the tent. Why he chose this particular evening to leave us all I never did quite understand – perhaps he'd had a premonition – but I took some small satisfaction from the fact that it rained at 3 a.m.

We all felt pretty ghastly next morning with Anna and I taking it in turns to sprint for the loo while the boys slowly packed up. Spirits were not lifted by a visit from the Obergruppenfuerher who cheered us no end by stating,

"Ze rule is zat you must go by 10 a.m. or pay for vun more day."

She also wasn't too pleased by our frequent use of her toilet block and when Peter tried to explain the problem she retorted frostily,

"Zen you must see ze doctor..."

"I AM A BLOODY DOCTOR," his voice resounded throughout the site. "AND YOU ARE THE MOST UNPLEASANT PERSON I HAVE EVER MET, CONGRATULATIONS!"

As they say, enough is enough.

We cycled only as far as necessary to be out of sight of this ghastly place before stopping to rest on a shady part of the bank. I was still being sick intermittently and felt absolutely drained, so we spread out the mats and dozed the morning away watching a tiny car ferry going back and forth across the wide expanse of water. By midday the nausea had eased and we slowly made our way the ten miles to Melk where we stopped for lunch. Melk was a lovely town dominated by a huge, ornate church built on a rocky spur overlooking the river and full of medieval squares and streets. Peter and the boys managed some bananas and fruit yoghurts but Anna and I only had some peculiar tasting fizzy liquid with a slightly bitter taste to it, which Peter had found in Melk's only supermarket. I wish I could have explored a little, but instead simply sat on the steps of a fountain longing for a comfortable bed and wondering how I was going to manage the afternoon.

To add to my misery, the path from Melk left the Danube for a few miles and climbed an agonising hill, up which cars and lorries roared leaving a blue mist of diesel oil behind them which was deeply inhaled with each gasping breath. The exercise on an empty stomach plus the pollution nearly finished me off and waves of nausea resurfaced once more.

A massive suspension bridge took us back to the north side of the river and some of the prettiest scenery so far as we meandered through the Danube Wine Country – I just wish I had felt well enough to really enjoy it. The path rose above the river which was always in sight and undulated through a series of picturesque villages connected by ranges of vine-covered hills. Each one seemed more charming than the last and on the wooded heights above them, majestic castles, sited as much for their romantic effect as any military purpose, glinted in the afternoon sun with flags fluttering from their turrets.

At one village we stopped in the cobbled square, while Krister and Ollie swung on the end of a long handled water pump next to a trough, eventually producing a gurgle of water from the spout. The frenzied creaking emanating from rusty pistons caused an old man in dark glasses to open the front door of his villa and feebly shout something before he slammed it and returned down the long hallway, the noise of his slippered feet and tapping stick gradually fading.

Near Goisbach we passed another bicycle trailer, towed by Lech Walesa's double, with two small boys pedalling like fury behind him.

The trailer was a work of art and had been hand made out of gleaming aluminium sheeting with a beautifully crafted towing hitch. It looked however somewhat ungainly as it lurched along behind 'Lech's' bike and he appeared to undergo some considerable strain, with sweat pouring off his forehead as each leg was forced down in turn. It was a tragedy that the hours of careful labour had been let down by two catastrophic flaws in design. Firstly, it was nearly five feet high and closely resembled the sort of duty free trolleys that air hostesses loath pushing down the middle of aeroplanes...

"Drink Sir, drink Madam? No I'm sorry but we've run out of tonic water, will bitter lemon do?"

There is always a never-ending supply of bitter lemon.

"Duty Free goods Sir? No, I'm sorry but the metal model of the Boeing 747 is no longer available – what about a man's wrist watch Sir?"

The air resistance alone would have been enough to bring the tears to his eyes but the second mechanical disaster was the wheels. These had a diameter of about 6ins, but the high centre of gravity of the towering edifice above them caused the whole affair to sway from side to side, alternately squashing the pathetic little tyres. We saw them several times over the next few days as we headed towards Vienna and would wave encouragement to the Dad who was literally putting his all into giving his sons an adventure to remember.

After making a detour through the beautiful medieval walled town of Durnstein, we stopped after a creditable forty-two miles at a crowded campsite in the large and important city of Krems. There was hardly a square foot free from caravans, enormous camping trucks and tents and as we circled around looking for a space we could sense the hostile gaze of the incumbent residents fiercely protecting their patch of territory and willing us to pass by. We had to go somewhere and eventually settled on a tiny corner next to the river between a small dome tent and a caravan, the owners of which were sitting outside enjoying a bottle of wine in the evening sun. Initial disappointment that we had picked on them, turned to surprise and then amazement as the trailer was unpacked and before long they were smiling and nodding at us. They even came over with a new box of matches for us when they saw that we were unable to light the stove.

Before long we had settled in and were also frowning at the new arrivals, willing them to go anywhere but next to us. The small tent on the other side was occupied by two friendly young Austrian lads on their first cycle tour, who listened open mouthed to our journey and insisted on Peter tracing it out for them on our maps, before inspecting our bicycles and baggage. We felt like seasoned veterans as our advice was absorbed with slow nods of the head and details were scribbled down in a little notebook. Like so many others we had seen on the Danube path, they were using mountain bikes with huge knobbly tyres which although fine for the odd quagmire, made cycling on tarmac at least twice as difficult as it need have been – the unnecessary effort generated throughout the world as a result of this simple fact is enough to bring tears to your eyes.

The simple solution would be to sell all mountain bikes with ordinary tyres but then this would detract from the reason why people buy them – in this sedentary age they want to somehow regain that primeval contact with the great outdoors without ever going there. Mountain bikes (the very name makes you wistful) with go anywhere tyres that spend most of their life in the garage or if they're lucky the local cycle path, 4x4 luxury jeeps (why are they called that? Are cars 2x2 and bicycles 1x1?) that every day brave the rigours of dropping the children off at school, jackets designed for the summit of Everest that have never strayed from the local shopping precinct – I must stop before I get carried away.

I feel that I have perhaps been a little hard on Austrian cuisine, so I will try to make amends. Still feeling delicate from the after effects of 'the bug', we walked over to the camp café as dusk was falling, since Ollie had spied a large pizza sign and would accept nothing else. A smiling, dumpy little lady behind the serving hatch was very apologetic.

"Bitte? Pizza? Es tut mir leid [I'm sorry]. Nein Pizza. Schnitzel? Es tut mir leid. Nein Schnitzel. Wurst? Es tut mir leid. Nein Wurst."

Well thank God for that – I couldn't face another sausage.

As we gloomily turned away however, she suddenly called us back with a,

"Ein augenblick [wait a moment]. Ich haben Suppe!"

I have a feeling that this soup had not been meant for public consumption at all, since it was absolutely delicious and obviously home-made. It was more like a stew than a soup, with tender pieces of meat, potatoes and carrots surrounded by a thick sauce and accompanied by hunks of fresh bread and butter. She nodded and beamed as the children, including Ollie, tucked in, making us feel like her personal guests – Marbach was all but forgotten.

Walking back to the tents feeling 100% better we couldn't help but notice a huge floodlit building several miles away on the other side of the river. Situated on the top of distant hills and bathed in a yellowish light, it appeared to be floating in the air like a cruise liner on a dark sea. A quick look at the map proved it to be the monastery at Gottweig – the Catholic church in Austria is a powerful and wealthy institution and we had passed many large, well maintained churches in complete contrast to the ones in East Germany and Czechoslovakia.

After a group photo next day at the request of the Austrian lads, a long detour through the centre of Krems eventually led us over yet another bridge to the quieter south side and a straight flat path which ran alongside the river for mile after mile. It was deserted apart from the occasional fellow cyclist and completely devoid of villages or even houses. With no traffic to worry about and the never-ending ribbon of water to hold our interest, we had a wonderfully relaxing morning, stopping only occasionally at one of the intermittent benches for a drink or piece of chocolate.

At intervals of several miles, the river would be interrupted by massive lock systems presumably capable of taking the monster barges which were still a regular feature, but this was the only evidence of habitation that we saw. We had a picnic lunch at a trestle table just downstream from one of these locks and not a single person passed during the whole hour that we sat there enjoying the fresh air, simple food and the wide expanse of sky all around us.

During the morning, Krister had been going slower and slower for some reason best known to himself, so that despite the ideal conditions we averaged less than 10mph. The others found this painfully slow and would forge on ahead, but inevitably they would have to stop and wait every so often in order for the slow ones to catch up. This process was becoming more and more frustrating and so to avoid a mutiny, Peter tried towing Krister with a piece of rope while Alexander pulled the trailer. It worked like a charm and within seconds we were whizzing along at 20mph with Krister grinning delightedly at the ride – within less than an hour of this exhilarating pace we had arrived at Tulln.

Tulln, unlike anywhere else on the Danube, had made the very most of its setting by creating lovely landscaped gardens all along the river edge. Columns, statues and flowering shrubs extended for nearly a mile next to the water, with the cycle path running slightly above it all on an embankment. The centre piece was an extraordinary series of fountains composed of boulders piled one on top of the other like strange totem poles. Water cascaded down from the top of each one and combined to form a broad, shallow stream at the base which gurgled away down a grating at one end. It was a fountain to get involved with, so taking our shoes and socks off we spent a happy hour paddling around and cooling off.

Tulln needed further investigation, so leaving the bikes locked up by the river we spent an hour exploring and shopping. This was certainly a town of lovely fountains, for in the market place stood another masterpiece of cascading water. From the rim of a carved stone basin about thirty feet in diameter, ten powerful jets of water curled towards another smaller basin, set on a raised central pedestal, in such a precise way that they all met exactly above it before overflowing back to the main pool. This fountain appeared on every postcard and guide book and was clearly a most famous local attraction – we bought a sticker showing it to add to our lengthening display on the side of the trailer.

The other famous attraction in Tulln is the Egon Schiele Museum near the riverside gardens. Egon Schiele was a prominent Viennese painter in the early 1900s (he died in 1918) and like the Viennese musicians of the same period produced works that the experts say require time, effort and intellect to understand. My instinctive response is that I haven't got the time, I'm too lazy to make the effort and my intellect will never be up to it – thank God.

Schiele's mother came from Cesky Krumlov and there is another small museum devoted to his work there.

Tulln also boasted a large and peaceful campsite and despite the fact we had only come thirty-three miles and it was still early, we decided to make the most of this pleasant little town and stop for the night. While checking in, we met an Australian couple with rucksacks who were in the middle of an Inter-railing holiday and had booked a chalet in the site for a few days. Amazingly it transpired that he was teaching in a Swansea primary school while on a year's exchange from Sydney – what a small world. Anna, not really paying attention to our conversation and seeing two large rucksacks which she immediately identified with Duke of Edinburgh expeditions, suddenly piped up:

"Gosh, did you walk all the way here? It's bad enough cycling!"

Although directed to a precise spot in a huge expanse of nothingness, we'd had enough of officialdom and found a quiet shaded spot reserved for caravans – tents are always given the grotty spots that nobody else wants.

We spent a restful afternoon here catching up on jobs and repairs including cleaning the bicycles and trailer, for tomorrow a short bend in the Danube would take us into the elegant city of Vienna and we wanted to look our best.

Chapter 12

Vienna

From Tulln, the path continued through quiet, low-lying country but although the day was bright and sunny, there was a stiff breeze, which of course was blowing directly against us. It was also blowing against the flow of the river which was raised into myriads of wavelets which slopped against the bank making a pleasant plopping sound. It was during a mid-morning stop for coffee at a cyclists' refreshment kiosk that Peter at last discovered the tiny piece of wire that had been responsible for Krister's daily punctures. Poor Krister, who thought he'd been doing something terribly wrong for all those weeks, was now at last triumphantly vindicated and spent the rest of the morning beaming delightedly as he continued to be towed along.

Just past Hoflein we stopped for lunch at a shingle beach where a small tributary flowed into the mainstream, forming a large shingle bank as it did so. Again there was a faintly tropical feeling to the surroundings and had we not been able to see the other side of the river, it would have done nicely for somewhere in the West Indies with exposed tree roots along the shoreline looking exactly like a mangrove swamp. The sun was hot and the wind had dropped, making us seek shade in the cool of an overhanging bank near a small lagoon almost enclosed by the finger of smooth white stones curving out into deeper water.

Fresh rolls with ham, cheese and tomatoes, peaches and apples for dessert plus a generous slab of Swiss chocolate left us feeling content as we watched the various wading birds picking their way through the shallows looking for morsels of food. After eating, we all went swimming in the clear water before drying ourselves on the warm pebbles, although I had to make do with my underwear following the loss of my swimsuit on the train from Kralupy. Our swim was a leisurely affair and consisted of wading out a little way from the shingle bank and lying back in the water which swiftly carried you several hundred yards downstream, whereupon you could stand up and walk back up the beach before repeating the exercise. So passed several happy hours until Peter announced:

"We should really get a move on and find a campsite close to Vienna."

As we neared the outskirts of this old capital of the Austro-Hungarian Empire, the quiet rural landscape began to give way to increasingly dense areas of population and the green cycle-path signs became more and more difficult to follow. I don't know if the people who put up signposts ever test the results of their efforts, but time and time again on our trip we would follow a series of signs with a feeling of ever increasing happiness and confidence only to find that they would suddenly stop, leaving us frustrated and bewildered. Despite learning the hard way to treat all signs with deep mistrust, we still couldn't help the spark of hope that they regularly generated in moments of despair. They are akin to the lights that Cornish wreckers are supposed to have set up on rocks in order to lure storm tossed ships into 'safer' havens, the unfortunates only realising at the last moment the fate that awaited them. So it was today that, when we were beginning to get worried, a sign appeared reaffirming that we were indeed still on the Donau Radweg and that a campsite was only 2km away.

"That's marvellous," crowed Peter. "And to think that you lot were beginning to doubt me!"

Sign followed sign – 2km, 1.75km, 1.3km – with an accuracy that was breathtaking. These efficient Austrians really seemed to be going overboard but of course the inevitable happened and they simply stopped at a busy junction where we could have taken any one of five possible directions.

"Just GREAT," Peter fumed after his third trip around the intersection, "I can't see another sign anywhere, although the cycle-path does seem to cross the river on that bridge."

Quick to take the credit when all is well, Peter's self-congratulatory comments gradually died away as we pedalled deeper and deeper into a maze of built up streets and dual carriageways until he finally conceded that we were lost. Occasionally an urban cycle path would appear which we would follow hopefully for a mile or so before it petered out – what an apt description – but nobody we asked knew of any "camping platz" and to be honest didn't seem too interested.

"This is hopeless," announced a weary tour leader after about an hour of us following him like a herd of sheep. "Let's take that major road over there and follow it south until we are clear of the city – it's far too busy here for a campsite."

The road he pointed out curved over the Danube which I thought we'd already crossed and although big, was fairly quiet and had a wide expanse of tarmac inside the white painted lines making it ideal for cycling. Off we went, glad to be escaping the claustrophobic urban mayhem and were soon speeding along comfortably at 20mph, remarking to each other as we did so at how friendly the car drivers were, since every one sounded their horn as they passed. Peter even started waving back and pointing at the GB sign thinking they were simply saluting a brave British achievement. We may have carried on for some time in this way had not one driver, more courageous than the others and in retrospect at great risk to himself, slowed down to our pace and with the window open shouted across the awful truth.

"VAT IN GOD'S NAME ARE YOU DOING HERE? ZIS IS ZE MAIN MOTORWAY TO WIENER NEUSTADT – BICYCLES ARE VERBOTEN!"

Muttering something presumably uncomplimentary about "Ze Engleesh," he roared off leaving us with no option but to turn round and cycle back the wrong way along what had turned out to be the hard shoulder, whilst enduring the flashing headlights and blaring horns of every car and lorry that passed.

"Well how was I to know?" said Peter defensively when we regained the urban mayhem. "If I had a little more help with the map reading these mistakes wouldn't happen."

"But you're the only one with a map," I retorted. "Who else can do it?"

Unable to reply to this devastating piece of logic, he glared at me before setting off in a determined fashion along a busy shopping street, his body language indicating that he didn't really care if we followed him or not.

The suburbs went on for depressing mile after depressing mile with smart shopping streets interspersed with scruffy tenement blocks from the doorways of which ragged Arab or gypsy children stared at us as we passed. You certainly see the whole of a city by cycling into it – both the good and the bad. At last Peter gave a shout and pointed at a big wheel a few miles away.

"That must be the Ferris Wheel," he said. "It's right in the middle of the city so if we're lucky we'll find a hotel."

The wheel loomed larger and larger until it completely disappeared due to the perspective of the mainly 19th century apartment blocks and office buildings that surrounded us. Passing a seedy bar and wearing only a bikini top and cycle shorts I was immediately volunteered to go in and ask for accommodation – to my eternal surprise I did so and marched into the gloomy, smoke-filled bar occupied by working class men having an early evening drink.

"Excuse me," I began, "can anyone tell me where I can find a hotel?"

The barman paused in his perennial polishing of glasses as the conversation died away and fifty pairs of eyes swivelled round to look at me. Well I didn't look that bad – seven weeks of cycling had produced a tanned, muscular figure set off to perfection by my current outfit and only marginally let down by the unflattering cycle shoes.

"You vant hotel?" leered a sweaty, bald-headed man as he got up from his seat. "I find hotel – you come viz me!"

"It's for six people," I replied, my voice squeaking slightly. "My husband and four children are outside."

Never has a change in intent been so rapid – after checking the truth of my statement by peering through the door, he now became our staunchest ally and co-opting two of his drinking chums, came outside to give Peter precise directions.

"Go left zen right zen left and valk two hundred metres and you vill find ze hotel Miramour – zat is best."

"Nein, Nein, Nein," interrupted the second man. "Ze hotel Miramour is too much schillings vor zese people – zey must go right zen left zen right and valk only one hundred meters to hotel Rudolph vich is half price."

"But ver vill zey put ze bicycles?" exclaimed the third man. "Hotel Rudolph is cheap but zer is nein garage."

"Vait a moment," said the first man. "Ve haf forgotten ze hotel Tabor – zat is cheap and has a garage."

After his colleagues had agreed, more complicated instructions followed and we left them on the corner, glasses of beer in hand, as they anxiously watched us depart. I'm not sure whether we ever did find the correct hotel, as I was thoroughly confused by this stage, but after a few fairly brusque rejections, we found one with three double rooms for £110 per night breakfast included – something of a feat for central Vienna in August.

The bikes and trailer were stored in a small, dank yard at the back of the hotel which was surrounded by high walls and overlooked by hundreds of dirty windows. The rooms were all on different floors and ours, at the end of a dark passageway on the third storey, was like the black hole of Calcutta. The room must have been built around the double bed, for it was virtually the only piece of furniture and there was no way now that it could be moved. The 8ft x 6ft box was windowless, airless and unfortunately for us the only one of our rooms with a shower, which occupied a tiny cubicle in the corner. This meant of course that within minutes of arriving, four filthy children were fighting for the right to first shower, divesting themselves of their clothing in the process, while Mum and Dad took refuge on the bed like shipwrecked mariners on a life-raft. Soon water was swimming over the floor, soaking piles of dirty clothes and making the atmosphere so steamy that it was difficult to breathe, let alone see.

"This is hopeless," I sighed from my perch on the bed. "Alexander – go and ask the manager if we can use another bathroom."

To my surprise he returned a few minutes later carrying a large key which opened a bathroom on the next floor containing an enormous cast iron bath set on clawed feet surrounded by mirrored tiles. When it eventually filled up, he wallowed in it like a film star for over an hour, singing tunelessly.

"Pleez make sure zat you haf ze keys," said the manager as we left to look for supper. "Vi only haf ze one set – it is best if vi look after zem."

I ought to have known that three sets of keys would be a recipe for disaster, but assuming that they were all safely on the board behind the counter we walked towards the Volks Prater where the famous Ferris Wheel was brightly lit up and revolving slowly in the darkening sky.

At the end of Stadtgutgaten and just before the Wien Nord U-Bahn station, we passed a colourful Chinese restaurant with some outdoor tables set up under a canopy on the wide pavement. The vote was unanimous – after weeks of fairly basic meals and picnics we would celebrate Vienna with a blow out Cantonese feast. The waitress was charming and dressed in a traditional Chinese embroidered smock and trousers, smiling and bowing as she took our order. The five course meal was delicious – undoubtedly the best so far – and so huge in quantity that despite excellent efforts all round, some was left. This of course was Peter's fault since he always gets carried away when ordering food, but to be fair this opportunity had not presented itself before and previous evening repasts had often left us feeling hungry.

How delightful to sit outside on a balmy night, watching the ever turning wheel with a feeling of pride and satisfaction that we had come so very far, that we were closer than ever before as a family and that we knew with an absolute certainty we would reach the goal we had set ourselves. It was almost a sadness to think that the end was nearly in sight.

Staggering slightly after mountains of crispy duck, ginger chicken, sizzling beef, steamed vegetables and bowl after bowl of noodles, we continued our evening stroll by crossing the road to the Volks Prater. This is the oldest amusement park in Europe with the famous wheel dating back nearly one hundred years being built by an Englishman, W. Basset in 1897. It consists of large wooden cabins, taking perhaps twenty people at a time, suspended on a wheel which takes them over two hundred feet into the night sky.

We of course had to have a ride since it is probably Vienna's most famous tourist attraction and were taken silently and rather eerily above the lights of the other fairground attractions until we could see the whole of the city spread out below us and even the twinkling planes making their approach to Schwechat Airport. The children tried out some of the more gruesome rides on our return to Earth but Peter and I avoided them like the plague, since the last one we had been persuaded to go on some years ago had made us sick and dizzy for at least a week.

"Aw come on Dad," Alexander would taunt. "It's really lush – you feel like you're flying. All the other Dads are coming."

Even this criticism wouldn't shake our resolve and off they would go to try yet another lethal-looking mechanical nightmare. Krister always surprised us, as although nervous by nature, he would follow his brothers anywhere and could often be seen in the front roller coaster car grinning delightedly as it hurtled towards the next loop, his hair plastered back by the slipstream.

11 p.m. – late for us – as we climbed the steps to the hotel and waited at reception for our keys.

"Ach so, vi haf Room 42, Room 26 und Room... but ver is Room 12?"

176

"Anna," I said resignedly, "you and Alexander are in 12 – what have you done with the key?"

"Alexander had it," came the automatic reply.

"No I did not," said an injured Alexander. "You were the last out – you always are. You take half an hour to brush your hair."

"Well at least I brush my hair – you look like a scarecrow most of the time."

The manager, understanding from this exchange that no key was likely to be forthcoming, shook his head in a depressed fashion and disappeared to get a screwdriver. Unfortunately, even taking the handle off and partially dismantling the lock failed to have any effect and we ended up standing in the street and peering up at the slightly open window about 15ft above the pavement. Like all good Austrian windows there was a huge wooden trough of geraniums bolted to the sill which effectively barred the way and undoubtedly would have been demolished by anyone climbing in.

"Mein Gott," raged the manager as he disappeared into the hotel, shortly to reappear with a large step-ladder. "Now vi must climb up ze wall – hold zis and pleese not to let go."

So saying, he gingerly climbed up while Peter, in his role as enthusiastic helper, put his foot against the bottom rung and made the odd encouraging comment.

"Nearly there now – that's it – careful of the drainpipe – what lovely flowers you have here."

The lovely flowers soon began to fall piecemeal from the sky as, leaning across at a dangerous angle, our hero began to unscrew the wooden trough from its mounts, knocking huge chunks of geranium off in the process. At last it was free and clutching it to his chest like a growbag in bloom, he began his precarious descent, covering himself with a mixture of water and compost in the process. Wanting to make some contribution to the problem, Peter very generously volunteered Ollie to climb in and retrieve the keys which Anna had left on the bedside table and within seconds the door was open. Leaving the manager to struggle back up his ladder with a now nearly empty geranium trough, we quietly slunk off to the oblivion of our black hole, hoping that our stay would not be marred by any further disasters.

Although we had picked this hotel out of desperation, it proved to be only a short walk from the old city of Vienna and therefore ideal as a base. Next morning, after a nice buffet breakfast, we walked down Taborstrasse and crossed a bridge over the Donau Kanal into the maze of alleyways and streets that make up the elegant heart of this city which is surrounded by a system of boulevards known as the Ring. Attempting to follow the river probably explained why we had got lost, for there are four main interconnected waterways – the Donau Kanal, the Donau proper, the Neue Donau and the Alte Donau – enough to confuse anyone. After only a few minutes of wandering, we emerged, quite unexpectedly, into the lovely square containing St Stephen's Cathedral whose spire soared high above us in a fine tracery of intricate stonework.

The cool interior offered welcome shade from another hot day and we sat in the front pew admiring the graceful and surprisingly light fusion of Gothic and Baroque architecture. The pulpit, carved in 1510 by Anton Pilgram, is without doubt a masterpiece and the most famous tomb is that of Prince Eugene of Savoy who finally defeated the Turks in 1697 and thus spared Europe from Islam.

The Hapsburgs it must be said were a strange lot – starting with Rudolf I in 1282 and ending with the First World War, the dynasty survived and prospered largely by judicious marriages, reaching its zenith under Empress Maria Theresa and her son Emperor Franz-Joseph in the 18th and 19th centuries. Their long rule must have given them an affinity with the ancient Egyptians, however, since like them they developed the most peculiar burial customs. Thus Hapsburg viscera are to be found in copper urns in St Stephen's crypt, their embalmed bodies in the Kapuzinerkirche five miles away while fifty-four Royal hearts are kept in silver urns in the Augustinerkirche. No wonder Franz-Joseph's son, Archduke Rudolf, shot himself at Mayerling – they all thought he was mad but perhaps it was the other way round.

Coming out of the cathedral, we walked through the alley behind it and stumbled across the house where Mozart lived as he worked on *The Marriage of Figaro*. It looked the same as countless other buildings, forming part of yet another 18th century tenement block and it took some imagination to recreate the atmosphere of that marvellous film *Amadeus* as the great composer worked into the night surrounded by tallow candles and empty wine glasses. Like his house in Prague, this is now a museum being cleverly identified for the tourist, as are other places of interest in Vienna, by red and white

flags fluttering above the front door. There was clearly so much to
see here that we began to wonder how on earth we could manage it,
for already our legs were complaining – perhaps we weren't used to
walking.

Parked in the cathedral precincts, were open horse drawn carriages
for tired tourists like us and after ascertaining the price – £60 for an
hour – we decided in another fit of extravagance to see the rest of
Vienna in a more comfortable manner. It was an excellent decision
and there is no better way to get a 'feel' for this very beautiful city.
Our driver was an amusing and well informed little chap who could
apparently control the horses while turning around to us in order to
describe all the various points of interest. This was no mean feat,
since the road was only slightly wider than the carriage wheels and the
odd parked car or traffic light had to be negotiated as well. The
highlight for us was driving up to the Hofburg Palace and then
through the magnificent carriage entrance, just as they must have done
for hundreds of years, before continuing on into the palace complex
itself past courtyards, gardens, fountains and statues.

"Vi are now in ze Heldenplatz," intoned the driver, giving the
right hand horse a deft flick with his whip which consisted of a piece
of string on the end of a stick. "On ze left side is ze statue to Prince
Eugene of Savoy vile on ze right side is ze statue to Archduke
Charles.

"Zis statue," he continued like a tape recorder, "is ze only horse
statue in ze Vorld vich stands on two back legs."

We had been having just a little trouble with his lefts and rights
because three of us were facing the direction of travel while the other
three were looking backwards, a bit like the Royal Family at Ascot.
This, combined with the fact that these directions were sometimes
given by him when he was concentrating on the horses and at other
times when he had swivelled round to talk to us, made the whole
situation thoroughly confusing.

"Nein, nein – ZAT statue is ze one on two legs," he corrected us,
noticing that half his customers were peering intently at the wrong
one. "Zis is now on my left," he continued as he turned round to talk
to us, causing the remaining half of his passengers to abandon the
correct statue and look at Prince Eugene.

"But that one's standing on its tail as well as its legs," complained
Ollie.

"Nein, nein you are looking at ze wrong vun. Archduke Charles is now on your right nein, nein not zat right but zis right – und he is on my left but ven I drive ze horses so," and with this he picked up his stick, "he is now on my right und Prince Eugene on ze left but only vor zose at ze back – OK?"

We all nodded dumbly and spent the rest of our trip frantically trying to calculate which side he really meant as he reeled off other places of interest. I gave up the unequal struggle and just followed everybody else, but I had my suspicions that they were doing the same, as periodically his monologue would be interrupted with a,

"Nein not zat side, ZIS side."

All too quickly we were back at the cathedral and with our heads spinning like a kaleidoscope full of images and facts, we thanked the driver and went to find a coffee. Old Vienna is a small area but so much had happened here and for a time under Maria Theresa it was the political and cultural centre of Europe. Beethoven, Mozart, Schubert, Brahms and Strauss all lived here and great museums, churches and palaces give ample testimony to a once glorious past. The carriage ride had enabled us quickly to pick out places meriting a closer look and the rest of the morning was spent looking at the Hofburg Palace and the imposing mirror pair of museums – the Kunsthistorisches and Naturhistorisches – separated by a large statue of the great Empress herself.

Walking east along the Ring we passed the famous Vienna Opera, now shrouded in scaffolding, before reaching the Karlsplatz, a small park full of interest and our immediate destination. The main reason for coming here lay in the fact that this was the site of the Brahms' Memorial, an imposing white marble sculpture showing the master late in his life with long hair and flowing beard, sitting in a chair looking down benignly at his visitors – I'm sure he would have smiled at the four young Hiltons as they posed for a photo at his feet. Other memorials littered the paths but the most imposing by far was the striking Karlskirche, built in 1716 as thanksgiving for the ending of a plague which had nearly wiped out the population in 1713.

Another very practical reason for coming here, was to take an underground to the Schonbrunn Palace, the famous summer residence of the Hapsburgs and known as the Austrian Versailles. We nearly missed the station for it was a thing of beauty in itself, blending perfectly with and even enhancing the elegant surroundings. Its proper title was 'Pavilion of the Transportation System' and was built in the early 1900s by the famous architect Otto Wagner in perfect Art Nouveau style.

Failing yet again to purchase tickets, we were whisked off on a clean, uncrowded train to Schonbrunn, another masterpiece of Art Nouveau by Mr Wagner, which was only five stops down the line. We emerged blinking into the midday light and following the crowds, were irresistibly drawn to the Palace and its extensive gardens. Destroyed initially by besieging Turks, Maria Theresa finished this most famous of palaces in 1743 as a home for herself and her sixteen children – Napoleon set up his headquarters here and received the Austrian surrender in 1809 – Charles I ended the Hapsburg monarchy by abdicating here in 1918 – and in recent times Kennedy and Khrushchev met here in 1961.

Our modest visit couldn't compete with these historical events, but as in Potsdam we felt a thrill just being there as a result of our own efforts. The park was a dazzling combination of red gravel paths and brightly coloured ornate flower-beds watered by sprinklers which jerked around in a circle, occasionally catching you unawares with a patter of drops which darkened the dust and released fragrant aromas from the petals. At one end of the park, completely filling the field of vision was the long, low, yellow facade of the Schloss itself while at the other, on a hill overlooking this timeless vista stood the Gloriette, a classical folly from which we could see a panorama extending over the park and castle to the historical centre of Vienna beyond. We sat there on the grass near the Gloriette for over an hour, talking about all sorts of things in a relaxed way that certainly wasn't matched by most of the other tourists, who scurried around worrying about their video cameras, guide books and the time that their coach was leaving – we had no such problems.

Although we had a close look at the outside of the castle, we decided against a guided tour, partly because of the expense but mainly because eighteenth-century interiors have never really appealed to us. They are certainly striking with very ornate gilded and inlaid furniture, mirrors, painted ceilings, oriental carpets, chandeliers and tapestries, but somehow I find it hard to imagine people living in these palaces and feeling genuinely at home. It is all so artificial somehow. A cultural philistine might say that if you've seen one such roped off collection of porcelain and portraits you've seen them all, but I couldn't possibly comment.

A snack lunch had left us all ravenous, so we had an early supper sitting at a table outside a baroque restaurant which had once been a lodge to the palace, from where we could gaze up the long, wide tree-lined drive guarded by its fine rococo wrought iron gate flanked by two obelisks. Fried cheese and cranberry sauce, salads, sauté potatoes, ice-creams, beers and lemonades at 5 p.m. may seem strange but who cares.

"What are we going to do now?" I asked Peter with my usual unshakeable optimism in his ability to provide an interesting itinerary day after day.

"Well how should I know?" he replied, rather irritably I thought. "I'm not a bloody Thomson's rep. Why don't you suggest something?"

"Well what I meant was, is there anything else to see; you know, anything interesting that we've missed?"

"There's a whole guide book of interesting things here," he sighed as he tossed it across to me, "but most of them will be shut now and shepherding you lot around is hard work."

Peter always seemed to get a trifle stressed planning our sightseeing days around these capitals, but I have to confess that I do expect one monument to follow another with maximum efficiency and minimum effort. Picking up the book, I started flicking through it from the back and had only gone two pages before shouting,

"Pierre!" – I've always called him that since we saw *War and Peace* together before we got married – "Pierre we've just got to see this!"

"What?" he replied suspiciously.

"MOZART'S GRAVE! – look, there's a picture of it here," I said excitedly and pushed the book across the table to him.

Peter groaned and shook his head slowly. "I was hoping that you wouldn't see that," he mumbled. "It's miles away and very difficult to get to and in any case he's not really buried there at all."

Strictly speaking he was correct. On December 5th, 1791 Wolfgang Amadeus Mozart died at 1 a.m. in his 1st floor apartment in the Rauhensteingasse at the age of thirty-six, shortly after completing his *Requiem Mass* which he knew instinctively was for himself. The cause of his death is uncertain, but Mozart had been seriously ill several times in his short life and probably had developed chronic renal failure as a result of repeated streptococcal infection, the final insult being a cerebral haemorrhage. Whatever the truth, his body was taken from his apartment at 2:30 p.m. to St Stephen's Cathedral for a short service – he was the Imperial Royal Kapellmeister – before being loaded on to a funeral wagon which was waiting to carry it to the cemetery of St Marx. His wife Constanze was in terrible financial straits and could only afford a third class funeral. The story is taken up by H.C. Robbins Landon in his book *Mozart's Last Year*:

"St Marx is a suburb of Vienna, a good hour's walk from the centre. None of the funeral party – we do not know the names of those who participated – wanted to accompany the corpse and no one, for years, cared to find out where Mozart was buried: as a result, we know only the approximate section of the cemetery under which, somewhere, music's greatest genius lies."

I can say categorically that none of us will ever forget the next few hours. The cemetery of St Marx, once a peaceful rural spot, is now a tiny island nearly suffocated by motorways, railway lines and a huge viaduct which completely separates it from its parent church. Even our guide book described it as:

"A bit isolated from the principal avenues of circulation," a phrase which would stand an excellent chance of winning the award, 'Understatement of the Year'. It took two hours of trains, trams, buses and walking through factories and cheap housing estates before we sensed that we were close. Finding ourselves in a rubbish strewn cul-de-sac with no apparent means of escape, Peter, with no prompting from me, went to ask help from a solitary middle-aged woman who was unpacking the boot of her car.

"Excuse me," he started. "I wonder if you can help. We're looking for Mozart's Grave?"

The incongruity of this request in these surroundings suddenly seemed so ludicrous to me that I started to laugh until I could hardly stand up. Anna also saw the funny side of it and before long we were holding on to each other for support while Peter continued to struggle to make himself understood, giving us frequent glares as he did so.

"Mozart's Grave?" Peter repeated to the uncomprehending woman. "St Marx's cemetery?"

"Ah Moseaart," she finally got the message and pointed to a small path we had missed.

"Moseaart Ja, Ja. Zwei hundert metres."

The two hundred metres led us through yet another factory's grounds to the green, tree-filled space of St Marx's cemetery – the only problem was that it lay on the far side of a motorway intersection that looked like Spaghetti Junction. We nearly gave up then, but it was so tantalisingly close that we persevered for another few miles until we discovered the one 'No Through' road that led to the cemetery gates. Unfortunately they were shut and locked.

"Oh my God," wailed Peter, grasping the iron railings like a convicted criminal. "I don't believe it – not after all this."

A high wall ran all the way round and there was no other possible way in. It was also nearly dark. Our luck appeared to have run out.

As we were turning to leave, a little old lady emerged from the shadows on the other side of the gate accompanied by a pair of tourists who she proceeded to let out with the aid of a large bunch of keys. Seizing his chance Peter, with his hands clasped together as though praying, implored her to let us in.

"Please," he begged, "please can we see Mozart's Grave – we've walked for miles and the children so want to and..."

The children had rapidly put on expressions of intense longing combined with extreme fatigue and with a resigned shrug she swung open the gate and we were in! The problem now was where to look. The cemetery was like a maze, with tall hedges and trees separating row upon row of gloomy graves, most of which were dominated by sorrowing marble statues or winged angels.

"Right," said Peter ignoring the first and most basic rule of survival, "let's split up and look for it – shout if you find anything."

It is difficult to describe the feeling of prickly menace that pervaded the atmosphere as we wandered up and down the unlit paths, our feet crunching on the gravel. It was the most atmospheric place I have ever been in and perhaps one of the most frightening as well. Within minutes we had become separated and completely lost, for the grounds were much bigger than we had thought and by now there was practically no light with only the occasional monumental memorial silhouetted against the inky sky.

"Alexander – Anna – Krister – Oliver – where are you?" I shouted, barely able to control the panic that was rising within me at the thought of being trapped in this unearthly place. Dead silence – the silence of the dead. This was the sort of place where psychic investigators would elect to spend the night with tape recorders and cameras, only to be found insane the next day.

I found it at last at the top of a broad path half a mile from the gate and surrounded by tall hedges. It was immediately identifiable as the only grave amongst thousands which was planted with fresh flowers, which were kept from wilting by a sprinkler dousing them with water drops every ten seconds. I know this to be a precise time, for it was just too short to allow for any proper attempt at photography without getting the camera soaked. The one shot I have got, as proof of our almost superhuman efforts, is blurred and dark since one eye was kept on the hose nozzle pivoting slowly towards me. Mozart loved practical jokes and I like to think he was having the last laugh at our expense.

One by one the children found us, with excited stories of being followed by ghostly footsteps and when we were all together once more, we literally ran down the path towards the small patch of indigo amongst the blackish green of the trees, which indicated the way out and civilisation.

Our journey back to the hotel took marginally less time than the one there, because Alexander spotted an overgound train or S-Bahn which on closer investigation went straight to a station near the Ferris Wheel.

Arriving at well past 9 p.m., we all went to bed with the exception of Peter, who decided to take his back wheel apart for the second time so far in order to replace yet another broken spoke. The manager, obviously not quite understanding what this entailed, cheerfully gave his assent for this to be carried out just around the corner from reception, in an area next to the lifts and toilets. Not only does the tyre and tube have to be removed, but also all the rear cogs, so that a new spoke can be threaded through and tightened up – the wheel can then be trued before replacing the tyre. This explains why Peter was still sitting on the floor surrounded by various oily bits with the bike upside down on its saddle and handlebars, when a coach-load of elderly Danish tourists arrived to check in.

By the length of the queue for the 'facilities' I don't think they had been let off their bus since leaving Prague and for one doddery, confused old man, this long wait and probably the sight of a bike mechanic hard at work outside the lavatory, proved to be too much for his self-control. When the door finally opened, it was clear that he had even surpassed my efforts in the campervans at Carmarthen – it was everywhere. A trail of brown footprints led back to a scene of absolute carnage, as he shuffled away holding up his trousers with one hand, while moaning quietly in Danish. Not surprisingly, his compatriots on seeing what he had done also shuffled away moaning quietly in Danish and I suppose it was just fate that dictated that Alexander should have stepped out of the lift dressed only in his pyjamas, at the precise moment that the manager decided to see what the problem was.

"Mein Gott – haf you done zis?" he asked Alexander accusingly.

"No it wasn't me – honest," he replied in the affronted, guilty manner typical of schoolboys. "It was like this when I got here, I just came to say goodnight to my Dad."

It was pointless explaining. Whatever Peter or Alexander said to him, he was convinced that they were responsible for the mess and from then on he became frosty and bad tempered – I think only a confession would have cheered him up.

We could easily have spent more time in Vienna, but cities were becoming less and less to our liking and we longed for fresh air and the open road once again. Our departure from the hotel next day was somewhat marred by a separate bill for use of the bathroom which we felt was unjustified and probably generated by Alexander's disgusting habits of the previous night. I refused to pay and we left on rather a sour note which was a pity, but then on the positive side we found a local laundry which washed and dried all our clothes while we were having breakfast.

Having gone horribly wrong coming into Vienna, Peter had carefully studied the maps in order to get us out with as little trouble as possible. Walking the bikes across the busy junction at Praterstern, we entered the Prater proper which is about the same size as Hyde Park and cycled down the central Hauptallee with hardly a car in sight. After several miles of tree lined roads and paths, we turned left over a high bridge which spanned both the old and new Danubes, being nearly blown over by high winds in the process, before picking up the Donau Radweg again on the far side – it was as simple as that. This north side of the river was hardly built up at all and with the strong breeze behind us, we sped along next to the rippling water until Vienna was just a dark smudge on the horizon.

The sky was blue and sunny with small clouds scudding across it driven by the same wind that was pushing us towards the border. Very few other cyclists were about and it felt wonderful to be by ourselves again. After a few miles, the path left the river and ran parallel to it on a raised embankment called the Marchfelddamm, which presumably had been built to prevent the Danube flooding the low-lying country to the North. It ran as straight as an arrow for over thirty miles and for most of this distance it was practically deserted with birds and the odd rabbit our only company. Lines of waving trees separated us from the river on our right, while on our left, marshes and fields stretched away to the horizon. Despite being mid-August, there was a definite autumnal feeling to the air and some leaves were even swirling to the ground as a result of the still strong breeze.

As we approached Hainburg and the end of the Donau Radweg, the surface of the path began to break up and for several stretches we had to cycle on loose gravel, an exhausting experience particularly for Peter, since the trailer slewed from side to side raising clouds of white dust and small stones would shoot out from our back wheels, stinging the rider behind. Crossing a bridge to the southern bank of the Danube where we would remain until we arrived in Budapest, Peter misjudged a small gap and caused a trailer wheel to collide with a bollard at speed. The whole contraption became airborne for a few seconds before landing with a sickening crash that signified major damage – the split was now nearly a foot long and gaped alarmingly. It was still towable – just – but only time would tell whether it could survive these last few days.

A campsite was marked on our map but it was simply an area of river bank set aside for tents with no other facilities at all – it was probably the most idyllic of all the places where we stopped. A strip of level ground with trees spaced at intervals and a cliff behind, looked out over the river which at this point was quite narrow resulting in an absolutely ferocious current. The town of Hainburg was about a mile distant and we were able to buy supper at the local shops, but the tents were surrounded by open skies and beautiful views, with water rushing past us only a few yards away – after the hustle of Vienna, it was paradise.

Moored to one of the trees near our tents was a home-made raft, but this was no simple affair. A wooden house with windows and a door had been built on a platform which itself rested on eight large oil drums – the roof of this house was flat and had a chair surrounded by potted plants perched on top, thus adding to the air of unreality. Deserted when we first arrived, it was apparent that 'the crew' had been shopping and they returned shortly afterwards laden with beer and vegetables, a strange combination that described perfectly their rather way-out appearance. Matted, fuzzy hair and beards, beads and bangles, bandannas and barefeet, shorts and T-shirts combined to form a group of Robinson Crusoe lookalikes. They were German and in the process of navigating their peculiar craft as far down the Danube as possible – even to the Black Sea if they could make it.

Despite the fading sun and their complete lack of navigation lights, they bravely cast off into the swirling current and starting a small outboard motor, crept sideways into the maelstrom. The reason for the chair on the roof became apparent as this was where the helmsman sat, controlling the struggling outboard with a long wooden pole while his companions paddled furiously with rough planks of wood. Barely managing to avoid shipwreck on a shingle bank, 'Kon Tiki' just made it to the centre of the river whereupon, on cessation of all propulsive activity, it was swept at an awesome speed downstream, controlled only by a steering oar at the stern. I have often wondered whether they made it.

We had a lovely evening sitting in front of the tents watching the setting sun and eating a very tasty pasta with diced ham, fresh tomatoes, peppers, onions, garlic etc. which I'd cooked in less than thirty minutes on our wonderful little stove. Wine for us, beer for the big children and fizzy apple juice for the little 'uns, followed by fruit yoghurts and coffee in absolute peace by this beautiful river is a memory I'll always treasure. Occasionally barges would pass – the ones heading towards Budapest would be swept past in a few seconds on the unstoppable current leaving us full of admiration for the man in the wheelhouse, but the ones going towards Vienna would take up to fifteen minutes to pass us, engines throbbing, for the same reason. There is a regular Hydrofoil service between these two great capitals and in spite of their rather clumsy appearance they skimmed along at high speed, seemingly unaffected by the turbulent flow.

We had noticed a young couple arriving on a tandem earlier on, and after supper, when it was nearly pitch dark, we introduced ourselves and started talking. They were Belgian and had started their tour in Budapest with the intention of cycling along the Danube path to Linz. A specialist Dutch coach company had driven them to Budapest, towing all the bicycles behind in a huge trailer and all being well, would pick them up in two weeks time at Linz, before returning to Amsterdam. This seemed to be an excellent way of organising a short cycle tour and since the coach company always arrived in Budapest on a Saturday, we made a note of their telephone number in Holland in the hope that they might have some spare seats. Getting home from Amsterdam would be easy. As well as this useful information, our new friends were also able to give us much advice on travel in Hungary and Peter spent a long time poring over various maps with the help of Emil and his torch.

Hungary we were told was different to any other country they had visited over several years of touring – it was cheap, colourful, old-fashioned, poor, rural, friendly and had excellent bread but no bananas or chocolate spread. The language was incomprehensible and there were steaming thermal baths everywhere.

Knowing that we would cross the border the following day, we zipped ourselves into our sleeping bags with the salutary thought that this would be our fifth and final country, what's more, it promised to provide a fitting end to many weeks which had been filled with interest and diversity.

Chapter 13

Hungary

It was so peaceful and restful here that we should have stayed an extra night, but Peter's excitement at the prospect of another frontier got the better of common sense and the rest of us reluctantly followed him out of Hainburg late the next morning. The Belgians had been off early, wobbling slightly on their tandem and full of sound advice from us about where not to stay in Vienna. Tandems always look rather fun and no doubt have their ardent supporters, but they do have problems as Emil was ready to point out.

"I have much mechanic failure," he confided. "Ze wheel plus ze spokes must have much strength for two persons and luggage."

Even so, their luggage was limited to rear panniers with tent and sleeping bags piled on top, which didn't seem much for two people.

"Also we have problem with carrying our bicycle on trains or planes – it is too big and they say no."

I could just imagine British Rail's reaction to one of these.

"But ze biggest problem is when we have shouts and argue at each other – there is nowhere else to go and we pedal many kilometres and I do not talk to her and she does not talk to me."

Images crossed my mind of a blazing row causing the tandem to weave and wobble for a few minutes, before an icy silence prevailed as they tried unsuccessfully to ignore each other's presence for the next hour.

"Well why do you use a tandem at all?" I asked him. "There don't seem to be many advantages."

"Aah, you don't understand," smiled Emil. "Sometimes we are in love very much and then it is so nice to be close and touch each other."

Typical Gallic emotional extremes I suppose – I would have thought that when you are "in love very much" the last thing on your mind is riding a bicycle. We'll never understand them.

A few miles West from Hainburg took us within sight of Bratislava, the capital of Slovakia, which appeared to consist entirely of blocks of flats and building cranes covering some low hills on the other side of the river. We wisely avoided visiting it, since a feature article describing a weekend break in this city, which I read in a Sunday paper after our return, was anything but complimentary. The food was awful, there was indeed nothing to see except flats and all foreigners were treated with deep suspicion – a hangover from the days when Bratislava was full of agents and spies. Instead we turned off the main road and headed south into flat rather bleak country where the borders of Slovakia, Hungary and Austria all meet near the Austrian village of Deutsch Jahrndorf.

Quiet country lanes took us to Kittsee where our map showed a small road crossing the frontier. There was indeed a border post here but the guard refused to let us across because we had British passports and these still hadn't been included on his list of desirable Nationalities.

"Nein zis eez not possible," he said. "Zis crossing eez not vor ze British but vor ze Austrians und ze Deutsch."

So much for the opening up of Eastern Europe. The Germans are everywhere, selling and buying but the Brits literally can't even get in through the front door. Feeling perversely rather proud, we turned around with heads held high and pedalled away to find a crossing point where we would be acceptable.

The weather was certainly changing and for a time became cold, blustery and rainy, necessitating waterproofs and jackets. Long straight roads through endless ploughed fields linked small villages consisting of only a few houses and although we were still in Austria, there was no evidence of wealth or affluence. Travelling parallel to the border, with an immense Norfolk sky above us, we stopped for lunch just beyond Deutsch Jahrndorf at the edge of a field full of maize and peculiar chicken-like birds which strutted around pecking vigorously at the ground. It was not one of our best lunches since Anna went off in a sulk down the road and my back tyre had disintegrated causing Peter to struggle for over an hour in his efforts to fit a new one – the new tyre had twisted in upon itself in storage but failing to notice this, he sweated and strained like the Royal Chamberlain trying to fit Cinderella's slipper on to the podgy foot of an Ugly Sister, before he realised what the problem was.

It was nearly 4 p.m. by the time we reached the main border crossing at Hegyeshalom which was marked by a stationary line of lorries and cars stretching back for over a mile into Austria. From the way that the drivers were lounging around eating, or even sleeping in their cabs, it was apparent that they had been here for some time. The average wait to enter Hungary by road, we were later told, is at least six hours and often longer, reflecting a deliberate attempt to obstruct trade from the EEC to the east. The political message seemed to be, "Help us economically and we'll allow your lorries through without fuss."

Hoping that bicycles would be exempt from this wrangling, we pedalled to the front of the queue and smiled encouragingly at the policeman who had a submachine gun slung round his neck and didn't smile back. Taking our passports, he carefully studied them upside down until reaching the photographs, which he then compared minutely with our actual appearance. The fact that I wasn't wearing sunglasses in my passport photo upset him considerably and I had to pose for him with glasses both on and off before he was eventually satisfied and laboriously stamped our entry permit.

We were in! Again, the advantages of a bicycle had been amply demonstrated as we headed away from the border – all other traffic was simply at a standstill. Our Belgian friends had suggested a campsite at the village of Lipot, but first we had to negotiate a large town with the rather ethnic name of Moson-Magyarovar. Cycling along the main road to it, we were somewhat surprised to see two young women dressed in stilettos, G-strings and flimsy shirts knotted loosely at the front, attempting to hitch a lift. Not that we could help it, but passing them so closely it was possible to see the tired, over made-up faces and the bruises on their legs that immediately identified their true profession.

"Good afternoon ladies," Peter called out as he crept by – his speed did seem to have dropped considerably. "Lovely day isn't it?"

More girls appeared ahead but before we reached them, an expensive Austrian registered car stopped nearby and after a rapid conversation which presumably was limited to, "How much?" they climbed in and he sped away. This is the one growth industry which the impoverished east is cashing in on as fast as it can. Village girls from Warsaw to Bucharest are drawn into Western vice as the only way of dragging themselves out of crushing poverty – our friends the Dutch play a major part here and many end up in the clubs and bars of Amsterdam. In return the west floods the bookstands of Prague and Budapest with lurid magazines containing images previously unobtainable behind the Iron Curtain. What must these poor people think of our way of life and I wonder how many are having second thoughts as to the wisdom of such rapid change.

Ominous thunderclouds darkened the horizon and distant rumbles filled the still air as we pushed on towards Lipot through almost medieval villages that had no shops or notice boards or any other sign of community life. Just beyond Halaszi we saw one of the most beautiful rainbows I've ever observed, with at least five colours easily visible as it arched right across the sky. Everyone we passed stopped to stare at us, turning their heads as they did so until we disappeared from view. We often waved or shouted a greeting and never did we feel in the least threatened by all this attention – on the contrary, the poorer the country the more we sensed the protection of the people whom we met. It was only in the cities that we were on our guard.

After a long and tiring forty-eight miles we found the small site at Lipot which my diary records as "the dirtiest, filthiest site we have ever been in". The shower block had not been cleaned for months and stank of sewage and stale urine, while the floor was covered with mud and slime. It says much for our determination to wash the dust and sweat of the road from our hair and bodies that we braved these horrors, but we did and as usual felt better for it. We managed to find a quiet spot for the tents and were watched with interest by another cycling couple who later became our great friends. We saw them again later that evening in the small restaurant across the road where we had an unbelievably cheap meal, but it wasn't until the following morning, after a night when the rain had thundered mercilessly down on our little tents, that we got into conversation.

David was French and Almut was German and they lived near Bordeaux in a small apartment. They had cycled through Czechoslovakia, although they had gone by train for some of the way and like us they were aiming to end their journey in Budapest. From what they said, we had made the right choice to come South to the Danube, for Slovakia had been difficult with delays of several days as they waited for the bicycles to be sent on a freight train from the Czech Republic.

"It always 'appens when bicycles go on a train," said David. "Zey keep them for up to four days – it 'appens in France, it 'appens in Germany and most certainly it 'appens in 'ungary."

This was most depressing news since our thoughts were now beginning to turn to methods of getting home again, with luck, complete with trailer and bicycles. It clearly was not going to be very easy.

Almut was sweet and quickly made friends with Anna who was only a few years younger, listening patiently to her as she went into graphic detail about how ghastly it was to holiday with your parents and younger brothers at the ripe old age of seventeen. Almut had also suffered with back trouble during their journey and now appeared to have sciatica affecting her left leg. They had brought no pain killers with them so out came Walter's magic pills again, some of which we gave her together with a few days supply of Brufen – thus fortified, we waved them off while we continued packing up, not really expecting to see them again.

Long, tree-lined country roads took us through idyllic rural countryside and quiet, sleepy villages to Gyorzamoly where we were fortunate enough to find a small bar which served food. There was no choice, but since several other such places we had tried had simply shaken their heads at us, it would have to do. The poor chap did his best and proudly presented us with six plates each containing a small curled up fish, which on investigation appeared to consist entirely of bones, a watery cucumber salad and a few soggy, cold potatoes. He anxiously watched us to see our reaction and assuming like everyone else that we were German said:

"Goot Ja? Goot fiske?"

Peter smacked his lips as though savouring a perfect fillet steak and beaming at the chef replied:

"Ja, fiske ist fantastisch – danke."

Relief spread over his face like sunshine and he tactfully withdrew so that we could enjoy the banquet in peace.

Gyor was an interesting old town with a fine square in which a market was in full swing, an impressive church and cobbled, winding streets. Being a Sunday it was very quiet and this influenced our decision to follow the Danube, or Duna as it was now called, via a main road to Komaron rather than risk the steep hills around Tatabanya. Our Belgian friends had warned us that these mountains were slow and difficult and if we had learnt anything over the past few weeks it was, "Stick to rivers wherever possible".

It was while we were sitting outside an ice-cream kiosk sucking a Magnum Weiss – a sweet white chocolate covered ice which the children were addicted to – that David and Almut whizzed past waving gaily, immediately recognisable by the blue plastic bags covering their sleeping rolls. This was odd, since they had left well before us six hours ago and should have been miles ahead by now. They didn't stop however and when we were eventually ready to start again, we determined to catch them up by cranking up our usual speed of 10mph.

"Is everyone alright?" shouted Peter over his shoulder as we sped along at 15mph.

"Well it's a bit slow," I replied. "Can't you go a bit faster?"

The gauntlet had been thrown down and hunching himself over the handlebars, Peter did his level best to leave us behind as he pushed our speed up to over 20mph. Every so often he would peer behind with a look of surprise that we were all still there and then redouble his efforts, the sweat pouring off his arms and forehead. The miles certainly sped by and in less than an hour we were approaching the outskirts of Komaron and spied David and Almut resting in a lay-by, viewing us with interest as we raced towards them sticking like glue to a now exhausted Dad.

"So we 'appen to meet once more," David smiled, ignoring for the moment the gasping sounds emanating from Peter.

"We 'ad not planned this road but we 'appened to be on ze wrong side of ze river and 'ad to take a small boat so 'ere we are."

They had made the mistake of not crossing the bridge at Gyor and had ended up at a tiny fishing village on a promontory in the Duna from which a friendly native had ferried them across in exchange for a packet of cigarettes – not that they smoked, but the Hungarian Forint was so worthless that cigarettes were always useful as a means of barter.

Sticking together, we all found the large campsite at Komaron, a large city whose road-bridge over the Danube formed an important border crossing with Slovakia on the other side. The site was large and clean with a covered swimming pool and kitchens for the preparation of food – the first we had been able to use since Denmark. The evenings and nights were now distinctly chilly and insects which always appeared at dusk, no longer seemed so prevalent – I had never before realised that seasons change with longitude as well as latitude. We camped separately at opposite ends of the site, almost as though there was an unwritten rule of the road that preserved our personal space and respected the need for peace after a long day. This sensitivity, which is very apparent when travelling, doesn't seem to apply at home where people think they can phone or drop in at any time regardless of what you might be doing. The communication revolution is seen as a great step forward with cellular phones making you instantly available wherever you happen to be – personally I have my doubts. Ask any doctor who carries a bleep and he will tell you that his greatest joy at the end of a shift is to get rid of it and thus be completely uncontactable.

We slept well and awoke to a bright, breezy day with leaves swirling around and the occasional hoot from the mainline to Budapest, which ran between the site and the river. On his way to the shower block to wash and clean his teeth, Peter noted a line of men carrying towels and toothbrushes waiting patiently next to a metal rod sticking out of the wall at waist height. The reason for this soon became apparent, when a camp official appeared promptly at 7:30 a.m. and ceremoniously placed one toilet roll on the rod, the free end fluttering in the wind. One by one the line shuffled forward with each man taking a few sheets of paper before disappearing into the nearest free loo. Clearly this was the ration for the day – one roll for an entire block and the early bird as they say.

David and Almut came over to say goodbye since they were planning to take a train to Budapest from the next station in view of continuing problems with Almut's leg.

"We 'ave liked you all so much," said David, "and we think your journey avec les enfants is INCREDIBLE. We would like very much to see you again and 'ave dinner with you."

Neither of us knew Budapest, but with the help of a map we agreed to meet on the Elizabeth bridge in three days time at 7 p.m.

"It sounds just like a James Bond film," said Peter. "Perhaps I should wear a carnation and carry a rolled up newspaper."

"Be very sure that we will be waiting 007," replied David. "If you 'appen not to be there, we will wait for half an hour before we 'ave to go."

And with that they pedalled out of the campsite, their blue coverings flapping in the wind.

We hadn't planned to be idle, but the morning drifted by while we did some shopping and changed some more traveller's cheques in the main bank.

"There's no point leaving before lunch," I explained to the children. "Let's sit down at that table over there and have something to eat before we leave."

Excellent crusty Hungarian bread, butter and a large pot of strawberry jam is absolutely delicious and can be thoroughly recommended to anyone contemplating an afternoon's cycling. Before you start this feast, however, make sure that you will be undisturbed – we had noticed the English caravan on our trips to the showers and they had obviously noticed us.

"Arfernoon heveriwon," announced a bald-headed man wearing nothing but a pair of swimming trunks that were three sizes too small. "Coodn't 'elp nowtising a fellow Brit – wear're y'all from?"

"Wales," began Peter. "We..."

"Oh Whailes – that's interesting that is. I knew sumun from Whailes once. Very, very wet Whailes is I boileve. Very, very wet."

"Well it's not that..."

"Yes, very, very wet. I sippose y'all pedalled them boikes from Whailes – not too wet around 'ere is it?"

"No, it's much drier and..."

"Well we've towed our van from Bearmingham rite 'cross Slowvachia and since we was in Bratislather, I sez lets do 'ungary and see Buddhapest an all. Are y'all going to Buddhapest?"

"Well we thought we might try and..."

"Gr-rate idea. You gotta see Buddhapest – d'you think y'all camp there too?"

"Well we plan to see what..."

"Ay, just the job. Well it's bin really grand chatting to y'all but I can see y'want to get on with lunch – ta ra."

Having had all our previous attempts to sink our teeth into the white, doughy, jam covered bread thwarted by this interlude, we set too with gusto and quickly departed before our friend thought up any further questions.

The road to Esztergom hugged the Danube for thirty-four miles and had it not been for the stiff head wind it would have been a very relaxing afternoon. The first we saw of this most beautiful of Hungarian towns when we were still some distance away, was the shimmering green copper dome of the cathedral rising high above the other buildings on castle hill. The sixteenth-century Renaissance basilica is the heart of the Catholic Church in Hungary and many of their Kings have been crowned here – St Stephen, famous from the carol, was born here in 970 AD and the remains of an ancient Royal Palace have been found. Many of the houses had once been elegant and substantial nineteenth-century villas built amongst a network of broad, tree-lined canals which were fed from the river. Sadly their glory was now fading rapidly, with peeling paint and weed-filled gardens a testimony to the lack of care and money – no signs of restoration here.

Crossing an old iron bridge across a quiet tributary of the Duna, we found a lovely campsite next to a broad shingle beach looking across at a cluster of Slovakian cottages on the other side of the main stream. The four star site had a distinctly end of season feel to it although it was still only August 15th, and we had a wide expanse of empty grass to choose from when pitching the tents. The river was wide here and at this time of day bathed in a wonderful golden glow as the sun began its journey to the western horizon, with the cathedral standing out as though floodlit by a celestial spotlight.

A short walk along the riverbank brought us to a rustic restaurant, with tables set on a big veranda under a vine heavy with bunches of white grape. The meal was pleasant enough, but what made the evening was the haunting Hungarian music played with breathtaking skill by two young musicians. One played a violin as he strolled among the tables, while the other sat at a cymballum which is rather like an open grand piano without the keys. The exposed strings would be struck with soft drumsticks to produce that shimmering, slightly oriental sound that is so characteristic of this country. We sat and talked and ate and drank and listened and looked out over the river to the fiery ball of light now dousing itself in the water so full of reflections in the still evening air. They played nearly all of Brahms' Hungarian Dances which practically had Peter in tears and then the violinist came round the tables asking for requests. On hearing that we were English he launched into *Over the Rainbow*, which nearly had me reaching for the hankies and he kept on repeating this until Krister gave him a 1000 Ft note which he carefully placed under his strings.

Esztergom marked the beginning of an extraordinary part of Hungary known rather romantically as 'The Danube Bend'. Having flowed down through the gorges of Austria, the Danube broadens again for over one hundred miles before encountering hills again at Esztergom. Here it is forced to turn sharply southwards through a narrow defile that is literally the gateway to Budapest and the rest of Hungary. Such is the strategic importance of the Danube Bend that it has been watched over for a thousand years by castles and fortifications, that stretch like the beads on a necklace along the forested hills that are still rich in game and wildlife.

We left early the next morning knowing that we had but to negotiate thirty to forty miles of this glorious scenery to arrive in Budapest – our destination. I think there was some excitement in the air but I don't remember anyone making a fuss about it as we quietly packed the tents away and checked our bicycles as we had been doing for the past two months. We were so used to this way of life now that perhaps we felt a little apprehensive about the prospect of returning to normality again.

Our pace was leisurely – there was no rush – and we savoured the unspoilt scenery with the trees already turning vivid shades of yellow and brown. There was no industry and very few cars to spoil our enjoyment – only rolling hills, white shingle beaches and a wide expanse of sky above our heads with the river, which had been our companion for so long now, still flowing purposefully towards its own destination near Istanbul. We rested for lunch at a particularly beautiful spot just below the citadel of Visegrad where the sun shone down on vine-covered hills and a small ferry plied back and forth across the shimmering waters. The far bank was now also Hungarian soil, Slovakia ending just outside Esztergom, so the crossing could be completed without the problem of border controls.

Visegrad in the 14th century became the seat of the Royal Court and for many centuries was the place where the Holy Crown of Hungary was kept. It was first used for the coronation of King Stephen on Christmas Day in 1000 AD and last used for Charles IV in 1916, so it is the oldest crown in Europe. Since only those crowned with it could be recognised as the true King of Hungary, it has had a chequered history and on one occasion was stolen from the treasure room in Visegrad castle on the orders of a medieval princess who used it to crown her infant son. Visegrad's golden age came under the civilising King Mathias in the 15th century who built a palace that was the envy of Europe with its beauty and learning. Legend would have us believe that Mathias entertained foreign envoys on a terrace overlooking the river, on which a red marble fountain stood flowing alternately with red and white wine. For centuries the palace was lost, but in the 1960s it was rediscovered at the foot of the castle and sure enough, on a terrace above the river, a beautiful red marble fountain was unearthed – now sadly dry.

A few miles from this peaceful spot, the river appeared to suddenly narrow, but in fact it had simply been divided into two by Sventendre Island which extends from near Visegrad to the outskirts of Budapest some fifteen miles away. At this point, hemmed in by substantial hills, the waters are forced southwards and continue in this direction until Belgrade, when once more they turn to the west. On the far bank was the town of Vac, famous for its massive prison where political opponents have been incarcerated for over two hundred years, most notably after the 1956 revolution when the cream of Hungary's intellectuals either fled or disappeared.

We were nearly there and Peter later admitted that at this precise moment he was thinking how lucky we had been to avoid serious injury after cycling such a long distance. The crash was quite spectacular with me hurtling over my handlebars followed shortly afterwards by Krister who lay in the middle of the road seemingly unable to move, his legs entangled in the twisted frame of his bike. The others stopped and still bunched in the middle of the road, stared at us with a vacant expression as a huge lorry thundered towards them.

"GET OFF THE BLOODY ROAD," screamed Peter who had left his bike and the trailer in a ditch one hundred yards ahead and was now running back towards us waving his arms like a referee at a football match.

I was only aware of an excruciating pain that closely resembled the time that Ollie had emerged into this world with the aid of a large pair of forceps and lay curled up on the tarmac groaning quietly to myself absolutely convinced that crossbars are not a good thing. Time stood still and it was only when the lorry was practically on top of us that we somehow managed to move, dragging the bicycles and panniers with us, helped by the uninjured who at last had woken up to what had happened.

It could have been much, much worse and after carefully examining the bicycles Peter announced in a relieved voice that apart from scratched paintwork, there was no permanent damage and we'd better be on our way.

"BUGGER THE BICYCLES," I gasped through gritted teeth. "I can't sit or walk let alone ride a bike – you are the most unsympathetic person I've ever known."

So we sat in the ditch for half an hour blaming each other for what had happened until the pain had subsided to a dull, throbbing ache. Then, only by standing on the pedals, was I able to maintain any sort of forward motion – sitting down was out of the question. After two miles of this peculiar progress we reached the town of Sventendre which lies just to the north of Budapest and is famed as a home to artists and sculptors, possessing more galleries and exhibitions than any other town in Hungary. Fortunately it also had a campsite and into this we limped at about 4 p.m. with 1460 miles on our computers.

Quiet, spacious grounds full of mature trees were deserted apart from a few determined Dutch families wringing the last few days from their summer holidays. The manageress was a smiling, very helpful lady in her late thirties who almost pleaded with us to make the most of all the facilities which included a huge swimming pool. The tents were pitched for the last time under a large beech tree against which we stacked the bicycles and I disappeared into the showers to bathe the rapidly expanding haematoma in my perineum.

Although forced to stop here because of the accident, we subsequently discovered that there was no nicer place to stay and Sventendre would form a perfect base for the exploration of our fourth and final capital city – Budapest.

Chapter 14

Budapest

We slept like logs and spent a quiet morning pottering around the campsite swimming and doing piles of dirty washing before cycling to Sventendre station in order to catch a commuter train to the centre of Budapest.

A few minutes unsuccessfully trying to make ourselves understood to the bespectacled charlady behind the ticket booth brought back happy memories of Czechoslovakia and East Germany and clutching thirteen – why thirteen? – very complicated pieces of paper costing approximately £1, we eventually boarded a train marked 'Batthyany Terrace' which we were assured was the terminus in Budapest.

The train rattled along through fields and vineyards with rolling hills and fields visible out of the right hand window. To Peter's delight, out of the left hand window could be seen the remains of Aquincum, the largest town in the Roman province of Pannonia and only rediscovered in the 18th century. Since then, excavations have brought to light a well preserved forum, amphitheatre, public baths, shops and paved streets not unlike those at Pompeii. The Danube was the north-east frontier of the Roman Empire and beyond here, on the Great Plain, only nomadic tribes lived grazing their flocks and wandering freely.

A ride of twenty-five minutes brought us to Batthyany Terrace, a station deep within a tunnel which connected with the underground railway system. The concourse was alive with gypsies and pedlars playing music or trying to sell anything from a bag of nuts to opera tickets – it was bedlam. Avoiding the plucking hands and strident cries we hurried down an escalator and caught a train to Keleti-pu, or the eastern railway terminus, where paradoxically we had been told that it was possible to book a sleeper to the west. We had already phoned the coach company in Amsterdam to be told that there were no seats, so a train home seemed to be the only alternative and it seemed sensible to sort it out as soon as possible.

Keleti-pu from the outside looked like a cathedral with soaring towers and intricate stonework cleverly masking the industrial reality within. Following the signs to 'Information and Tickets' we entered a cool, air-conditioned room where two women, one young and pretty and the other old and not so, sat behind a glass partition while attempting to deal with the requests and problems of a long queue of travellers. When Peter's turn eventually came he of course got the old one, who apart from being visually unremarkable spoke only a few words of English.

"I would like to go to London," he mouthed slowly through the small aperture. "Can you help us?"

"No Longdong," she replied shaking her head emphatically.

"Oh, well can we go to Paris?" Peter persisted – anywhere west of here would be an advantage.

"Pahree is OK," she said, consulting a large book of time-tables as she did so. "You can go on the Orient Express."

Of course, the Orient Express went all the way from Istanbul to Paris via Budapest – why hadn't we thought of it before?

"Fantastic," beamed Peter. "We'll have two adults and four children please in the sleeper leaving for Paris on Sunday."

It took some time for this request to be converted into action but eventually, with much drawing on pieces of paper, understanding slowly dawned and six tickets were laboriously written out by hand before being pushed through the grill. The cost was 107,000 Fts. – about £670 – which left us reeling slightly.

"Oh, by the way," Peter said, almost as an afterthought as we were leaving, "we have six bicycles – is that OK as well?"

More shrugs and pointing followed and it became clear that baggage of this type was dealt with by a different department on the other side of the station. Since the rest of the queue was by now getting decidedly restless, we thanked our travel agent and set off to look for it.

We eventually tracked it down at the end of a passage near platform fifteen, passing in the process a row of trains with romantic destinations like Athens, Belgrade, Moscow and Istanbul displayed in large letters on overhead boards.

The director of baggage and bicycles was not a happy man and sitting at a scruffy desk wearing a shirt that may have been dark blue or possibly a very dirty white, he seemed weighed down with the burden of his immense responsibility. Signalling us to wait, he lit another cigarette and taking a deep, sighing puff, placed it on the edge of an ashtray already overflowing with butt-ends while he examined out tickets.

"Paris?" he looked up at us. "Bicycles?"

The emphatic shaking of his head from side to side told us that we had a problem.

"Komm," he beckoned and levering his not inconsiderable bulk from the chair, waddled over to a large time-table on the wall. Picking out a train from Budapest to Krakow, he pointed out a little bicycle symbol along with others indicating that there was a dining car and couchettes. Moving his finger to the Orient Express it was obvious that there was no such little bicycle symbol.

"Paris no goot," he repeated before sitting down, picking up his smouldering fag and pointedly ignoring us – the interview was clearly over.

He didn't object to our studying his time-table, however, which was quickly scanned for any more bicycle symbols in the hope that we would find one associated with a train going West – Krakow was not really very helpful. Germany appeared to be our only hope – there were two bicycle trains, one to Frankfurt and one to Dortmund and a quick look at our European map showed us that Dortmund was much closer to home.

"Dortmund OK?" Peter asked timidly as another cloud of smoke added to the deepening haze in the room.

"Ja, ja, ja," came the irritable reply. "Dortmund OK," and with that he turned his back on us and disappeared into a little office slamming the door behind him.

Fortunately we were allocated the young, pretty one on our return to the ticket office and progress was more rapid. Explaining the problem with our bicycles, the Orient Express Tickets were torn up and another six to Dortmund were prepared by hand and pushed under the grill. She had written out all the various stops along the route, one of which was Cologne and another look at the map showed Cologne to be even closer to the Channel Ports than Dortmund. Was there a train from Cologne to Ostend? With a resigned sigh that was echoed by the queue, she consulted a huge book of railway time-tables and was forced to admit that there was indeed. Splendid – would she mind ever so much writing the ticket again?

We slunk away clutching the third set of tickets knowing that we could never return.

It was still necessary to buy bicycle tickets from our chain smoking friend, so back we went, hoping to at last finalise our journey home and forget all about it while we relaxed for a few days in Budapest. It was not to be.

"Hello," ventured Peter in an ingratiating tone, while proffering our tickets for his inspection. "Can we have six bicycle tickets to Cologne please?"

"Cologne? COLOGNE? COLOGNE EEZ NICHT GOOT."

"But you said Dortmund OK," protested Peter, his voice cracking slightly. "The Dortmund train stops at Cologne."

"Dortmund OK, Cologne nicht OK."

"But that's ridiculous," Peter unwisely continued. "It's the same bloody train."

Fortunately we were all able to escape in good time, as with a bellow of anger the director of baggage and bicycles struggled out of his chair with what can only be described as murder in his eyes and lunged towards us.

So there it was. We were stuck with six tickets to Cologne with no apparent means of getting the bikes home, let alone the trailer which we hadn't yet dared mention. There was no question of going back to either office and surviving, so we walked out of Keleti-pu and down Rakoczi Street towards the Erzsebet or Elizabeth Bridge where in an hour's time we were due to meet David and Almut.

Contemporary Budapest, lying astride the Danube, only came into existence in 1873 by the merger of the separate towns of Buda on the hilly West side and Pest on the East side where the vast flat lands of the Hungarian Plain begin. Unfortunately over 70% of the city was destroyed by bitter fighting during the Second World War and most of the rebuilding has not been very sensitive. Pest, where we were now walking, is recognised as the busy commercial centre of the city and is full of shops, cafés and offices. It was grimy and noisy with a density of traffic unlike anything we had seen before, which included Rome and Athens. Six lanes of clapped out cars, pouring smoke from their exhausts, hurtled along in an unbroken stream with horns blaring and brakes squealing. It was difficult even to speak. Trams with clanging bells added to the cacophony and we held hands tightly to prevent getting lost in the swirling crowds on the narrow pavement. Cycling here would have been suicide.

At the bottom of Rakoczi Street spanning the river was the Elizabeth Suspension Bridge named, I was delighted to see, after an elegant Hapsburg Empress who was one of the most beautiful women of her day. The bridge, like the road, was a mass of traffic but on the opposite side we could just make out David and Almut leaning over the railing looking up at the floodlit statue on Gellert Hill. Weaving dangerously through the cars, Peter crossed the road and creeping up behind Almut whispered softly in her ear,

"The name's Bond, James Bond."

"You CAME!" she exclaimed with a delighted smile. "But where are Liz and the children?"

Soon we were all reunited and swapping stories about what had happened since we last met. They were staying in a university room and had already spent a few days exploring the sights. Tomorrow they were leaving on the regular hydrofoil to Vienna from where they would take the Orient Express back to Paris – minus, of course, the bicycles which would follow by freight train at a later date.

"But," said David, "tonight we 'ave to 'ave dinner with you and to toast your arrival after a most extraordinary voyage."

So we wandered through the back streets of Pest, still chatting away excitedly, until we came to a quiet restaurant that had been recommended to our friends as cheap and authentically Hungarian. Pest used to be a city of cafés and the great poet and patriot Petofi organised the bloodless revolution from such establishments in 1848, which marked the beginning of the War of Independence against the Viennese government. Having stirred his countrymen to action, Petofi died in battle at the tender age of twenty-six.

White-aproned, moustached waiters dragged two tables together and covered them with starched clothes and silver cutlery before taking our orders in German from Almut. Fans swished round above our heads and a copper samovar full of hot water bubbled gently in the corner. The far wall was painted with a huge mural depicting a rural scene of rolling hills and autumn trees presumably in an effort to distract the diner from the labyrinth of buildings outside. We had a lovely evening with them, drinking and laughing and eating while the dusk deepened to night and the regulars came in to have a coffee or a meal and of course, read the newspaper. David was not optimistic about our troubles at Keleti-pu.

"Even if you 'ave tickets for ze bicycles," he said, "zey will not be at Cologne when you arrive there. You must wait three per'aps four days. It 'appens in France, it 'appens in Germany and most certainly..."

"It 'appens in 'ungary," we all chorused together.

We had to run to the underground station to be sure of getting back to Batthyany Terrace in time for the last train to Sventendre and said an emotional goodbye to David and Almut at the top of a long flight of steps leading down to the platforms. Although we had only known them for a short time, they were kindred spirits and shared our view that it is the simple things in life that bring the most pleasure. We had just clicked with each other, as I'm sure most of mankind would, if freed from politicians, nationalistic fears and the vested interests of big business.

At Sventendre we found our bikes still locked up outside the station, but minus all the cycle computers except mine; the sensors had been left behind however, rendering them useless to the thief as well as us. It was our fault of course, but a shame that the record of the children's achievement should have been removed when they had been building upon it day by day for so long. Perhaps my recent glowing feeling about mankind was misplaced after all – it was probably due to all that beer.

The following morning we awoke to leaden skies and a continuous drizzle. It was also miserably cold, but our Buffalo jackets kept us comfortably snug as we huddled together in the covered washing up area to have our breakfast. The last of the Dutch were hitching up their caravans as piles of fallen leaves swirled around in miniature eddies, making a melancholy rustling noise as they did so. A sad-faced woman with long hair and broken teeth, who looked about sixty but was probably much younger, spent hours every day brushing the leaves into neat mounds only to have her efforts destroyed by the elements. She was also responsible for cleaning the showers, toilets and basins with the aid of a metal bucket and a single brown tattered rag which would be wrung out slowly and methodically by hand after completion of each job – I never did use the basins after observing this and made sure the shower ran for a good few minutes before stepping in.

There was little point in mooching around at the campsite, so we walked back to Sventendre station, not daring to leave the bikes there again and caught a train into Budapest for a day's sightseeing. Not over-impressed with Pest, we had decided to explore Buda which retains much of the atmosphere of an old Baroque town and is more interesting. Surfacing at Batthyany Terrace we found ourselves opposite the impressive Hungarian Parliament building on the far bank of the Danube and walked along an embankment still glistening with rain towards the Chain Bridge. This early suspension bridge, made from jointed iron strips rather than cable, was the first permanent crossing of the Danube and the two ornate stone pillars bearing the load are more akin to triumphal arches than bridge supports. It was designed and built by an Englishman, William Tierney Clark in the 19th century and if you wish to see it without travelling too far, he built an exact miniature copy which to this day spans the Thames at Marlow.

In need of some warming cheer on this dank day we had an early lunch of goulash soup and thick, white bread in an otherwise deserted café and thus fortified, continued along to the short funicular railway which would take us up to Castle Hill and the Royal Palace. On the traffic roundabout close to where the wooden carriages began their journey up the steep gradient, a large concrete 'zero' stood on a stone plinth. All distances in Hungary were measured from this point and the diminishing kilometre signs we had seen over the last few days – e.g.: Budapest 175km – led to this precise spot.

The train ride lasted less than five minutes and as we ascended a near vertical incline the whole panorama of Budapest gradually spread out below us. At the top, a wide stone terrace ran in front of the Palace enabling us to dawdle and appreciate the wonderful vista. Way below us the Danube gently curved through the city spanned by five bridges of completely different designs, almost like a textbook of mechanical engineering. To our left lay the green expanse of Margaret Island named after a medieval princess who was confined to the now ruined convent and later became a saint, while on the far bank rather like our own Houses of Parliament stood the Hungarian version. Opposite, wreathed in a hazy polluted fog, the flat expanse of Pest merged on the horizon with the 'puszta' or barren land stretching away until finally it meets the mountains of Transylvania. To the far right the Danube widened again, branched out and left several islands in its wake, some of which appeared to be the sites of major industrial plants. On our immediate right was Gellert Hill, a rugged rock topped by a huge statue of the saint who in the 11th century was cast into the river by the pagan Magyars as thanks for his attempts to convert them to Christianity. Under our feet, winding defensive walls spiralled down to the narrow lanes and church spires of Buda and a short walk along the terrace took us to the Castle District proper with the old burgher's quarters – beautiful Baroque houses with yellow plastered walls and the Matthias Church, which is a sort of Hungarian Westminster Cathedral containing the remains of Kings and Statesmen. Under Turkish rule from 1526-1686, during which many of Buda's famous baths were built, the church became a mosque with its tower serving as a minaret.

The ground under this area is honeycombed with tunnels driven deep into the limestone, and these have often provided a refuge from the ravages of war – the last occasion being the Russian siege of 1942. Two floors below the Ruszwurm, a lovely Biedermeier Café, a skeleton in chains was found when explorers lit up the corridors where no man had stepped for over two hundred years.

Meandering through the palace courtyards we emerged on the far side near one of the most visually impressive statues I've ever seen. Fashioned out of bronze, it had been cleverly set against a huge niche in the palace wall which acted as a backdrop and somehow managed to portray an entire story frozen in time. A waterfall cascaded down a rocky mountainside, forming small pools at various levels which overflowed into the main stream before ending their journey in a large marble basin. The body of a stag, noble in death, lay to one side with an arrow protruding from its chest, while the huntsman who had shot it stood at the head of the falls, crossbow in hand. Several hunting dogs, tired from the chase, lapped water from one of the pools while other members of the party rested on the rocks, looking back in admiration at the marksman. At the bottom, a small man wearing a leather cap raised a hunting horn to his lips sending an imaginary, triumphant note echoing around the glade and through the forest beyond.

We sat and looked at it for ages while Ollie and Krister climbed amongst the various life-size figures, adding even more reality to the already vivid scene.

We walked down from Castle Hill to the Danube Embankment once again and searched for a telephone box. Today was the dreaded day when my 'A' Level Photography results were due and by now

Brian would have picked them up from the college and be in possession of the awful truth. I had never done an 'A' Level before having gone straight into nursing and in a funny way it was something that I had always felt guilty about – how could I persuade my children to do something that I hadn't attempted? So from scratch, in over less than nine months, I had struggled with essays and projects culminating in the paper itself, where of course, I had answered all the wrong questions.

"Brian – is that you – it's Liz... yes we're all fine... we're in Budapest... Oh the house is fine too – I'm so glad... and you're fine as well? That's marvellous... Er Brian, I don't suppose by any chance you've got my... you have?... I'VE PASSED."

The shout echoed around the small park where we had stopped causing startled glances from passers-by while the others breathed a sigh of relief – the rest of the day wouldn't now be ruined by me moaning about how unfair life was. On the contrary, I was walking on air and it couldn't have been a nicer present with which to end our odyssey.

We celebrated at the same restaurant where only the night before we had dined with our friends, before catching the train back to Batthyany Terrace and our connection to Sventendre. It was while waiting for one of these trains, that we had a most depressing conversation with a young American woman who was studying in Budapest.

"Hi ya," she grinned on hearing us talking. "Where're y'all from? Oh England? Not too many English 'round here," she continued in a condescending way. "Nope, we jus' about got this place sewn up."

"What do you mean?" I asked, genuinely perplexed.

"Well jus' what Ah say," she said smugly. "We can jus' do anything we like becawse these here people think us Americans know everything; we know about business, we know about music, we know about science, we know about teaching, we know about money; we jus' know everything."

I was taking a rapid dislike to this over-confident know-all.

"They think," she went on, "they think that they're jus' failures an we're jus' a success an Ah'm having a ball. What is more, it's so dirt cheap Ah reckun Ah could stay here for years impressing 'em all – they jus' luv' it."

"Perhaps you don't know everything," I said stiffly, the anger rising within me.

"My dear," she replied like a scene from *Gone With The Wind*, "that doesn't matter at all. The important thing is they THINK Ah do."

This attitude was typical of the Americans that we met and as she had said, Budapest and also Prague to some extent – was full of them. The general feeling was that they had won the ideological war and were therefore entitled to the 'spoils' from the ignorant east before clearing out, taking their profits with them. America seems to be entirely driven by money – perhaps someone ought to tell them that there is more to life.

After a freezing night in the tents, we decided to spend the day exploring Sventendre which proved to be packed with interest and thankfully lacking the bustle of the capital. Situated on the Danube, its winding streets, alleys and flights of steps ascending Castle Hill, its pastel coloured houses and vineyards lend the town a distinctly Mediterranean air. Looking down from the defensive wall circling the thirteenth-century church one sees picturesque rooftops and atmospheric little courtyards as well as nearly a dozen church towers – evidence that Sventendre was once inhabited by people of substance. In fact many of the families are of Serbian descent, fleeing here in 1690 after the crushing of an insurrection against Turkish rule. By an extraordinary coincidence today – August 19th – was the feast day of the cathedral's Serbian patron saint, which meant that families from miles around had gathered for a day of dancing, music and festivities.

Parking our bikes in the main square, we meandered through the cobbled streets drinking in the atmosphere and dawdling in the shops and numerous outside stalls as we admired the usual displays of pottery, embroidery and walking sticks. A confectionery shop was selling detailed little marzipan figures of animals, brightly coloured and obviously handmade, so the children had one each and spent the next few minutes describing to each other which bit of anatomy they had just consumed. The sun made an appearance at coffee time and we sat outside sipping delicious frothy cappuccinos near the market cross while we watched the world go by and wondered if our journey home would be straightforward.

That evening we came back to Sventendre and had a lovely meal in a restaurant which had once been a merchant's house. Inside it was lit by flickering candles and rugs covered the walls and floors, giving a faintly oriental effect which was again enhanced by a group of talented musicians. The violinist was a huge man, with arms like shovels and fingers like cucumbers, but he managed to extract the most beautiful sounds from his instrument which looked like a toy tucked under his hairy chin.

We kept on having to remind ourselves that we had cycled here; cycled to this far off land with its eastern customs, dark swarthy people and romantic sounding names; cycled across five countries from the islands of Denmark to the plains of Hungary; cycled 1500 miles, caring for and looking after each other all the way with hardly a disagreement. The waiter simply didn't believe us and who can blame him – even I had to look out of the window into the dimly lit square to make sure that those were our bikes leaning against the wall.

Saturday August 20th – our last day in Budapest – was spent looking at the National Museum and Art Gallery as well as some of the other sites we had missed on our previous visits. Walking from the station, we were as usual, immediately accosted by shifty looking individuals wanting to change money. They always worked in pairs and would surreptitiously expose a wad of Forints while looking around furtively for the police.

"Pleez Mista," they would whisper. "Change zis for Deutschmark or Dollar; good price, much Forints."

Driven by spiralling inflation and a ready supply of forged notes they would target anyone remotely resembling a tourist and over the past few days, we had become adept at fending them off. Today, however, Peter's patience snapped – he was getting very anxious about meeting the director of baggage and bicycles once more – and he gave the next hapless tout an earful.

"I do not want your filthy money," he snarled. "Just piss off and leave us alone comprenez vous, PISS OFF."

Again, the tactic of shouting loudly in English appeared to pay off, as with a malevolent scowl in our direction the mobile cashpoint joined his friend to wait for their next victim.

The National Museum is an imposing building and in 1848 was the site where Petofi stirred up massed resistance by reciting one of his verses – perhaps they just didn't appreciate poetry. The Museum in Prague, as we had seen, was also the focus of their revolution under Vaclav Havel and there is little doubt when our slow-witted citizens eventually do something about our appalling government, it will all start on the steps of the British Museum.

Just inside the main door and on the left, two soldiers with bowed heads and rifles at the slant, stood guard over a door opening on to the strong room containing the crown jewels.

In the centre, under a thick glass cover and resting on a purple cushion, was the Holy Crown of Hungary dating back nearly a thousand years and the embodiment of the nation. It was clearly of eastern manufacture with jewels on the end of golden chains hanging from the diadem rather like the champagne corks on an Australian hat. At the top of the crown was a bent golden cross which appears on all known images of the crown since the Middle Ages, signifying that the King was also the protector of the faith. Around the side were enamelled portraits of the saints with the large staring eyes so characteristic of this period. Taken by the Americans at the end of the last war, it was only returned from Fort Knox in 1976.

Unlike the enormous shuffling queues at the Tower of London when we took the children to see the British equivalent, we had the room to ourselves and spent a long time examining this wonderful relic while trying to picture the turbulent history it must have seen.

The rest of the museum was equally impressive and had been laid out in a series of rooms which told the history of Hungary in chronological sequence. Thus starting with geology and the fossil record, we moved through the various stone ages noting the appearance of finely crafted flint spearheads and the emergence of pottery. Copper and Bronze working was represented by fine collections of axeheads aged to beautiful greens and browns behind their protective glass but the bulk of the displays were devoted to the period when Hungary south of the Danube was a large Roman province.

This surpassed anything we had seen before; the whole of Roman life was here, with textiles, glassware, fine pottery, statues, children's toys and incredibly preserved armour. All this paled into insignificance compared with the collection of gold jewellery which was housed in a huge strong room guarded by massive steel doors. It was dazzling, with necklaces, brooches, earrings, bracelets and small figurines glowing like only gold can in the bright halogen lights. There must have been hundreds of kilograms of the stuff – the bullion weight alone would have been worth millions of pounds let alone the artistic and historical value which was incalculable. The workmanship of contemporary pieces simply cannot match the aesthetic skills of those craftsmen working two thousand years ago. What also comes across strongly when looking at ancient objects, is the zest and optimism these people had for life; it may have been short but they seemed to make the most of what little time they had.

Next stop was Hero's Square, the largest open space in Budapest and capable of holding half a million people between the two colonnaded buildings on either side – the Palace of Exhibitions and the Museum of Fine Arts. A gigantic statue of Stalin stood here before it was demolished by demonstrators on 23rd October 1956 – the start of the Hungarian Revolution. The most recent major gathering was in the summer of 1989 when the remains of Imre Nagy, the Prime Minister executed after this revolution was crushed, were laid on the steps of the Palace of Exhibitions before being reburied with his companions.

In the centre of the square, at the base of a huge obelisk and enclosed protectively by statues representing the greatest figures of Hungarian history, lay the Tomb of the Unknown Soldier, its eternal flame flickering in the afternoon light. Standing guard over this, were two soldiers who every few minutes performed the most peculiar set of steps and contortions with their rifles. The choreography was as complex as a ballet and looked utterly ridiculous in such solemn surroundings – after twirling and stamping in an incomprehensible fashion, the finale of the show consisted of them hurling their rifles to each other so that they could be caught and thrown back again like some sort of weird beach game.

The rest of the afternoon was spent in the Fine Arts Museum looking at a large collection of Impressionist painting as well as the largest number of El Greco's outside Madrid. Although I hate El Greco, I am forced to admit that for someone living in the middle ages it is nothing short of revolutionary – what must his friends have thought of this man who was stylistically several hundred years ahead of his time? As well as paintings, this Museum housed a delightful little Egyptian collection which although small, was very representative of the period and very well displayed. Much of Hungary's art has been looted by successive occupations and it is a wonder that anything has survived at all. What impressed us, was the enthusiasm with which they were trying to rebuild their heritage and the very positive attitude that seemed to prevail.

On this upbeat note we returned to Sventendre thinking of all the marvellous things we had seen and learnt. Hungary was indeed very different from the rest of Europe and in some ways is more of a cultural cross-roads than Istanbul would have been – it is truly the place where east meets west.

Back at the campsite, I started to prepare a huge pasta full of tomatoes, fresh vegetables and diced sausages, while Alexander had the bright idea of making a fire, since the evenings were now distinctly chilly and it would be a most cheerful way to bring to an end our roving, outdoor lifestyle. Soon the boys had collected a mound of dry wood and with a little help from the remains of our stove fuel, produced a merry blaze in no time at all. As dusk fell and the bats flitted by, we sat around it on wooden seats eating our supper, talking quietly and drinking a very palatable Hungarian white wine. Sparks flew up to join the myriad of twinkling stars above our heads as the children poked sticks into the flames before waving them around like wands. Comfortable and warm, our faces bathed in the light from the fire, we drank some more wine and reflected back on the places we had visited and the people we had met.

Tomorrow we would start our journey home, bringing to an end this unique, shared experience that had been entirely of our own making and which no money could ever buy.

Chapter 15

Homeward Bound

Our train didn't leave until 5:30 p.m., so the morning was spent packing up for the last time and throwing away as many non-essential possessions as we could. By this stage, the foam rolls had disintegrated along with some of our clothes, so they went into the bin followed by the remains of our dehydrated food which Alexander had manfully carried all this way.

"That was a bit of a waste of effort," he complained as about 5kg of noodles and soups were chucked out. "I could have brought my Game Boy after all."

We were thoughtless to dispose of them in this way, as later on we noticed the cleaner picking through the rubbish and carefully removing the unopened packets – Western throwaway habits seemed to be returning, despite the fact we had yet to leave.

The weather was cloudy, blustery and overcast with hardly anybody else left on the site which would be closed for the season in a few days time. A middle-aged man who spoke fluent English came over to wish us bon voyage and stayed to have a long chat; he had fled Hungary with his parents and many, many others following the revolution of 1956 and this was the first time he had plucked up the courage to return. He had taught English in a German school for thirty years but had never forgotten his childhood in Budapest and the frantic escape to the Austrian border on the night when the arrests began.

Peter went to the reception to settle our bill and also to ask for a note in Hungarian which he could show to the bicycle man in the hope that it would ease our passage.

"How much do we owe you?" he asked the woman when she had written out what was hopefully going to be our passport to freedom.

"Pleez, can I ask you something?" she replied, shutting the door of the office and looking through the window in case anyone else was in earshot. "Can I ask you to pay me in Sterling if I settle your account in Forints?"

"But we don't have any Sterling," Peter replied. "All I have is a traveller's cheque."

"Well perhaps you can owe me the money," she continued. "Perhaps my daughter will come to England next year and you can give the money to her."

"If that is what you want," Peter agreed with a puzzled look on his face "then of course we will give the money to her. But next year is a long way away – how can you trust us?"

"You are an Englishman and a doctor," she smiled. "I trust you."

So we gave her an IOU and promised to help her young daughter if she ever turned up in Swansea – she was only twelve. Since the ending of Communism, inflation had been running at 20% and there was no longer full employment. People were confused and worried as they saw their savings and security disappear – obtaining as much foreign currency as possible was an effective way of maintaining a nest egg. It transpired that she had been doing this all summer and was owed money by Dutch and German campers as well as by us. A market economy is brutal, ensuring the survival only of the fittest, which usually means the most ruthless and corrupt in society and certainly not the most caring or hard working. Entrepreneurial businessmen rise to the top in every Western country proving beyond doubt that money is God and if so, He's probably a Deutschmark.

Midday and we cycled off, waving to our helpful but sad-faced friend, who pulled her jacket ever closer to keep out the keen wind which as usual was demolishing the neat piles of swept leaves. Up the long hill to Sventendre station and our attempt to transport everything into the centre of Budapest by train rather than risk the busy suburbs – we had noticed sections of some carriages marked with bicycle signs and dividing ourselves into two groups we loaded everything on to a waiting train, heaving the trailer up from the platform. There wasn't much room for anyone else by the time we'd finished, but reckoning that the worst the guard could do would be to throw us off, sat with innocent expressions hoping that this wouldn't happen until we were nearly at Batthyany Terrace. Indeed, he wasn't very happy and charged us extra, but he didn't evict us and soon we were pulling into Budapest – so far so good.

There was no way we could possibly negotiate the escalators on the underground, so were forced to laboriously carry everything up a long flight of steps into the daylight of the embankment. From here an easy ride on a cycle-path led us to the Szabadsag bridge which took us over the river to Pest. Even though it was a Sunday, the traffic had only slightly diminished and we pushed the bikes most of the way to Keleti-pu through the series of back streets behind the National Museum.

The director of baggage and bicycles was nowhere to be seen, and seizing our opportunity, showed our tickets to a porter who was dozing quietly on a bench. Shrugs and smiles followed before he returned to his siesta.

"What about offering him some money?" I suggested in desperation.

We didn't have much Hungarian money left, but finding 200 Fts – about £1.10 – Peter waved these in front of his nose, gave him the note from the lady at the campsite and pointed again at the bicycles and our tickets. The effect as they say was dramatic. Stuffing the notes into his pocket he was transformed into our devoted helper and within minutes had organised bicycle tickets and labels which were attached to the crossbars. The trailer was a bit more of a problem as it needed customs clearance and the custom's office was nearly a mile away. Undaunted, our ally commandeered a little electric truck on to which the trailer was loaded and beckoning Peter to join him, shot off into the melee of passengers waiting on the platform, sounding the horn continuously.

I watched them disappear into the crowd, the trailer flag waving gaily as little old ladies struggled to get out of the way before they were mown down – there was no question of him stopping. The occasional royal wave from Peter would have been a nice touch but he was too busy holding on.

"Don't forget to take out some clothes and our washbags," I yelled after them, not sure whether he had heard me in the pandemonium. He hadn't.

Left alone with the children, I had time to study some of the other inhabitants of this busy station. Many were young with headbands, rucksacks and ethnic jewellery, travelling on student railcards and seeing the cities of Europe. Some were young soldiers in uniform with serious faces and smartly pressed khaki shirts, perhaps dreaming of the day when they too would be free to laze away the summer with an olive-skinned girlfriend. Others were elderly and smartly, even elegantly dressed as they looked disdainfully at the seething mass of humanity around them – it was never like this in the old days. Preying on these people like sharks on a shoal of fish, were the pickpockets and spivs offering anything from a hotel room to the partner of your dreams and perhaps both. They were easily recognisable by the way they stood relatively still while everyone else bustled to and fro, until having selected a victim, they would move in for the kill often under the pretext of asking directions. Hesitation would be fatal, as once a conversation was established, it became increasingly likely that the gullible would be taken in – the only safe option was to ignore them completely.

The strident blaring of a horn and the agitated movement of the crowd told me Peter was on his way back several minutes before I saw him. The trailer was now sealed with a stout piece of wire from which hung several impressive lead discs bearing the official stamp of Hungarian customs. We now had clearance to leave the country – the only problem was that apart from the few clothes we were wearing, everything else we possessed was in the trailer, which might just as well have been on Mars. It could not now be opened until customs clearance in Cologne.

"That's just great," I exploded. "Didn't you hear me tell you to take out our clothes and washbags?"

"Look," Peter retorted, "it's a bloody miracle we're leaving at all – I was nearly shot!"

Customs had apparently resembled a border post in Mexico with a heavily moustached officer sleeping peacefully in a chair, hat over eyes and feet on desk. Annoyed at having his slumber disturbed, he had initially refused to even look at our trailer but when pressed by our friend – who clearly felt that he hadn't quite yet earned his bribe – he had grown even more angry and drawn his pistol. It probably wasn't even loaded and was just his way of emphasising a point, but that's easy to say with hindsight. Stirred by the commotion, a more senior officer arrived, ticked off his subordinate with a volley of abuse, briefly looked into the trailer and having sealed it with the wire, laughingly sent a rather pale Peter on his way.

The Budapest-Dortmund sleeper was already waiting and we quickly found our compartment with its six berths – it was a German train and was absolutely spotless, with smoked glass windows and air-conditioning. It was a different world, completely insulating us from the noise, smells and bustle of Keleti-pu which we could watch in a detached fashion through the window. Leaving the children to fiddle with all the various dials and switches that controlled the lighting and temperature, Peter and I spent our last few Forints on some supplies for the journey which amounted to six bananas and a bottle of pineapple juice, unwisely assuming that there would be catering facilities on the train.

We returned just in time to see our bicycles and trailer being loaded into a freight wagon at the front of our train and relieved that they were at least starting with us, settled down with the children to enjoy the luxury of being transported nearly one thousand miles without any effort at all. Promptly at 5:30 p.m. the carriage imperceptibly began to move and slowly gathering speed, drew away from the station – we were on our way.

After a wide loop to the south, we crossed the Danube again and headed west, following part of the route we had taken. A few hours later we arrived back at Esztergom and then Komarom, Gyor and Hegyeshalom appeared in succession as the evening wore on and the low sun lit up the countryside with a warm glow. At the Austro-Hungarian border there were long delays for passports but to our delight, the bikes remained securely locked in the freight wagon as we approached Vienna – perhaps we had got away with it after all.

At Vienna, amidst a lot of clanking and shunting back and forth of various carriages we were able to look out of our window and see the brightly lit Ferris Wheel still slowly revolving in the night sky – it was strange to think that we had been enjoying the view from up there only a few weeks before. Shortly after leaving Vienna, the conductor came around with a large key and let down each of the couchettes with a resounding crash – clearly it was bedtime and with rumbling tummies, for indeed there was no dining car and one banana each doesn't go far, we climbed into the berths and tried to get some sleep. Anna found a suspect mark on her pillow and examined it closely for at least fifteen minutes by the light of her reading lamp, convinced that the sheets hadn't been washed since the last occupants.

My memory of that night is of rocking, jolting and rattling with the bright lights of stations flashing past our curtained window, or the screeches of other trains reaching a crescendo and fading again as they hurtled past on the opposite track.

We awoke early next morning to find the train running along the west bank of the Rhine under a grey and cloudy sky, with the occasional squall of rain pattering on the glass. On the far bank, villages nestled at the bottom of steep slopes covered with vineyards and where the river made a detour around rocky bluffs, turreted castles could often be seen occupying the heights. Over the next hour we were taken on what amounted to a high speed Rhine cruise and indeed the original conveyances of such a journey could be seen steaming gently in both directions on the dark, brooding waters.

It was charming, but our enjoyment came to an abrupt end when we realised that the wagon containing all our bicycles had completely disappeared at some point during the night. It had 'appened as David said it would and we now had nothing but six cycle helmets and a pannier full of sandals with which to survive the next few days.

We pulled slowly into Koln – Cologne – at 9 a.m. having taken just under sixteen hours to cover the same distance that had taken us over five weeks on the bicycles – an aeroplane would have done it in two hours and no doubt in a few more years it'll be faster still. Speed, however, isn't everything.

If you have to be stranded in Germany, then Cologne is almost an ideal spot. The railway station is an enormous covered area with shops, banks and restaurants and is situated right in the middle of the city next to the soaring Gothic Cathedral which is literally only a few yards away. Feeling rather at a loss to know what to do, we trooped into a smart café and ordered six delicious cappuccino's which arrived in big mugs with a good inch of cream, froth and chocolate on the top. These lifted our spirits almost instantly and deciding to wait until midday before checking to see whether or not the bicycles had arrived, set off to explore.

This central area was virtually completely pedestrianised with the cathedral surrounded by a broad flagged terrace which led off to the various main shopping streets on one side and the Rhine on the other. It was a hive of activity and obviously the focus of this city's life. Smart young ladies in well tailored suits carrying slim plastic shopping bags bearing the name of expensive outfitters, strode purposefully along wondering if they could justify to themselves the purchase of yet another pair of shoes. Businessmen in dark suits and black leather moccasins had a more preoccupied air as they hurried by, perhaps worrying if they could afford their wife's increasing credit card bill. Japanese tourists snapped away at the cathedral with huge camera bags hanging round their shoulders and smaller money pouches protruding from the front of their belts like early pregnancies. Stalls sold cheap jewellery and yet another mime artist, this time wearing dungarees and welder's goggles and sprayed from head to foot with silver paint, managed to give a passable rendition of a robot. Through all this bustle swerved skateboarders and roller-bladers wearing the required baseball cap back to front and earphones blasting out music that even we could hear. A display of religious posters extolled the path of True Righteousness and explained how 5 Dm could keep an African family alive for a month, while next to them beggars held out their hands and asked for the price of a sandwich.

Crossing a pedestrian walkway, we chanced to look down into the small cave-like area below. There, amid mounds of litter and soft drink cans, was a village of cardboard boxes and crude canvas shelters with the inhabitants either lying in sleeping bags or scavenging through the ordure. It was like a scene from after a nuclear holocaust when people survive in the remnants of their previous civilisation – no hydrogen bomb, however, was responsible for this state of affairs, which can now be found in every apparently thriving city in the western world. We hadn't seen it in Prague or Budapest – Calcutta may have an excuse but I don't believe that Cologne or London has.

Returning to the station restaurant for a very nice, and for us unusual, lunch of chicken salad and curries, we watched a rather lonely man carefully order his meal before eating it slowly and meticulously accompanied by half a bottle of white wine. He had no one to talk to, so spent the time between courses carefully arranging his place setting and wine glass which he kept looking at critically as though unsure whether to have a sip now or wait for the food. It was a ritual which may well have occurred every day – I hope that I never have to eat alone.

The baggage office was easy to find and staffed by a helpful bearded man who somehow seemed out of place – perhaps we just weren't used to helpful baggage officials.

"Nein, I haf no record of bicycles from Budapest. Per'aps vi must vait for three maybe four days. I am sorry. You can come tomorrow again?"

Yes we could come tomorrow again. It would be the highlight of our day as there was nothing else to do. At least he showed that he cared and feeling a bit happier because of that, we walked back to the tourist information office to ask about hotels.

I have never been tempted to use these places before but this has obviously been a mistake. In response to the question:

"Do you know a cheap hotel within walking distance of here that has a family room for six people for anything from one to seven nights?"

The young man behind the desk scanned a list before making a telephone call. Yes there was such a hotel for 210 Dm per night – about £80 all in – and could we go there now? It was as simple as that and armed with a map we quickly found it on the far side of the railway station in a quiet side street.

Hotel Constance was run by a pleasant young woman with two small children who listened wide-eyed as she explained our journey to them. The rooms were perfect, consisting of a large basement bedroom and bathroom for the children connected to our master suite by a spiral staircase – as an enforced base it wasn't bad at all but how long could we afford to wait? With food and other essentials, our daily bill would easily be over £150 and not having a clue as to how much money was in our account, I was waiting with some trepidation to see if our next credit card transaction would be refused.

In the hall near the reception desk was a series of black and white photographs depicting Cologne before and just after the war. The destruction wrought by bombing was terrible and in one picture the damaged cathedral spire could be seen jutting up from a sea of rubble without a single building standing.

Showers were followed by a doze on our beds and thus refreshed we went out to look for supper. The cathedral precincts were even more alive now than earlier and we watched with interest a street show involving acrobats and jugglers. The climax of this occurred when, with the aid of a stepladder and a rather dozy member of the audience, a member of the troupe mounted a ten feet high unicycle and pedalled it around the square juggling five hoops as he did so – it was a tour de force.

The children had suffered withdrawal symptoms from pizza deprivation during the past weeks and it was impossible to pass a Pizza Hut without them dragging us inside for a feast of mozzarella. Further along the street, a friendly young man was making delicious looking pancakes on a broad iron skillet and still feeling ravenous, we each had one covered with lemon and sugar served rolled up in a paper cone.

At an intersection in the pedestrian precinct stood a huge, shiny granite monolith about fifteen feet high with water cascading down its sides from an invisible hole at the top. The water flowed slowly, forming a moving, shimmering skin over the surface of the stone before disappearing into small drainage holes at the base. We could walk right up to it and pressing our hands against it, wash the sticky sugar away from our fingers. The children had been given helium filled balloons from Pizza Hut and soon discovered that if these were covered with water they would sink to the ground under the small increase in weight, only to rise slowly again as the water evaporated.

Thus absorbed, we stayed near this unusual fountain for some time listening to the haunting sounds of a Peruvian pipe band, who were playing in the doorway of a big department store, until it was time to go back.

The breakfast next morning was delicious with hot rolls, coffee, eggs and jams served in a light airy dining room. After cereal for weeks and weeks, luxuries like boiled eggs and unlimited coffee were wonderful and we were the last to leave what we considered to be a banquet.

Our friend in the baggage office shook his head sadly as he saw us coming towards him.

"So sorry but zere is no bicycles last night, you can come tomorrow again?"

Yes we could come tomorrow again, and the next day and the next day. Freight in Germany is only transported at night so there was no point in returning until the following morning.

"Come on," I said. "Let's just forget the bikes and cheer ourselves up by going shopping."

Anna's eyes lit up at this point but all the boys groaned; shopping is always the answer to a girl's blues, but seems to be the cause of most men's. On this occasion, however, it was essential. We all needed a change of clothing and what better excuse than to buy it. With all the time in the world we browsed happily in the main shopping street comparing prices and bargains before settling on very reasonable tracksuits for the boys and masses of underwear and tops for the girls. A toothbrush each completed our immediate requirements and with boys looking like a visiting athletics team, we turned our attentions to the cathedral.

Begun in 1248 it was the most ambitious building project of the middle ages but work came to a halt at the beginning of the 16th century and it wasn't completed before 1880 - just sixty years before the RAF blasted it to bits. The interior was huge, being supported by fifty-six massive pillars and above the high altar was the famous reliquary of the Three Kings, a masterpiece of 13th century goldsmith's work, made to house relics of the Three Kings including Charlemagne – brought to Cologne from Milan.

Behind the cathedral, a maze of medieval streets full of Bier Kellars and smart restaurants led to the wide promenade which bordered the Rhine. Very broad and full, the waters would sweep north towards Arnhem before turning west and entering the sea near Rotterdam. Moored alongside the promenade were long pleasure boats displaying advertisements for mini-cruises or day trips and we watched one crab in sideways to its berth, the throttles juggled skilfully by the captain so as to keep the bows pointing into the strong current.

Finding a kiosk selling kebabs, we bought six pieces of pitta bread stuffed with lamb, salad and spices and ate them sitting on a bench looking out over the river with all its interest and activity. Only three months later, this whole area would be lying under several metres of flood water after the wettest winter on record, combined with melting snow in the Alps, causing the Rhine to break its banks. The cathedral, on slightly higher ground, just managed to escape. Every year the climate appears to break new records – wettest winter, driest/hottest summer, windiest November, coldest February – is it really deteriorating or are we simply obsessed with statistics?

We returned that evening for a stroll to find the cathedral beautifully floodlit with a pale green light which had the effect of endowing it with a soft patina of age, rather like an ancient bronze. The pleasure boats were making ready for their evening dinner cruises and through the glass picture windows we could see tables set with starched white clothes and set with fresh flowers. Passengers were already sipping cocktails and scanning the menus, no doubt torn between the fillet steak and the salmon – it looked a wonderful way to spend an evening but we could never afford it and in any case, after what we had done and seen, it somehow seemed too ostentatious.

Like little boys leaving the window of a sweet shop, we turned away and walked over one of the big Rhine bridges stopping in the middle as we did so to watch the barges heading south from Rotterdam. By now it was quite dark, but presumably with the aid of radar, these monsters passed below us in a never ending stream missing the bridge supports by only a few metres. Often we could look into the cabin below the wheelhouse and see the crew watching television or reading, surrounded by a homely collection of potted plants and soft furnishings. At the stern a small car would be suspended from derricks, ready to be lowered on to the quayside at their next port of call.

The Rhine rises near Lake Constance, not very far from the source of the Danube and the thought crossed my mind that if these two major waterways could somehow be linked, it would be possible to travel by boat right across Europe – no doubt greater brains than mine have considered a Rhine-Danube canal.

Wednesday August 24th. Our bearded baggage man greeted us with a broad smile and his thumbs in the air – our bikes had arrived! The wire around the trailer had been removed and the lock forced by Austrian customs in their efforts to find cocaine but otherwise all was well. Rushing over to the ticket office, we bought six bicycle tickets to Ostend and just managed to catch the 11 a.m. train, heaving everything into an otherwise empty freight car behind the engine – as long as we kept going they were safe from disconnection.

As we thundered through the flat Belgian countryside we drank coffee served by a friendly young man who pushed his little trolley past us every thirty minutes.

"More coffee?" he would ask hopefully for the tenth time as though on commission.

Four hours later, having passed through Brussels without losing the bikes, we arrived in Ostend with the wind howling and the rain drizzling – yes, we were certainly close to home. £130 for tickets to Ramsgate and a few minutes later we were queuing in Line One as the rain continued to fall. Car drivers pointed and stared at us as they had done ten weeks before in Harwich, but unlike then we just ignored them – we had nothing to prove now and didn't really care what they thought.

Peter thought the crossing only took just over an hour and leaving at 5:30 p.m., with the bonus of an hour converting to British Summer Time, would leave us plenty of daylight to find somewhere to sleep in Ramsgate – we had even thought of a campsite if the rain stopped.

Nearly five hours later, the loading ramp dropped on Ramsgate quay to reveal a pitch black, rainswept night with container lorries thundering through the port sending up clouds of spray.

"Well," I laughed at Peter, "I can see that your standard of planning has been consistent throughout this little jaunt of ours; WELL DONE!"

I used the term 'Well Done', almost as a form of abuse and he had been congratulated in this fashion more than once. He hadn't done badly though and I know he had felt the responsibility of bringing us all home safely much more keenly than I had. After all, it was his idea and he had quietly mentioned to me more than once that he'd never forgive himself if we came to any harm. Taking no chances at this late stage, we pushed everything on the pavement up the long winding road that leads from the port to the town of Ramsgate itself. Leaving the children huddled on the promenade, we went into a nearby pub to ask for advice before trying the hotels which the barman suggested.

The first was one of these flashy places so beloved of businessmen on expense accounts. A young, over made-up receptionist with a badge proclaiming her to be a 'Customer Services Manager' viewed our dishevelled appearance with distaste and said certainly we could have a room without breakfast for £30 each – she seemed rather surprised when we left. The next one we tried was cluttered, warm and friendly, being run by a smiling middle-aged Irish lady.

"Oi've only got the one room but you're more than welcome to it – come on in out of the rain. Oi'll see if Oi can find somewhere for them boikes."

Fetching the children, we heaved everything into a basement bar and made ourselves comfortable in our room – Alexander volunteered to sleep on the floor while the rest of us divided ourselves between the bunks and the large double bed, while the rain continued to thunder down outside.

The night was somewhat disturbed by the clanging of bells and the whooping of distress rockets outside, but it was only while we were all having a blissful English breakfast the following morning that the cause of all this was pointed out to us from the window of the dining room. Far out in the bay, smoke drifted from a burning ferry from which all the passengers and crew had been evacuated during the night. In fact it was the ferry that we had been on making its return trip; the boys of course were mortified.

"If only we'd been on that!" moaned Ollie. "It would have been so lush being winched into a helicopter."

We were lucky to leave Ramsgate unscathed, since the following day a loading ramp collapsed killing five people as they disembarked from another cross-channel ferry.

Settling our monstrous bill of £48, we left this pleasant place with,

"Good luck t'you all and God Bless," ringing in our ears as we cycled back to the port to await the arrival of Brian and the van which would take us home.

There he was smiling and waving to us almost as though he had just dropped us off – was it really ten weeks ago that we had last seen him?

"Did you think we'd make it?" I smiled at him.

"I never had the slightest doubt," he replied, shaking his head slowly as he looked at each of us in turn. "Whatever are you going to get up to next?"

228

EPILOGUE

October 1994 – another rain-lashed Saturday afternoon in our suburban house. Anna was upstairs washing her hair while the boys were playing the latest version of Mortal Kombat complete with blood curdling grunts and shrieks. Peter was laboriously practising a piece set by his new piano teacher and, surrounded by piles of damp washing, I was sinking into my usual winter depression. One thousand five hundred miles on bicycles from Denmark to Budapest had obviously not changed our way of life, it was no longer even a topic of conversation, so what had it achieved?

We had certainly sampled the sights of four major European capitals along with thousands of other tourists – interesting yes, educational undoubtedly, but what set it apart?

I think the real difference was that our summer had not been a holiday in the true sense at all, but was more akin to a medieval pilgrimage. We didn't actually crawl on our hands and knees the last mile to a relic filled shrine in Budapest, although seeing the stupendous Royal Crown was a good alternative – but I think we nevertheless must have shared many of the emotions experienced by travellers to Canterbury, Jerusalem and Santiago de Compostela hundreds of years ago. Long journeys over many weeks by foot or horseback used to be common occurrences, often undertaken several times in the average lifetime and would be considered to be among the main events in that life along with marriages, births and deaths. They would also have been wonderful topics of conversation.

"D'you remember Simon, the time we got caught in that storm on the way to Canterbury in 1240?"

Travel is so easy now and yet so unsatisfying. Stepping out of a plane or even a train gives very little idea of the distances covered – there is no sense of accomplishment and perhaps this leads many people to search for ever more exotic destinations.

"I've been to Bali/Maldives/Goa," when all they've really done is to turn up at an airport and sit on a seat.

A pilgrimage is different – the route and destination are not really that important. It is the **doing** that matters.

Firstly it's a form of escapism from routine. Whether a thirteenth-century serf tilling the fields, a housewife, a doctor or a schoolchild, life is bound to have a tedious, repetitive side to it and I think it is an unusual person who does not dream of getting away from it all. I suppose that annual holidays and weekend breaks serve this purpose in our strange modern society to some extent, but they can have their own problems. The short time and great expense mean that hopes may not always be fulfilled and in any case, there is no sense of being in control when everything is organised for you.

The long period we were away for enabled us to unwind and completely forget the stresses and strains of our normal lives, while seeing things in a sharper and more balanced perspective from far away. We had no expectations other than that we would have to rely totally on ourselves.

Secondly the journey itself was important. There was a daily sense of achievement with difficulties overcome and progress made, no matter how small. Staying in one place, however pleasant, could never have given us this feeling of satisfaction. Having a meaningful destination gave us a finite objective or end point with which the pilgrimage could be said to be complete but it was the journey itself that really mattered.

We hoped that the children would realise in their lives that however difficult a task might first appear, patience, perseverance, courage and time can accomplish almost anything.

We became fitter and leaner and appreciated simple things – ordinary food, water, a shower and a good road surface. Luxuries such as beds and clean clothes gave us immense pleasure – in essence, we stopped taking life for granted.

We learnt that people in general are kind, caring and eager to help a traveller, as they have been since time began. We met some wonderful individuals, some very poor and we realised that good or evil has nothing to do with nationality.

We developed a deepening scepticism about the benefits of 'Americanising' eastern Europe, as indeed were the inhabitants themselves and we have a unanimous and lasting loathing for the motor car.

Lastly and most importantly, it taught us something about ourselves. It gave us immense pride both as individuals but also as parents of four very brave, cheerful and determined children. We did it together and whatever happens in the rest of our lives, we will always be able to look back and think about those wonderfully free days when we were all so close to each other, in body and in spirit, for so long. It is a sadness that it will probably never happen again.

In his marvellous autobiography *Dear Me*, Peter Ustinov likens the mind to a prison cell from which there is no escape. All you can do, he advises, is to furnish the walls as comfortably as possible with pictures and images which can be looked at and taken down, time and time again. I know that our adventure has provided us with a mental photograph album which we can all leaf through in the years to come, when perhaps the weather outside our cell window is dark and dreary.

Let's forget the washing for a while and just remember.

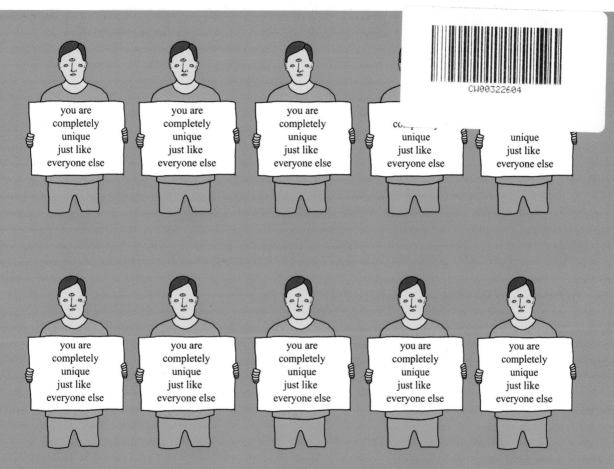

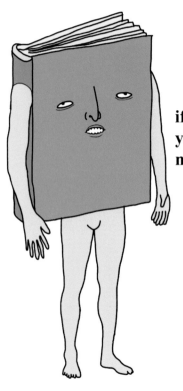

if you read me
you will feel
more positive

i am so depressed

this book is dedicated to all of my friends
and my mum

Motivational Quotes to Help You Be More Positive

chris (simpsons artist)

Copyright © Chris (Simpsons artist) 2015

The right of Chris (Simpsons artist) to be identified as the author of this work has been asserted in accordance with the Copyright, Designs and Patents Act 1988.

This edition first published in Great Britain in 2015 by
Orion
an imprint of the Orion Publishing Group Ltd
Carmelite House
50 Victoria Embankment
London EC4Y 0DZ
An Hachette UK Company

1 3 5 7 9 10 8 6 4 2

A CIP catalogue record for this book is available
from the British Library.

ISBN: 978 1 4091 5876 9

Printed in Germany

The Orion Publishing Group's policy is to use papers that are natural, renewable and recyclable and made from wood grown in sustainable forests. The logging and manufacturing processes are expected to conform to the environmental regulations of the country of origin.

Every effort has been made to fulfil requirements with regard to reproducing copyright material. The author and publisher will be glad to rectify any omissions at the earliest opportunity.

www.orionbooks.co.uk

introduction

if you wake up in the morning time
and you dont like what you have become

then it is up to you to change yourself
and become the person who you truly wish to be

what have i become

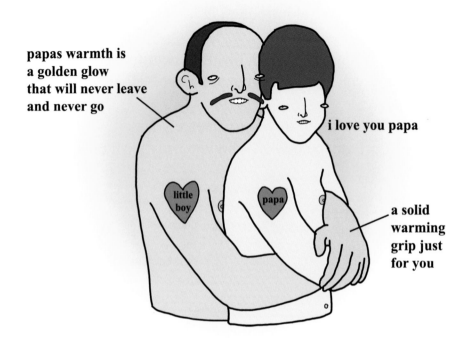

a fathers love will always
keep you warm

a apple a day keeps the doctor away

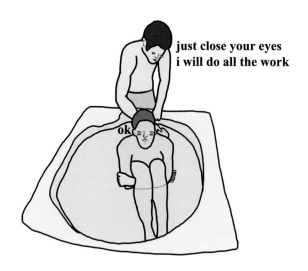

washing a mans back will make yourself feel like
you are good at something for once in your life

be happy while you are living

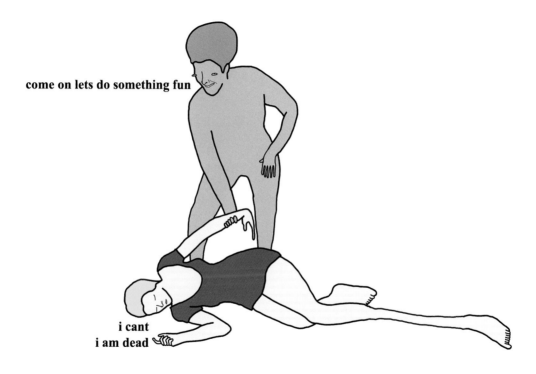

because it is almost impossible to do when you are dead

everyone is looking for something
maybe it is you

nothing says i love you
more than the warm breeze of a fire burning
underneath a blanket of stars

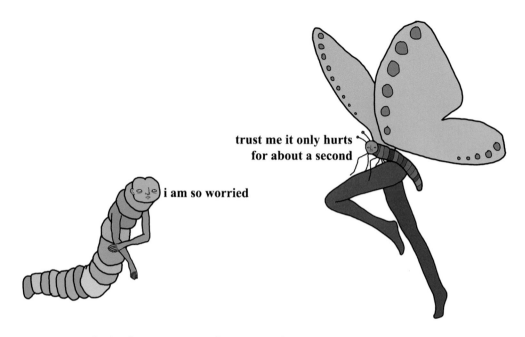

it is important for people to try new things
because if you dont try new things then you might not
become a butterfly at the end of it and if you dont try
anything new then you might just be a caterpillar
for the rest of your life

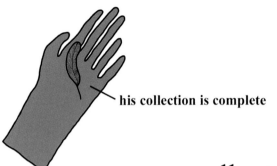

his collection is complete

this one reminds
him to smile

collect feathers
to keep yourself positive

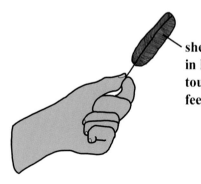

she will keep this one
in her bag so she can
touch it when she
feels depressed

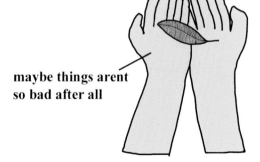

maybe things arent
so bad after all

he is crying because
he has found a photograph
of his wife sharpening a
pencil for his son on his
first day of school

eye spit

it is ok to cry sometimes because tears are
just sad spit that comes out of your eyes

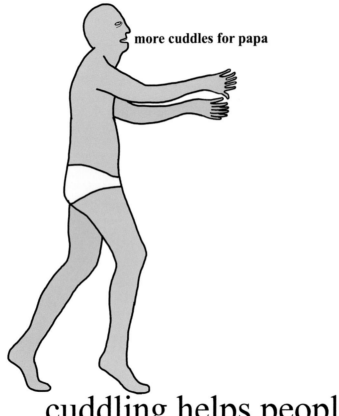

no confidence
because he is deaf

sits on a chair all day
touching his face

afraid of his own thoughts

pathetic

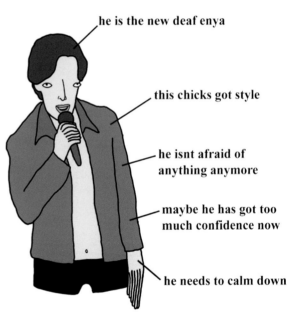

he is the new deaf enya

this chicks got style

he isnt afraid of
anything anymore

maybe he has got too
much confidence now

he needs to calm down

why dont you become
a pop singer to give
yourself a bit of confidence

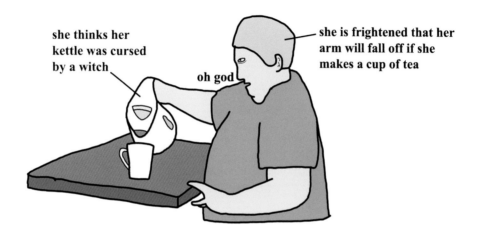

do the things that you fear most
because they probably arent as
scary as you think they are
inside of your head

thank you for saving my life

it is fine

a true friend is someone who will rescue you from a drought
without even thinking about their own safety

dont have favourites

because everyone has favourites

and if you have favourites then you are the same as everyone else

and if you are the same as everyone else then you wont be anybodys favourite

jesus christ
he is massive

he is so large

600 years ago today on a cold north pole night something magical happened under a star that shined so bright that is right it is the birth of our lord saviour baby jesus christ. a lot of people sometimes always forget the true story of christmas time so pull up a seat or borrow a stool from a friend and listen to the tale of the newborn king. when mary was lay in her bedroom on christmas eve feeling really excited for it being christmas day a angel whos name is called gabron floated down from heaven to tell her that while she was sleeping the other night santa claus laid an egg inside of her and mary said i cant believe it and then gabron did a massive screaming laugh that sounded like someone rolling a barrel of children off a roof and he said well we will see about that haha and then he tapped his finger on his nose 3 times and he did a slow motion wink and then he completely vanished into a puff of steam and then mary ran over to her boyfriend josephs house and she told him that santa claus had laid an egg inside of her and joseph said he couldnt believe it and mary said i know it is the one thing i least expected to happen and then suddenly a bright star whos name is called north appeared

in the sky above them and he told them to follow him quickly before it is too late so mary and joseph climbed onto a donkeys back and they galloped after the star which led them to a barn in the middle of the north pole and he said this is where you are going to have your baby and mary said are you actually kidding me this place is so disgusting and it stinks of camels and the star said i know but it is the best i could do at this short notice and joseph said fair enough this will do i suppose and he looked at mary and rolled his eyes and then the star said good and it disappeared into the darkness and then 3 wise men came to the barn because they heard there was some sort of birthing going to be happening and joseph said they could watch if they each give mary a gift so they gave mary some gold earrings a 6 pack of frankfurter sausages and a olly murs cd because those are the things that she enjoys the most and then as quickly as a christmas wish mary starts pooing the egg out of her bum and one of the 3 wise men bursts out laughing when he sees the top of the egg coming out of marys bum and his laughing makes the other wise men burst out laughing as well and joseph kept on looking at them and tutting and then he said either you three just shut up or just stand outside of the barn because you are putting my mary off laying her egg and then mary did one last thick deep push and the egg completely slid out of her bum and landed on the barn floor and cracked open and baby jesus slowly climbed out of the egg and when joseph sees jesus he cant believe how big he is and he screams jesus christ he is massive and that is why they decided to call him jesus christ because it is what everyone always says when they first see the size of him and as mary and joseph and baby jesus and the three wise men all lay in the barn cuddling each others legs they hear the sound of sleigh bells high above their heads and at that very moment they knew that the spirit of christmas will forever live on inside of each and every single one of us for as long as baby jesus name is remembered and that is why on christmas eve santa claus lays an egg down everyones chimneys so they will always be reminded of that magical night when mary laid our lord saviour baby jesus christ out of her bum and into our hearts.

suck your stomach
in and out really
quickly to locate
your air sacks if
you cant find them

listen to your air sacks
like you are having a
listen to the sound of
your mums sack
when you was inside
of her when you was
a little boy

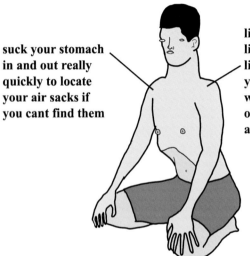

dont forget to breathe

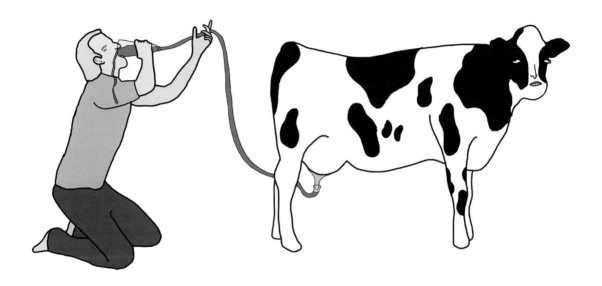

try and drink a smaller
amount of meat

delicious wet soup

eating soup in the rain is like eating
a sandwich that grows with every bite

it doesnt matter what type of shape
you are because all that really matters
is what type of shape your eyes make
when he tells you that he loves you

every
shadow
is a friend

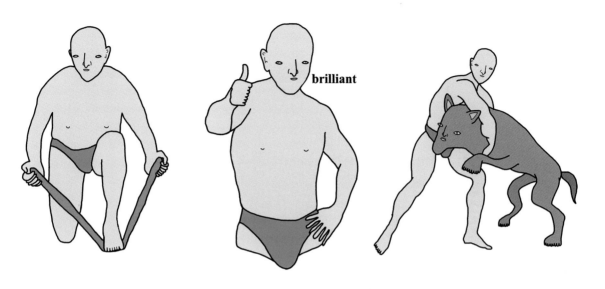

brilliant

exercising will help you
live for longer and it will also help
you build up strength to finally capture
the wolf that killed your wife

dont eat wool

yum

it will just clog up your stomach

why

and you will die

i dont care what you say
i am wearing it
i am nearly 29

if you want to make outfits out of bits of cloth
that you found in your loft then you should
just do it because you are a grown man
and it is your body not your mums

butterflys dont taste of butter
they just taste of flys

never be sad
because somewhere there is someone
who is falling in love with your smile

wear some gold lipstick to
make yourself look and feel great

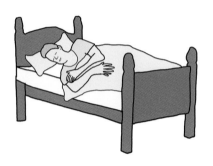 

gold isnt the most important thing in your life
the most important thing in your life is
your family and your friends and your wife
and i think that it is better for a person to live their life happily
in a wooden bed and be remembered than it is to spend their life
feeling sad and be buried in a golden coffin and be forgotten

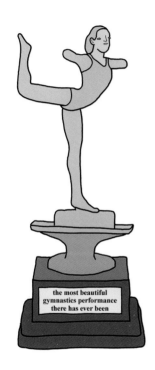

the most beautiful
gymnastics performance
there has ever been

dont think about all of the
things in your life that you cant
do for yourself just think about all of the
things in your life that you can achieve
if you just start believing in yourself

a new hairstyle is a great way to make
yourself feel young again

happiness is different for everyone

some people like eating ham

**the ham gives
him a powerful
feeling that he
cant control**

and some people like putting ham
on their face and pretending to
be a killer from a film

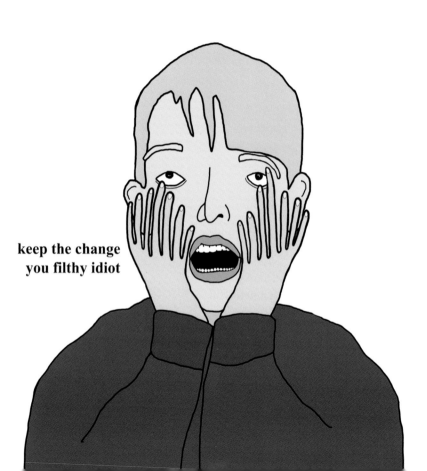

keep the change
you filthy idiot

it is everyones favourite family christmas film about child neglect and torture that is right it is home alone. i have done a picture of the main character from home alone and his name is called kevin but everyone just calls him kev the slev because he is always making spit go down his chin to make people laugh and if you havent seen home alone before then you should have a watch of it tonight or tomorrow night because it is really good and my best bit in it is when kevin pours a can of coke on to his pizza and he says to his mum to clean it up and then his mum says ugh kevin you are such a disease and then she locks him in the loft and his cousin wees on him when he is sleeping and then his family all decide to go on holiday and they leave kevin in the loft on his own because he is the most unpopular one in his family and when he wakes up in the morning time he realises that everyone is gone and he goes in to his mum and dads bedroom and he stares at himself in the mirror for ages and he keeps on saying why and then he sees 2 robbers outside of his house and he hears them saying that they are going to rob his house at 9 o clock on the dot and kevin says yeah right are you hell going to have a rob of my house you homeless idiots so he sets up loads of some traps in his house so that he can kill the robbers and then when it is night time he trys to make himself something to eat but all that he can find in the cupboards is plastic so he has to eat plastic for his christmas dinner and it made me feel really sorry for him because he was nearly crying because it was so sharp and it was cutting his throat when he is swallowing it and he kept on saying so sharp and then he hears the robbers trying to get in to his house so he goes in to the kitchen and he says to the robbers that if they come in to his house he will kill them and the robbers just start laughing and they say ha ha you cant kill us you are only 5 years old and we are both 20 years old and then kevin says ok then you asked for it and he puts a flame thrower with a knife on the end of it out of the door and he flames them and he slashes their legs with the knife as well and the robbers have to put their faces in to the snow to cool themselfs and then the tall robber stands on a nail and it goes right inside of his foot and it is so disgusting and a massive spider comes out of his mouth because he is screaming so much and then when the robbers are lay on the floor kevin goes up to them and he starts laughing and he makes loads of spit go down his chin and he says you messed with the wrong 5 year old and then the police come and they arrest the robbers and kevin says that was close and then he goes to sleep because he is so tired and starved and when he wakes up in the morning time he goes downstairs and he stands in his living room and he looks at a picture of himself for about a hour and then he hears some footsteps behind him and he says i know them familiar footsteps and he turns around and it is his mum and she says merry christmas kevin and he says merry christmas mum and she realises that she does like him after all and then right at the end kevins dad finds a gold tooth on the floor and he says to kevin did you loose your gold tooth and kevin says oh yeah i wondered where that thing went to and he puts his gold tooth back inside of his mouth and then there is a close up of kevins face and it goes in slow motion and he says merry christmas in a really deep voice and then the film just ends and it really is the best christmas film that there has ever been.

having a walk next to a friend
in the darkness of night is better
than having a walk on your own
in the lightness of day

it is better to say goodbye in peace
than to say hello in pain

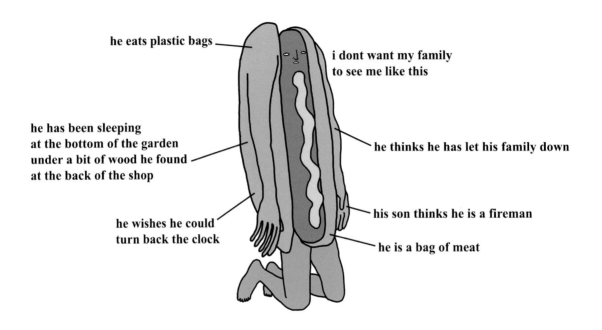

talk to your family about how you feel
they wont be angry at you forever

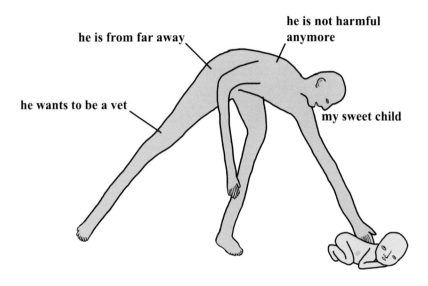

he is from far away

he is not harmful anymore

he wants to be a vet

my sweet child

if you see it then it can be yours
so just go over to it and pick it up

if you feel sick just be sick
if you love someone just tell them

if you love something never let it go

if you love something so much then you
should never let it go because it is the most
tiniest of things in your life that make the
most biggest difference and sometimes you
dont even realise it was even
there until it is gone

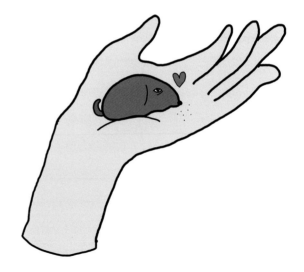

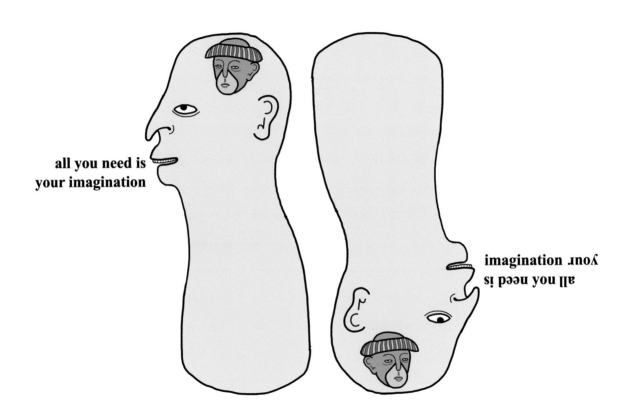

all you need is
your imagination

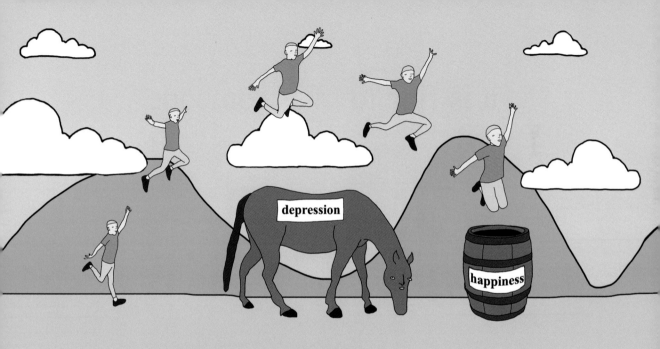

jump over depression like you are
jumping over a massive brown horse
into barrel of happiness

it is fine to miss someone

because it just means you remember
all of the beautiful things about them

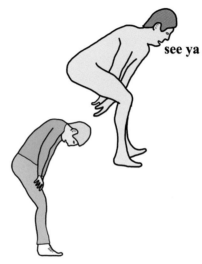

see ya

you can do it
just go for it
jump over a little boys head

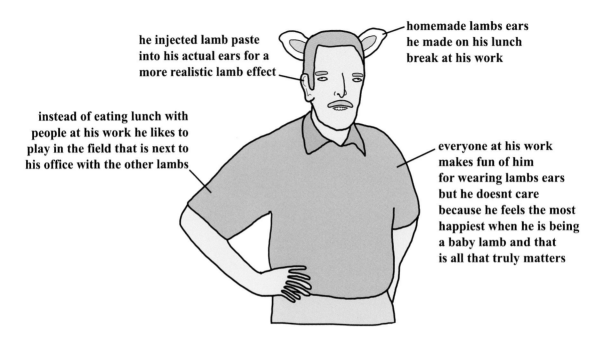

he injected lamb paste into his actual ears for a more realistic lamb effect

homemade lambs ears he made on his lunch break at his work

instead of eating lunch with people at his work he likes to play in the field that is next to his office with the other lambs

everyone at his work makes fun of him for wearing lambs ears but he doesnt care because he feels the most happiest when he is being a baby lamb and that is all that truly matters

if you want to be a baby lamb
then just be a baby lamb

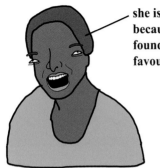

she is laughing because she found her favourite cloth

he is laughing because he saw a shoe shaped like a little boy playing a fiddle on top of a hill

laugh more

she is laughing because she loves looking at pictures of pinecones on her computer

he is laughing because he has such tiny ears

positive thinking

life is a massive firework
so sit on it and aim it for the stars

this little baby
who is so tiny and small
is going to make the biggest
and most massive difference
to the world of anyone of all

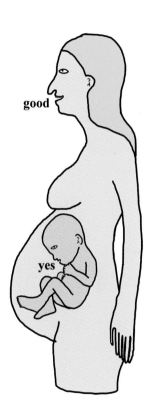

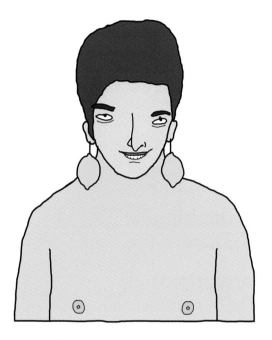

when life gives you lemons
make some lemon earrings

maybe you will win the lottery
and you will get loads of money
and everything will be ok again

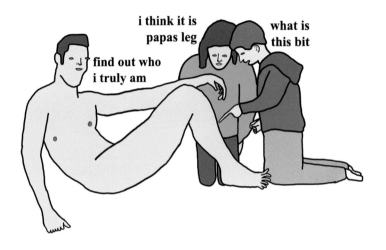

let your family explore your body

be more positive

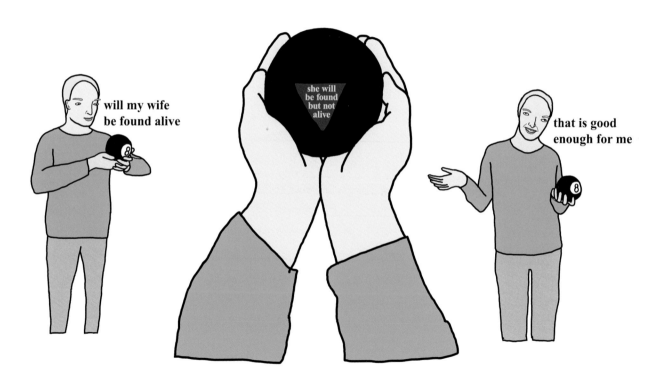

life begins
at fifty

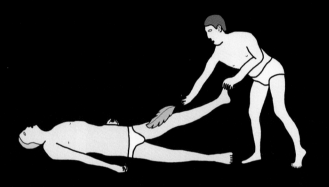

no feeling on all of the earth
is as true as the feeling of a man
tickling another mans legs
in complete darkness

it is more important for children to look up to the silver stars in the sky
and wonder about all of the beautiful things in the universe
than it is to look up to a star in a magazine and wonder where
they got their silver crop top from

if he feels stressed he just goes outside
and he milks his hen and then he feels
back to normal again

hens milk tastes
like wet eggs
it is delicious

milking a hen is a good way to relieve stress

love

can

be

found

in

the

most

strangest

of

places

make one wish every day

he wishes he didnt
have to wear a nappy
to his wifes christning

because today just might be the day that it comes true

hahahahahahahaha

a hill is a perfect place
for you to rest your head

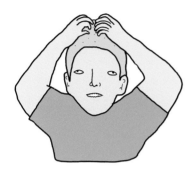

so what if you have nits

they are just hair pets

a man who doesnt love pancakes
is a man who has completely
given up on life

his arm shrunk
when he fell asleep
in the rain

passionate
about
life

he paints his arm like
a puppys paw and he
tours around schools
letting children stroke it

who
gives
a hell

just because your arm has shrunk
it doesnt mean your heart has to shrink as well

free willy

is it a bird or is it a plane no it is a massive black dolphin jumping over a little boy that is right it is the film that is called free willy. if you havent seen free willy before then i feel really sorry for you because you are missing out on the greatest love story ever told about a little boy called jesse who falls in love with a massive black dolphin called free willy and my best bit in the whole of the film is when jesse is lay next to the swimming pool sun bathing and he is watching free willy just floating around like a big wet slug and jesse says to him what is wrong big guy but free willy just looks at jesse all sad and he doesnt say anything and jesse says that it is getting late and he has got to go back to his house because his mum will be wondering where he is again so he rollerblades back to his house and when he is sleeping at night time free willy slithers into jesses bedroom and he whispers to jesse if you love me then you will help me escape from the swimming pool and jesse cant believe that free willy can talk and free willy says yeah well it is hard to talk under water dont you know haha and he does a massive deep laugh and then him and jesse just look at each other for about 20 seconds and then free willy leans over jesse and he kisses him on his lips and it is so romantic and jesse says ok honey i will help you escape so the next morning jesse steals his mums gun and he takes it to the swimming pool where free willy is being kept and he shoots the lock on the main door of the swimming pool and loads of water goes everywhere and free willy manages to climb over a metal fence but there is loads of rocks in front of the sea and free willy screams damn it i knew it i ruddy knew it and jesse looks at free willy and he says you know what you have got to do and free willy nods and he says i know honey but i dont want to leave you and jesse says if you love me then you will be free because that is all i want you to be so free willy takes a massive run up and then he leaps out of the water and into the air and over his true love and as he splashes down into the sea his floppy weak fin goes completely stiff and healthy again and jesse screams thats my willy thats my willy thats my willy willy willy and then there is a slow motion close up of jesse picking up a dead fish from off the ground and kissing it and then the film just ends really suddenly and i think that to risk your own life for the person who you truly love is what true love is all about no matter who you may be even if you are a little boy or a massive black dolphin.

i hope emily and the children will forgive me for being so old

if you are really old then why not tie a cat or small goat around your face with some wire to make your family like you again

One day we will meet again
and on that day our smiles will
stretch for as far and wide
as the distance that we were apart

put your thumb up if

he is putting his thumb up
because a girl in his class
let him borrow a pencil

he is putting his thumb up
because he hasnt been sick
all over himself today

you are feeling confident

she is putting her thumb up
because the doctor said
that her bowel infection
is slowly getting better

he is putting all of his thumbs up
because he is singing a confident
rhyme about a mouse
inside of his head

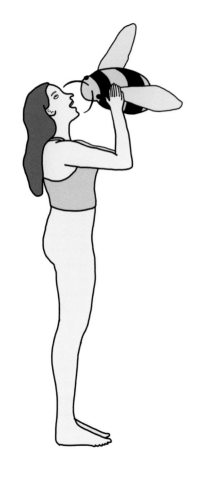

who cares
if your son is a bee

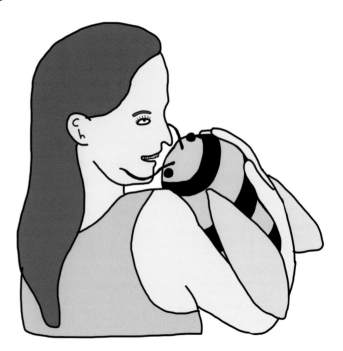

take me to my wife

his son found him in the woods
after being lost for nearly a year

merry christmas dad

the most important gift of all
is spending christmas with your family

let me taste your leg

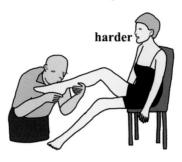

harder

your precious gentle leg

precious leg

the most precious leg that i have
tasted in 465 years

why must
things be
this way

if you dont like the way your life is
then why dont you do something about it
instead of kneeling down with no clothes on all day

sucking up quiche out of a bumbag through a glass pipe will definetly give you the motivational boost that you have been searching for all of these years

be quiet for a moment and you will see
such beautiful things around you and me

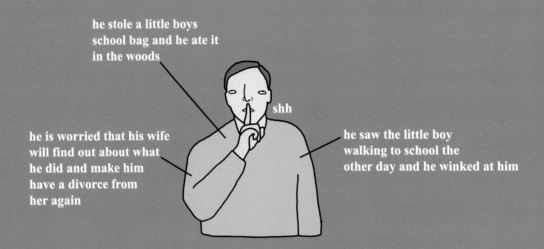

people dont have to find out about your secret
that you have been hiding for the past year and a half
so stop worrying about it constantly

the soothing smell of friendship
is the only thing that you truly need

some people dont deserve you in their life at all
so just say to them get out of my life and never come back
i have had enough of you

twin sisters

together forever and never apart
i will love you forever
inside of my heart

i am the lord
of the rings

he is thirsty for rings of all shapes and sizes and his bum bag is filled with secret surprises that is right it is sonic the hedgehog the blue haired squirrel from the 3d family adventure game that is called sonic the hedgehog and the deaf prince of egypt. if you like the type of games that are about jewellery and bum bags then prepare yourself to go on a bum bag filled adventure of a lifetime and right at the start of the game it shows sonic the hedgehog standing behind his school with some boys from his class and he keeps on looking at his bum bag and smiling at it and all of the boys think that he is actually in love with his bum bag or something and then after about 5 minutes sonic slowly unzips his bum bag and it is filled right to the top with loads of quiche and he says to the boys do you think i can suck up all of this quiche out of my bum bag through this glass tube and they all look at sonic and they say do it if you want to do it mate but we are honestly not bothered if you do it or not and sonic says well i can do it so easy without even trying and his friend scott says fair enough sonyan if you want to do it then just do it but stop constantly going on about it to us every single day because it is just getting annoying now and then sonic says haha well read it and weep you bunch of cloth helmets and then he kneels down on the ground and he puts the glass tube over the quiche and he starts sucking it up out of his bum bag and all of the boys are just looking at each other and saying what is the actual point of him doing this and sonic was sucking it up so hard that he actually looked like he was having a quiche fit because his whole body was shaking so much and then once he had swallowed up every last taste from out of his bum bag he stands up and he says now that is how you unleash the quiche and a boy who is called jamie says well done sonic you just sucked up a massive slab of your mums quiche from out of your bum bag congratulations you must feel so proud of yourself and sonic says yes i do feel proud actually it is more than any of you idiots have done today and then sonic looks at his wrist and he says oh would you look at that it is time for me to go and collect some delicious golden rings haha and then he runs off over a hill and after about 2 minutes the boys get a text on their phones from sonic and it is a picture of him pretending to be crying and he is wiping his tears away with loads of gold rings and then on the last level of the game sonic the hedgehog has to battle the deaf prince of egypt who is played by teen throbsticle zac efron from the the film grease and sonic must defeat him or the world will be destroyed and turned into a paste and with every kick and slap to zac efrons deaf egyptian face a golden ring falls from the sky and then as quickly as a blink of a dolphins eye sonic jumps up into the air and he screams see you in hell zac efron and then he turns his legs turn into electric whisks and he slams them right into the side of zac efrons neck and his neck completely bursts open and the whole of the sky starts raining pure liquid gold like a beautiful golden shower falling right out of gods throat and then when the world has been saved and sonic has buried zac efron underneath his castle there is a shot of sonic standing on top of a mountain looking out over emerald city and he is smiling to himself and then he does a massive slow motion scream and loads of golden rings and quiche come flying out of his mouth and all of the villagers bellow eat the quiche and they spend the golden rings on new clothes and ipads and they all live happily ever after until the end of time.

dont be sad that it is sunday
just be happy that you arent dead

damn you to hell
swiss cheese wheel
you have ruined my life

this was the worst
decision of his life

even the inventor of
the swiss cheese wheel
gets depressed sometimes

his dad bought him a couple of internets for a joke when he was 15 but who is laughing now dad

he didnt know what was real life anymore

his family tried to put him in a home but there wasnt any internet there so he escaped when it was at night by digging a hole in the wall with a dongle

online

now look at him

rest in paste

do you want to end up like this

spend less time on your computer or you will turn into some sort of internet paste and your family will have to bury you inside a plastic tube

you are what you eat

you

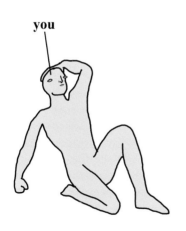

you in a month

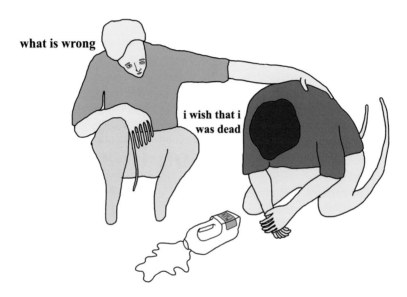

dont cry over spilt cow juice

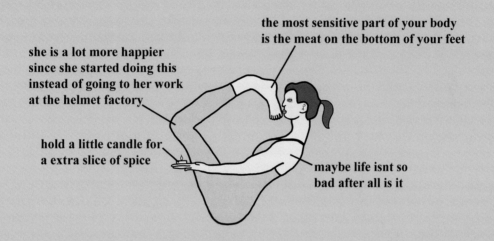

the most sensitive part of your body
is the meat on the bottom of your feet

she is a lot more happier
since she started doing this
instead of going to her work
at the helmet factory

hold a little candle for
a extra slice of spice

maybe life isnt so
bad after all is it

spoil yourself once in a while
because you deserve it

stop
worrying
so much

he is worrying because his wife went to portugal 5 years ago and he hasnt heard from her in about a week

he is worrying because everyone at his school thinks his mum is a prostitutes

he is worrying because he cant remember where he left his newborn son

he is worrying because his family doesnt want to visit him anymore because they said he smells of fireplaces

a friend is a person who will always be there
for you when you really need them to be

this could be you

if you can actually be bothered getting out of your bed

and floating around the sky for a whole day

the inside of a brain

dont ask her
about it

he just lies there
every single night
frightened to move
and terrified to ask

sometimes the less you know about your wife
the better your life will be

why was i born a train

them things and at the start of the film it shows thomas the tank engine being born in a thunder and lightning storm and his dad who is the fat controller and his mum who is the main woman train at the train station are really frightened because they were told to never have a baby together and the fat controller even swore on his mums life when he took the job that he would never get any of the trains pregnant not even one of the small unused ones that they keep around the back and the train elders said to him that if he ever gets any of the trains pregnant then his first son will be born cursed with the body of a train and the legs and arms of a man and the fat controller said you got it there will be no pregnant trains around here haha trust me but then along came thomas and my best bit in the whole of the film is when thomas the tank engine

it is everyones favourite childrens film about a man who is trapped inside the body of a steam train that is right it is thomas the tank engine from the hit family film that is called thomas

the tank engine and the curse of fat controller. if you like films that are about curses and trains then prepare yourself to go on a train journey of a lifetime because it is about both of is a teenager and he is fed up because he hates being a trains gender teen because he is really sensitive about his massive long mens beige legs and all of the other trains make fun of him and they call him thomas the rank engine and they spit on him all of the time as well and it makes him feel really fed up and then one day his friend henry says to him thomas have you ever thought about trying out for the local gymnastics team because you would probably be quite good at it and thomas said yeah right who would want me on their gymnastics team i am a freak and then henry says oh go on just give it a go there is no harm in trying and thomas says fine i will try out for the local gymnastics team because anything is better than being spat on all day here by these bunch of idiots so thomas goes to the village hall where the gymnastics team practice and he crawls in through the door covered in spit and he says i would like to join your gymnastics team and the gymnastics teacher walks over to thomas and she takes one look at him and she says you want to join my gymnastics team and thomas says yes and she says but you are a train and thomas says i know i am a train but i have got the heart of a man and she taps her bottom lip with her pen 3 times and then she nods her head and she says ok then lets see what ya got kiddo and then she points to a boy who has got a ghetto blaster on top of his head and he puts on the number 1 gymnastics song of the year that is called lucky boy by the daft punk experience and thomas the tank engine goes into the middle of the room and then he slowly stands up on to his hind legs and everyone cant believe how massive he actually is and everyone was saying that he was nearly about as big as a train and then thomas says here goes nothing and then he jumps up into the air and he does a massive sideways gymnastic spin and he blows loads of glitter out of his head chimney and everyone starts cheering and shouting come on and as he stood there in the middle of the room under the blanket of glitter slapping his massive long mens beige legs together in time to the music he finally felt free for the first time in his life because he had found a place where people accepted him for who he truly was and then right at the end of the film there is a shot of thomas the tank engine standing on top of a hill and he screams freedom in a really deep voice and then he stabs a massive sword into the ground in slow motion and then the film just ends really suddenly and it gave me such a fright.

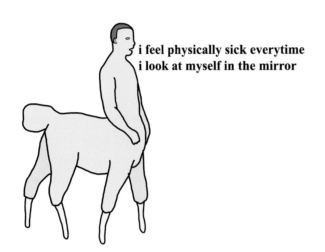

i feel physically sick everytime
i look at myself in the mirror

you cant even tell
you look fine

talking to someone
about your problems
can instantly make you feel better

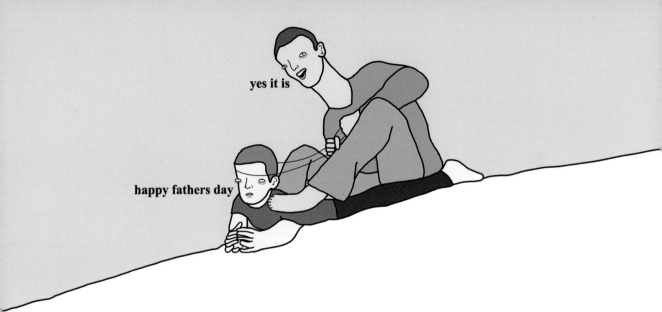

sometimes dads need
to have a bit of fun too

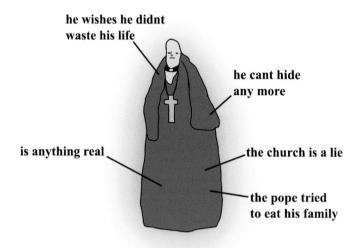

he wishes he didnt waste his life

he cant hide any more

is anything real

the church is a lie

the pope tried to eat his family

wish until it hurts

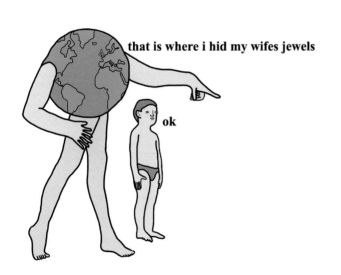

open your heart

and let the world

show you all of its secrets

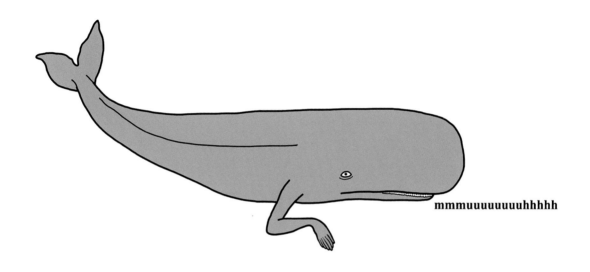

mmmuuuuuuuuhhhhh

there is nothing more beautiful than the
relaxing sound of a whales song

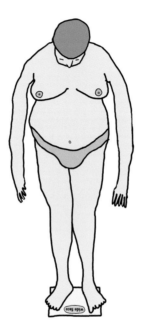

you are not fat
you just have a really wide face

mums are the creatures that hold the world together
and if it wasnt for your mum then you probably
would have never even been born

i am watching you

remember that the christmas robin is watching your every single move
right now so make sure you are being good or else santa wont be climbing
through your letterbox this year

if you cant beat them

just eat them

give me all of your bee syrup now

bee syrup

please dont take it from me my wife is pregnant

whole of the film is when winnie the poo is standing outside of his college in his red coloured crop top with his traditional no trousers on and he is making loads of people laugh by sucking syrup off the top of a teachers car and then gargling with it to the theme tune of mtvs sweet sixteen and all of his friends was saying that it was so funny and his friend ross even said that it was probably one of the best things that he has seen in about half a year and then tigger who is the main idiot at the college was going around telling everyone that he is going to punch winnie the poo in the back of his head after college when he is not looking because he hates him so much but it was so obvious that he is just jealous of winnie the poo for getting all of the attention from everyone and then after college tigger goes to punch him but winnie the poo senses his

it is everyones favourite film about a syrup addicted bear that is right it is winnie the poo and his cousin piglet from the hit family film that is called winnie the poo and the chamber of syrup. if you havent seen winnie

the poo and the chamber of syrup before then you might as well just be blind or deaf or both because you are missing out on a action packed adventure that will haunt you for the rest of your life and my best bit in the presence and he instantly turns around and slices tiggers spine with a bit of plastic that he found next to a fence and then winnie the poo goes on top of tigger on the ground and he does a massive screaming laugh right in tiggers face that sounded like a train full of bees smashing into a school and then before tigger could even say why cant i move my legs winnie the poo had completely vanished and then when it was at night time winnie the poo goes over to piglets house and he says for piglet to give him all of the syrup that he has got and piglet says you cant have it because my wife is pregnant and it is all that she can eat right now and winnie the poo says pregnant shmegnant i dont give a flying hell if she is pregnant or if she is just fat i just want to have all of your delicious golden bee juice inside of myself and then he slowly walks over to piglet and he kisses him on his forehead and he says my sweet cousin in a really light voice and then he looks at him for about 5 seconds and he does a half smile and then he slaps him right across his face and he bends forward and he licks piglets face where he was just slapped and he says give me your bee syrup now you salmon coloured dwarf and piglet says you need help mate you have got a serious syrup problem and winnie the poo says shut up no i do not and piglet says eh you do realise the reason everyone calls you winnie the poo is because you actually stink of poo because you never wash because all that you do is drink bee syrup all day and tigger said he actually saw you eating your own poo out of a napkin in the college car park as well and then winnie the poo just grabs the jar of syrup out of piglets pale pink palms and he runs out of the house and as he is running away he screams jumanji and then right at the end of the film there is a shot of winnie the poo sitting in the woods looking at a photograph of him and christopher robin in italy next to the eiffel tower and the camera goes really close up on winnie the poos face and he starts laughing and loads of bees fly out of his mouth and it lasts for about 5 minutes and then the screen just goes completely black and writing comes up that says winnie the poo hasnt been seen for nearly 2 and a half years and then a lightning bolt goes across the screen and it smashes the writing up into loads of little pieces and then the film just ends really suddenly and it really is one of the most action packed films that has ever been made about syrup and if you have children of your very own or if you can find a child just for a day then you should definitely have a watch of it with them when it is the summer holidays because trust me you will not regret it not even a slice.

if at first you dont succeed
give up and try something easier
or move abroad

he has been trying to
pull his head off for a
week now but he just
cant quite do it

his family keep telling
him there is no point
trying to pull his head
off because he will
never be able to do it

he saw a man
do it in a film

he says he is going to do it
even if he dies trying

he did it

it is fine to be curious about things

(turn to the next page if you are feeling curious today)

it looks like someone is
feeling a little bit curious today

i know

kiss this page
to make yourself
not feel so alone
anymore

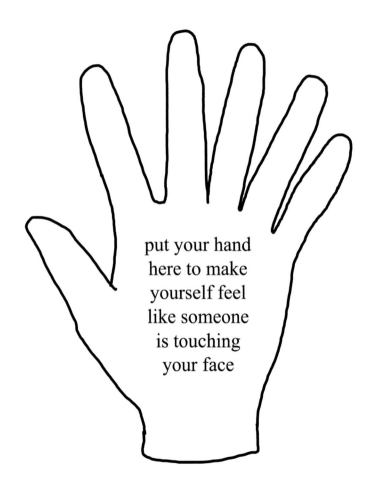

put your hand
here to make
yourself feel
like someone
is touching
your face

outroduction

now that you have finished having a read of this book
i hope that it has made you feel more positive about yourself

and remember that whenever you may feel sad or a bit down about your life
then just pick up this book and hold it next to your face and let the
pictures and words stroke your whole body and tell you
that everything is going to be ok

because i believe in you
and you should do too.

love from your friend

chris (simpsons artist) xox

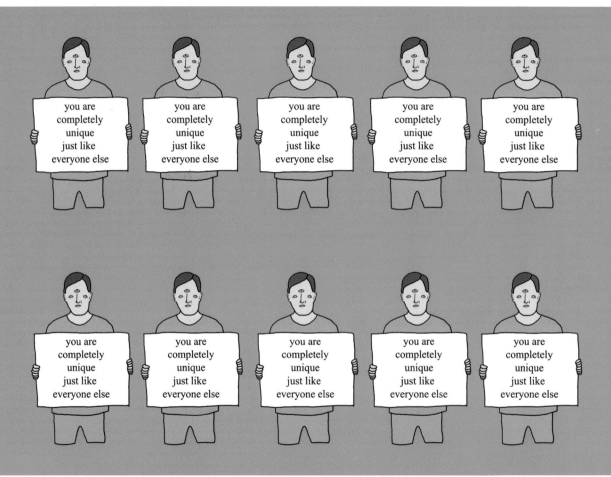